Gender, Race, and Power

Examining IR through an Intersectional Lens

Joyce P. Kaufman
Whittier College, Emerita

Kristen P. Williams
Clark University

ROWMAN & LITTLEFIELD
Lanham • Boulder • New York • London

Executive Acquisitions Editor: Michael Kerns
Associate Editor: Elizabeth Von Buhr
Sales and Marketing Inquiries: textbooks@rowman.com

Credits and acknowledgments for material borrowed from other sources, and
reproduced with permission, appear on the appropriate pages within the text.

Published by Rowman & Littlefield
An imprint of The Rowman & Littlefield Publishing Group, Inc.
4501 Forbes Boulevard, Suite 200, Lanham, Maryland 20706
www.rowman.com

86-90 Paul Street, London EC2A 4NE

British Library Cataloguing in Publication Information Available

Library of Congress Cataloging-in-Publication Data
Names: Kaufman, Joyce P., author. | Williams, Kristen P., 1964– author.
Title: Gender, race, and power : examining IR through an intersectional lens /
    Joyce P. Kaufman, Kristen P. Williams.
Description: Lanham, Maryland : Rowman & Littlefield, 2025. | Includes
    bibliographical references and index.
Identifiers: LCCN 2024030551 (print) | LCCN 2024030552 (ebook) |
    ISBN 9781538182116 (cloth) | ISBN 9781538182123 (paperback) |
    ISBN 9781538182130 (epub)
Subjects: LCSH: International relations—Social aspects.
Classification: LCC JZ1251 .K38 2025 (print) | LCC JZ1251 (ebook) |
    DDC 327—dc23/eng/20240716
LC record available at https://lccn.loc.gov/2024030551
LC ebook record available at https://lccn.loc.gov/2024030552

Contents

List of Textboxes   v

Preface   vii

Abbreviations   xi

1 Intersectionality and IR   1
   Starting with the War in Ukraine   1
   Intersectionality   5
   Mainstream IR Theories: Realism, Liberalism, and Constructivism   6
   Critiques of Mainstream IR: Race, Gender, and Empire—And
       Intersectionality   9
   Conclusion: Overview of Chapters 2–6   14

2 Intersectionality and Issues of War, Peace, and Security   17
   What Is War?   18
   What Is Peace?   20
   War and Peace from an Intersectional Perspective: Human Security   23
   The Women, Peace and Security Agenda and UNSCR 1325   25
   Critiques of UNSCR 1325: Intersectionality Matters   28
   Case Study: Northern Ireland   31
   Conclusion   43

3 Intersectionality, Human Rights, and Humanitarian Intervention   45
   Human Rights as a Concept and a Norm   46
   Women and Their Impact on the UN Charter and UDHR   49
   UDHR and Human Rights from an Intersectional Perspective   52
   Case Study: CEDAW   56
   Humanitarian Intervention and the Responsibility to Protect (R2P)   60
   Conclusion   67

4 Intersectionality, the Global Economy, and Issues of Development 69
IR Approaches to the Global Economy 72
Gendering Development: WID, WAD, and GAD 77
Case Study: COVID-19 85
Conclusion 95

5 Intersectionality and the Environment 97
Development and Evolution of International Environmental
Politics 99
International Relations and the Environment 102
Intersectionality and International/Global Environmental
Politics 104
Case Study: Climate Change 110
Gendering Climate Change and Global Governance 112
Conclusion 115

6 Examining IR from an Intersectional Perspective 117
Lessons Learned 117
Answering the Questions 119
Intersectionality and the Case Studies 119
Conclusion: The Challenges and Possible Next Steps 121

Glossary 123

Notes 127

Index 161

About the Authors 173

Textboxes

2.1   Selected UN Security Council Resolutions Growing from
      UNSCR 1325   25
3.1   Universal Declaration of Human Rights Preamble   47
3.2   Bandung Conference and Human Rights   51
4.1   Globalization   70
4.2   Global Restructuring   76
4.3   Gendering the Global Economy and Leading the
      International Financial Institutions   80
4.4   Sustainable Development Goals (SDGs)   84
5.1   Women and Gender Constituency at the UNFCCC:
      "A Just Framework for Action"   113

Preface

This book is the latest step in an intellectual journey that we started together in December 2000 when we both attended a lecture given by Cynthia Enloe, during which she asked the audience to think about where are the women in their research. That led to our first collaboration, an article titled "Who Belongs? Women, Marriage and Citizenship: Gendered Nationalism and the Balkan Wars," *International Feminist Journal of Politics*, in 2004, which in turn led to our first book together, *Women, the State, and War: A Comparative Perspective on Citizenship and Nationalism* (Lexington Books, 2007). A number of other books, articles, and papers followed that reinforced the importance of injecting feminist perspectives into our research, both individually and collectively.

When Michael Kerns, an editor at Rowman & Littlefield with whom Joyce had worked, approached us at ISA in 2022 about doing a textbook on gender and international relations (IR), we thought about it and convinced Michael that rather than do that, given the plethora of books that already examined the topic, we would prefer instead to tackle a text on looking at international relations through an intersectional lens. Our argument was a simple one: While there are many books that look at aspects of gender and international relations and some that look at race and IR, there were very few that we were aware of that interrogate a broad intersectional approach to the field. After doing a literature review, Michael concurred and we went to work. Neither of us had done much work on intersectionality to that point, and both of us immersed ourselves in the literature on the topic so we could better understand why this approach is an important one and what can be gained by using an intersectional analysis or methodology. Since both of us had often taught introduction to international relations courses as well as upper-division IR seminars to undergraduates, from that starting point we worked on developing an approach that would be accessible to undergraduates or even graduate students, emphasizing especially the ways in which injecting intersectionality could broaden our understanding of basic issues central to IR such as war and peace, security, human rights, the economy, and the environment. To make the approach especially accessible and relevant, we wanted to emphasize case studies that would help illustrate how an intersectional approach can lead to better understanding of these issues.

The result is this text. We open this book with a case study of Russia's invasion of Ukraine in February 2022 to illustrate how "traditional" IR approaches would analyze this event versus what is gained by using an intersectional approach. We continue with an overview of mainstream IR theories—realism, liberalism, and constructivism—in order to frame our work and all that follows. We then offer critiques of these approaches and introduce alternative approaches to studying the field. Each of the subsequent four chapters delves in depth into an important topic in the field of IR using an intersectional analysis to contrast with the more traditional approaches. Each chapter includes a case study that illustrates our points. We conclude with what we have learned and the admonition to consider looking at various issues in IR through an intersectional lens. We are clear that we are not dismissing the traditional approaches, which have contributed greatly to our base of knowledge, but rather of the importance of considering an alternative approach.

We presented aspects of this book in its early stages at various professional conferences and appreciate the feedback we received from discussants, fellow panelists, and members of the audience. That goes back to a presentation of our preliminary work at ISA in Montreal in 2023, APSA in Los Angeles in 2023, and ISA in San Francisco in 2024. In addition to an initial proposal review, Michael sent early drafts of our chapters to four reviewers, who offered feedback and comments not only about the book as it existed at that point but also helpful suggestions based on how they would integrate such a book into their own teaching. Our thanks to David Andersen-Rodgers, California State University, Sacramento; Hollis France, College of Charleston; Colette Mazzucelli, New York University; Elisabeth Hope Murray, president of the International Network of Genocide Scholars; Jennie Woodard, University of Maine; and other reviewers who chose to remain anonymous.

Both Michael and his then-assistant, Elizabeth Von Buhr (who has since been promoted), were extremely helpful with the literature review and provided feedback on various versions of the draft. We looked to Michael especially for guidance as to how to draft a basic text on this topic that could be useful to faculty teaching a range of topics where this book might be an appropriate fit. We very much appreciated Jehanne Schweitzer (senior production editor) shepherding the manuscript from start to finish. We thank them and all the others at Rowman & Littlefield who helped bring this book forward.

We were delighted to have the opportunity to work together once again, and, as always, the collaboration has been an intellectually exciting and fruitful one. Both of us have benefitted greatly from the chance to explore IR in a different way. That said, each of us also knows that a work such as this, which can be time-consuming and challenging, would not be possible without the support of our families throughout the process. Joyce owes a debt of gratitude to her husband, Robert B. Marks, who has been a supportive partner through this latest endeavor as he has on all previous books. Kristen thanks her husband, James Culhane, and her children, Anne and Matthew Culhane-Williams, for their ongoing support. We dedicate this book to all of them and to all IR scholars and researchers who are struggling to find ways to understand an increasingly complex international environment.

Abbreviations

BPfA	Beijing Platform for Action
CEDAW	The Convention on the Elimination of All Forms of Discrimination Against Women
COP	Conference of the Parties
EU	European Union
GAD	Gender and Development
GATT	General Agreement on Tariffs and Trade
GFA	Good Friday Agreement
HDI	Human Development Index
ICC	International Criminal Court
ICTR	International Criminal Tribunal for Rwanda
ICTY	International Criminal Tribunal for the former Yugoslavia
IHL	International Humanitarian Law
IMF	International Monetary Fund
IPE	international political economy
IR	international relations
IRA	Irish Republican Army
NAP	National Action Plan
NATO	North Atlantic Treaty Organization
NGO	non-governmental organization
NIWC	Northern Ireland Women's Coalition
OHCHR	Office of the High Commissioner for Human Rights
R2P	Responsibility to Protect
SAP	Structural Adjustment Program
SDGs	Sustainable Development Goals
UDHR	Universal Declaration of Human Rights
UNFCCC	United Nations Framework Convention on Climate Change
UNIFEM	United Nations Development Fund for Women

UNSC	United Nations Security Council
WAD	Women and Development
WID	Women in Development
WPS	Women, Peace and Security agenda
WTO	World Trade Organization

Chapter 1

Intersectionality and IR

STARTING WITH THE WAR IN UKRAINE

On February 24, 2022, Russia launched a full-scale invasion against Ukraine, a country that had been a republic in the former Soviet Union decades earlier. The Russian government argued that it was simply reclaiming land that it rightfully owned, extending a conflict begun some eight years previous with Russia's invasion of Crimea. In utilizing a "nationalist narrative," President Putin claimed that the invasion was necessary for the protection of Russian speakers living in the Donbas region of Ukraine.[1] The view of most of the world, however, was that the invasion was an unprovoked act of aggression, a violation of international law and the norm of state sovereignty, the bedrock of international relations between states since the 1648 Treaty of Westphalia that ended the Thirty Years' War in Europe.

Ukrainian forces, under the leadership of President Volodymyr Zelenskyy, mounted fierce resistance, as the Russian invasion threatens Ukraine's very existence as an independent state. With arms and support from the United States, the European Union (EU), NATO, and other countries, Ukrainian troops have made several counteroffensives to push Russians out of the north and toward the east, where bloody fighting has continued along the front line.[2]

NATO, the Western military alliance that was formed in 1949 explicitly to counter the Soviet Union, has been renewed and strengthened, with Russia once again seen as the immediate threat. Russia's aggression spurred a new round of NATO expansion, as Sweden and Finland applied for membership to the security alliance, both with strong geopolitical incentives to seek safeguards against Russia.[3] Finland was admitted to NATO on April 4, 2023, and Sweden became a member on March 7, 2024.[4]

1

As of this writing, the war so far has been bloody and brutal, with millions of Ukrainians fleeing west, mostly to neighboring Poland and to Germany. As one set of scholars assert, "The movement of forced migrants and refugees fleeing from the war in Ukraine that began in February 2022 represents Europe's most significant wave of migration since World War II. At least 7 million people are estimated to have left the country in 2022."[5] In order to ensure that there are military forces available to fight, Ukraine passed a law at the start of the war prohibiting men between the ages of eighteen and sixty from leaving the country except under exceptional circumstances. Andrews et al. collected data in the spring and summer of 2022 that showed "this wave of migration . . . [was] overwhelmingly female" and that "women [were] often migrating with children."[6] As they further noted, "The fact that many women are traveling with children—usually but not always their own—affects their needs upon arrival and their ability to meet the challenges of resettlement."[7] Many respondents "said that they only left Ukraine to keep their children safe," often leaving their husbands and other family members who remained in Ukraine.[8] Those who fled after the invasion "have been taking the most vulnerable family members out of the country—children, older people, or those who need medical care."[9]

Race also matters when considering those fleeing, with "reports of Black people being refused at border crossings in favor of white Ukrainians, leaving them stuck at borders for days in brutal conditions."[10] The data also show that many of those Ukrainians (both women and men) who fled to Poland or Germany were highly skilled professionals, white-collar workers, or had some experience in the service sector. Of those who went to Germany, approximately three-quarters had higher education degrees and nearly 20 percent had some vocational training; more than 85–90 percent were under sixty years old.[11] This tells us something about class, as well as the economic status and ages of the refugees.

As many women fled Ukraine, others stayed, either because they wanted to or had no choice. As *New York Times* columnist Nicholas Kristof reported in December 2022, "Ukraine is a traditional and sexist society caught in a grueling artillery war with Russia, so the last person you would expect to see in an army uniform is a grandma." And then he quoted a woman, Mariia Stalinska, as saying, "We need to defend our children. If not us, who?" At the time Kristof wrote the article, about sixty thousand women were in the Ukrainian military.[12]

Why are we starting this text on IR and intersectionality with the war in Ukraine? Because a case study of the Russia-Ukraine conflict is one that lends itself to analysis by political scientists, including international relations (IR) scholars, as well as historians, sociologists, and psychologists.

From an IR perspective, the conflict involves two sovereign states, one of which has invaded another in violation of international law. The conflict also relates to how we understand the balance of power in Europe, given the geographic location of the two states, as well as the larger balance of power in the international system. Many countries, including the United States, are providing aid to Ukraine. Other states, such as China, have made statements indicating their "independent and impartial position."[13] That said, the leaders of both China and Russia "see the other as a critical partner in reshaping what they see as an American-led world order hostile to their aims." China has not condemned the Russian invasion and, in fact, "has continued to bolster its economic, diplomatic, and security ties with Russia."[14]

International organizations such as the United Nations (UN) and the European Union have responded to the conflict. The UN General Assembly has called for an end to the war and demanded that Russia withdraw immediately from Ukraine.[15] The EU has made clear its support for Ukraine and condemnation of Russia's invasion.[16] More specifically, the EU has placed economic and individual sanctions on Russia, including prohibitions on particular technologies and industrial goods. It has also provided humanitarian assistance and military support to Ukraine.[17]

Yet, as noted above, there is a gendered aspect of the war, as evidenced by the massive refugee situation, with primarily women and children fleeing Ukraine to safety in other European countries. In this way, women (and children) are viewed as victims in need of protection. While other Ukrainian women have joined the military to fight, they still experience gender-based discrimination. Additionally, it is telling that there are no women delegates from either Russia or Ukraine at various peace talks that have been held to date.[18] In maintaining and promoting the traditional gender role of protector, all men aged eighteen and above are eligible for conscription, while men under the age of sixty cannot leave Ukraine. Not all men want to fight and yet are "shamed by crowds" because they want to leave the country.[19] In Russia, "women, feminist and LGBTQ+ activists have been at the vanguard of anti-war and anti-Putin resistance" and in doing so, according to Valerie Sperling et al., "they're challenging a regime that relies on patriarchy for the legitimacy of its leader."[20]

This exceedingly brief description of the Russian invasion of Ukraine makes clear that the conflict is more than just two states' militaries fighting. Understanding the dynamics at play is important if we are to get a more complete understanding of this conflict, such as the impact of the war on both countries' economies, the ways in which the discourses of nationalism and national identity are prominent, and the continuation of traditional gender roles but also in what ways these traditional roles are changing (i.e., Ukrainian women in the military). An analysis of the conflict also reveals how class and race matter in the context of who is permitted and also who is able to leave, seeking safety away from the violence. In essence, if we care about the people caught in wars and conflict zones, an intersectional analysis is necessary in examining the major issues in international relations, including war and peace, for a fuller understanding. And yet, only recently have IR scholars published works that present a broad intersectional approach to the field.[21]

Make no mistake: The paradigms that have dominated the field have been important in providing a foundation upon which IR scholars could address major questions, such as why do countries go to war or devolve into civil war, and what does "peace" really mean? We are not discounting the role that these paradigms play, nor the knowledge they have provided as we study these issues. Rather, in this volume we build on that work as well as the work of feminist scholarship that broadened the IR field by focusing on women and the role of gender, and on postcolonial scholarship that examines the impacts of colonial rule that reinforce global hierarchies of power. The evolution of feminist and postcolonial approaches that are explicitly intersectional—that include multiple categories, such as race, ethnicity, class, religion, sexuality, and even age, as well as women and gender—have enriched our understandings of issues that are salient in international relations. Thus, this book interrogates the traditional IR theories and the issues that the field studies, including war, peace, security, the environment, human rights, the global economy, and development, to demonstrate that a more comprehensive and holistic understanding of these issues can only be found by utilizing an intersectional analysis.

We begin with a brief presentation of intersectionality, followed by a discussion of the international relations theories (realism, liberalism, and constructivism) that dominate the discipline. In many ways, this is the logical starting point; we cannot begin to understand in what ways an intersectional approach enhances our understanding of critical IR topics without addressing the limitations of the traditional study of the field. International relations as a field of study has often lagged in examining how and why factors such as gender, race, ethnicity, sexuality, class, and religion matter. The next section discusses scholarship on race in international relations, feminist IR, and postcolonialism. These three approaches to the study of IR help us to answer the main questions that we seek to address in this volume: What does traditional IR miss by not including intersectionality in addressing critical issues? How does an intersectional approach change and, in fact, broaden our understanding of international relations and the international system? We conclude this chapter with a brief description of the remaining chapters of the book.

INTERSECTIONALITY

Kimberlé Crenshaw coined the term "intersectionality" in the late 1980s. In an analysis of US courts and their rulings in sex and race discrimination cases, she argued for an intersectional analysis, noting that "Black women can experience discrimination in ways that are both similar to and different from those experienced by white women and Black men."[22] She further asserts, "The paradigm of sex discrimination tends to be based on the experiences of white women; the model of race discrimination tends to be based on the experiences of the most privileged Blacks. Notions of what constitutes race and sex discrimination are, as a result, narrowly tailored to embrace only a small set of circumstances, none of which include discrimination against Black women."[23] In the end, "because of their intersectional identity as both women *and* of color within discourses that are shaped to respond to one *or* the other, women of color are marginalized within both" (emphasis in original).[24]

Building on Crenshaw's work, scholars across many disciplines, including political science, history, sociology, anthropology, and psychology, have utilized intersectional analyses. For such scholars, as noted by Ange-Marie Hancock, intersectionality is "a normative theoretical argument" as well as "an approach to conducting empirical research." Hancock points out that as an approach, scholars analyze "the interaction of categories of difference (including but not limited to race, gender, class, and sexual orientation)" and "the interaction of such categories as organizing structures of society, recognizing that these key components influence political access, equality, and the potential for any form of justice."[25] Notably, these categories, "while operating according to distinct logics, are interdependent and interrelated."[26]

In essence, framing questions along a single axis (i.e., race-only, sexuality-only, class-only, or gender-only) rather than multiple axes remains problematic.[27] As Wendy Smooth asserts, "Studies illustrate how singular axis framing can result in a failure to represent subpopulations of women who are often the least empowered and most vulnerable segments of already politically marginalized groups. . . . Further, single axis models limit the extent to which representatives are held accountable for 'showing up' on behalf of *all* women" (emphasis in original).[28] As will be demonstrated later in the chapter, postcolonial feminist IR approaches interrogate "how gender, sexuality, race and class are *co-constituted* within the production of the international" (emphasis added).[29]

MAINSTREAM IR THEORIES: REALISM, LIBERALISM, AND CONSTRUCTIVISM

Realism

The field of international relations, established in the nineteenth century, came into its own after World War I as nations began to gain their independence from empires. In a 1961 article, "Is International Relations a Discipline?" Morton Kaplan wrote, "International relations broke loose as an independent discipline during a period in the 1920s when idealism was high and the urge to solve practical problems great."[30] Yet the international relations discipline really became prominent after World War II when theorists such as Hans J. Morgenthau tried to understand what led to major catastrophes such as the one the world had just experienced and, in so doing, hoped to be able to avoid repetition of those in the future. For Morgenthau, and the realists who followed him:

> Domestic and international politics are but two different manifestations of the same phenomenon: *the struggle for power*. Its manifestations differ in the two different spheres because different moral, political, and social conditions prevail in each (emphasis added).[31]

Moreover, Morgenthau made clear: "Whatever the ultimate aims of international politics, power is always the immediate aim."[32] But more than that, in his words, "All history shows that nations active in international politics are continuously preparing for, actively involved in, or recovering from organized violence in the form of war."[33] When he originally published *Politics Among Nations* in 1948, the world was recovering from one war and settling into another, a cold war, that would dominate international politics for the next forty-plus years and would indeed be a struggle for power.[34]

And yet, while power is central to the field of IR, as Daniel Drezner remarks, "scholars cannot agree on how to define or measure it."[35] Consequently, when we consider different theories, paradigms, or approaches in the discipline, in the study of international relations, three main theories dominate: realism, liberalism, and constructivism. These theories, along with others in the field, have differing views about how power, as a concept, matters in international relations.

Realist theory has a long history. One can consider, for example, Thucydides's *History of the Peloponnesian War*, about 400 BCE, in which he writes about the wars and politics of the Greek city-states. In *The Art of War*, Chinese general Sun Tzu (500 BCE) wrote about Chinese military strategy. In essence, for realists it is the study of war and peace—high politics—that is most important. Economics, trade, and domestic issues, considered "low politics," are relatively less important.[36]

Realism in both its classical and neo-, or structural, variants focuses on the state, as the state is considered the primary unit of analysis.[37] Further, for structural (or neo-) realists, the anarchic international system—in which there is no political authority above states—and the distribution, or balance, of power among the major states matter in accounting for state behavior as states seek to ensure their security and survival.[38] In addition to the anarchic international system and the balance of power, realists share other assumptions: "States are prone to conflict, not cooperation"; and "states that prioritize cooperation or economic gain over security will not fare as well in the international system."[39] Moreover, for structural realists, states are unitary, rational actors, in that domestic actors and politics are not important relative to the anarchic international system and the distribution of power. A state's relative power, rather than its absolute power, or its position in the international system relative to other states means that each state focuses on ensuring its own security, whether that is through building up its military or forming alliances with other states.[40]

Morgenthau and other realist theorists gave rise to a number of important political thinkers and approaches to understanding international relations. Realist theory influenced the approaches taken by American policymakers such as George Kennan, who was the architect of the US Cold War foreign policy of containment, and Henry Kissinger, who was first national security advisor and then secretary of state under President Nixon. And realist thinking, many believed, seemed especially appropriate to understanding the political dynamics of the Cold War and the constant struggle for power between the United States and the Soviet Union.

But this approach also carries with it weaknesses or limitations, which subsequent theories try to address. By focusing on security and competition between states, realism cannot account for cooperation between states or that international relations is a variable-sum game (rather than a zero-sum game in the realist world) in which all states can benefit. Like the realists, as will be discussed below, liberalism (including neoliberalism) considers the state the primary unit of analysis, but also recognizes the importance of other actors, including international institutions, that provide a way for states to cooperate.[41] As Drezner summarizes, "For liberals, institutions are the mechanism through which actors can amass more power without triggering negative feedback."[42]

Liberalism

International institutions such as the International Monetary Fund (IMF) and World Bank, both of which were created during the Bretton Woods Conference in 1944 during World War II (and will be addressed in more detail in chapter 4), provide examples of the role that such institutions can play for state cooperation. In creating the IMF and World Bank, the Western liberal democracies restructured the economic system to their benefit. Those two institutions helped promote monetary cooperation that was perceived as important not only to the postwar reconstruction efforts but also to the stability of the international economic and financial systems. These institutions, in turn, were considered essential for building and maintaining the liberal international order.[43]

One aspect of liberalism is the notion of the "democratic peace." Theorists such as Michael Doyle drew on the work of Immanuel Kant (writing in 1795, *Perpetual Peace*) and Joseph Schumpeter to conclude that although liberal democratic states do engage in war, specifically when they are attacked and/or threatened in some way, they have established a separate peace among themselves.[44] The argument is that in a democracy, the public holds leaders accountable. If the leaders decide to go to war, then the voting public can vote them out of office if they oppose the leaders' policies. Moreover, democratic states have shared norms that include solving disputes peacefully, and such states also recognize the benefits from cooperation with each other.[45] While the reality is that democracies fight as many wars as authoritarian states do, they rarely go to war against other democratic states. "No major historical cases contradict this generalization, which is known as the *democratic peace*" (emphasis in original).[46]

Realists critique liberalism in several ways. They assert that international institutions reflect the distribution of power, and that such institutions "are based on the self-interested calculations of the great powers, and they have no independent effect on state behavior." Given that, such "institutions are not an important cause of peace."[47] Realists also provide a critique of the democratic peace theory, noting that, in fact, democracies do fight each other, as evidenced by the War of 1812 between the United States and Britain or Wilhelmine Germany fighting France and Britain in World War I.[48] Nonetheless, liberal theory offers an alternative approach to understanding international relations that stresses cooperation between states and moves beyond the competition that characterized the Cold War period.

Constructivism

Emerging as an alternative to realism and liberalism in the 1990s, constructivist thinkers argue that state identities and interests are socially constructed. And because they are socially constructed, they can change, although such "social processes . . . require considerable amounts of time to change."[49] Political scientist Alexander Wendt, one of the first to define and advocate for this approach, describes it as follows: "Social theories which seek to explain identities and interests do exist. . . . I want to emphasize their focus on the social construction of subjectivity. . . . I will call them 'constructivist.'" For constructivists such as Wendt, as the title of his article asserts, "anarchy is what states make of it."[50]

According to Karen Mingst, "The major theoretical proposition that all constructivists subscribe to is that state behavior is shaped by elite beliefs, identities, and social norms. Individuals in collectivities forge, shape, and change culture through ideas and practices. State and national interests are the result of the social identities of these actors." Because of these assumptions, social constructivism, more than the other two traditional theoretical approaches, "has opened new substantive areas to inquiry, such as the roles of gender and ethnicity, which has been largely absent from international relations approaches."[51] As will be discussed next, other IR theories and approaches have challenged the assumptions and conclusions of the mainstream theories, noting their limitations.

CRITIQUES OF MAINSTREAM IR: RACE, GENDER, AND EMPIRE—AND INTERSECTIONALITY

While the mainstream IR theories take into account the role of international institutions and democracy (liberalism), how state identities and interests can change (constructivism), or the anarchic structure of the international system (realism), at their most basic these theories are concerned with the struggle for power, particularly the major states in the international system. In response, critical theories, including the works of feminist and postcolonial theorists, examine "the nature of hegemonic discourse. All critical theorists share a desire to challenge privileged forms of neoliberal power."[52] As Drezner makes clear: "Critical theory recognizes how power informs and structures social relations."[53] In this section we discuss briefly the various approaches to IR that center on race and gender, which in turn underscore the necessity of an intersectional approach to the study of IR.

Race and IR

The field of IR and its mainstream theories focus on states, anarchy, and the balance of power among the great powers in the international system, but they have not really examined race and racial hierarchies.[54] The neglect of the connection between race and international relations, however, has not always been the case. Kelebogile Zvobgo and Meredith Loken note that initial works published in the late 1800s and early 1900s "invoked race as the linchpin holding together colonial administration and war. Belief in white people's biological and sociological supremacy offered a tidy dualism between the civilized and the savage that justified the former's murderous exploitation of the latter." Moreover, in the late nineteenth and early twentieth centuries, they indicate that academic journals as well as research institutions studied race and international relations.[55] For example, the first academic international relations journal was the *Journal of Race Development*. Its first issue, July 1910, included articles such as "The Point of View Toward Primitive Races" and "Our Philippine Policies and Their Results." Subsequent issues included articles titled "The Indian Problem and Imperial Politics" and "A Worthy Example of the Influence of a Strong Man Upon the Development of Racial Character."[56] Zvobgo and Loken assert that the journal "advanced racist treatises, including on the inability of 'native races' to develop states without colonialism." At the same time, they note that W. E. B. Du Bois and others wrote critiques about European mercantilism in the journal.[57] Less than a decade after the journal was established, it was renamed the *Journal of International Relations* (1919), followed three years later by a further name change in 1922 to *Foreign Affairs*. With these changes, the journal's content changed as well, no longer focused primarily on race and IR.[58]

It is also important to recognize the role of Black IR scholars, many of whom were faculty at Howard University in the mid-twentieth century, writing about race and IR, particularly in the context of anti-colonial revolutions following World War II.[59] As Bianca Freeman et al. assert, "The critique of IR's race blindness begins with the Howard School."[60] Such scholars explored the "relationship of racism to imperialism."[61] But mainstream IR theory did not continue to focus on race and "stopped engaging with the subject altogether."[62] As Roxanne Lynn Doty states, "International relations scholars in the late 1960s and early 1970s raised the issue of race in international relations and offered some fruitful directions in which to proceed. . . . Yet, interest in race was not sustained and never did cut to the heart of IR as an academic discipline."[63] As will be discussed later in this section, it was the work of postcolonial scholars in the 1990s and 2000s that centered race and colonialism again in the discipline.[64]

Suffice it to say that scholars in major academic journals continue to call for analysis and study of race and IR. One example is the January 2022 special issue of the journal *International Affairs*: "Race and Imperialism in International Relations—Theory and Practice," guest edited by Jasmine Gani and Jenna Marshall. Fifteen articles include works titled "The impact of colonialism on policy and knowledge production in international relations," "Race and racism in the founding of the modern world order," and "Between mobile corridors and immobilizing borders: race, fixity, and friction in Palestine/Israel."[65]

In the "Forum" in the *International Studies Review* journal in 2021, "Stripping Away the Body: Prospects for Reimagining Race in IR," the editors write: "Through our examination of race in this light [material-spatial-temporal relation of power] issues of gender effortlessly emerge alongside the study of race."[66] Importantly, this special forum also makes clear the need to utilize an intersectional analysis. As one of the contributors, K. Melchor Quick Hall, contends, "An intersectional lens names the locations of multiple oppressions, which pushes the IR gaze away from heads of states and government halls of power to consider other subjects."[67]

Feminist IR

In the late 1980s and early 1990s, feminist scholars began to critique mainstream IR theories, noting the masculinist bias in the field and challenged the binaries of male/female, public/private, masculine/feminine, and protector/protected.[68] As J. Ann Tickner declares, "Feminists also emphasize that, rather than introducing gender into IR, they are revealing how gender is already embedded in the theory and practice of international relations."[69] While there are different kinds of feminist approaches to IR (including standpoint feminism, liberal feminism, radical feminism, and postmodern feminism), most IR feminist scholars consider "gender as the relational construction of individual masculine and feminine identities, where masculine identities are preferred over feminine ones, and are a signifier for power relations of domination and subordination among individuals and collectivities more generally."[70] In effect, all feminist IR research utilizes a gender analysis to account for issues such as war and conflict, trade and economics, and the environment.

With regard to feminist approaches to security, rather than focused narrowly on the security of the state, as is the case with mainstream IR theories, security can be understood more broadly to include domestic violence, economic security, environmental security, and human security. Moreover, feminist security studies highlight the ways in which gender is implicated in state-building and nationalism, militarism and militarized masculinity, and sexual and gender-based violence in wartime. Works focus on women's roles in conflict—as peace activists, and as victims as well as perpetrators of political violence. Feminist IR scholars have also examined the ways in which post-conflict reconstruction is gendered, often a period of time in which there is a gendered backlash and domestic violence increases following the end of formal hostilities.[71] As noted above, feminist scholars broadened the conception of security to include economic security. In bridging feminist security studies and feminist political economy, Jacqui True analyzes the violence and insecurity women experience during times of both war and peace, noting the gendered economic and social inequalities faced by men and women.[72]

Feminist scholars have also focused on the ways in which the global economy is gendered. As Anne Sisson Runyan and V. Spike Peterson assert, "the gendered division of labor positions men and women differently; . . . women's domestic, reproductive, and caring labor is deemed marginal to 'production' and analyses of it." Moreover, "orthodox models and methods presuppose male-dominated activities (paid work, the formal economy) and masculinized characteristics (autonomous, objective, rational, instrumental, competitive)."[73] Clearly, there are trends in the global economy that illustrate the consistent biases against women. Tickner remarks: "Women have not been left outside of global restructuring; they are participating while remaining invisible."[74] Many of these topics regarding the global economy will be explored in more detail in chapter 4.

Feminist scholars increasingly recognized the limitations of the single axis of gender in their analysis—that women are not a monolithic group. Writing nearly two decades ago, Leslie McCall observed, "Feminists are perhaps alone in the academy in the extent to which they have embraced intersectionality—the relationships among multiple dimensions and modalities of social relations and subject formations—as itself a central category of analysis."[75] Importantly, "the growth of intersectional frameworks marked a shift in the gender and politics literature."[76] As V. Spike Peterson argues, "*the privileging of masculinity does not privilege all men or only men*. . . . Gender . . . pervades language and culture and devalorizes *all* feminized statuses, including those occupied by subordinated men." She concludes, "Diverse hierarchies are linked and ideologically 'naturalized' by *feminizing* those who are subordinated. I understand this insight as key to advancing intersectional analysis" (emphasis in original).[77] In other words, "gender cannot be understood in isolation from other identity categories and relations of inequality, recognize that there are multiple genders, as well as sexes, in part because race/ethnicity, class, sexuality, and other cultural variations shape gender identities and performances."[78]

In paying attention to intersectionality in the context of the global and national economies, for example, feminist scholars have considered "how hierarchical structures of class, race, and gender cross and intersect with national boundaries" to account for "the global division of labor."[79] In considering intersectionality and peace and security, an intersectional analysis of the UN's Women, Peace and Security (WPS) agenda is telling (see chapter 2 for more on the WPS agenda). Since 2000, when the first UN Security Council resolution (Resolution 1325) that recognized the impact of war and conflict on women (including sexual and gender-based violence) and called for women's participation in peace negotiations was passed, women have been categorized in particular ways. As Sarah Smith and Elena B. Stavrevska demonstrate, "Women and girls are generally already always assumed to be vulnerable . . . , but in trying to account for different sets of experiences, the WPS resolutions frame some women and girls as more vulnerable than others."[80]

Postcolonialism

The major European powers and then the United States[81] conquered countries in Asia, Africa, and Latin America to extract their resources as well as impose their political and legal systems, and often culture and religion, on the Indigenous peoples. While the European states governed differently and "faced varying levels and types of indigenous resistance over time and place," the result was that "colonialism's impact has been both complex and contradictory."[82]

Recognizing the impact of colonialism in the contemporary period, as explained by Sheila Nair: "Postcolonialism examines how societies, governments and peoples in the formerly colonized regions of the world experience international relations."[83] The historical experience of European colonialism and empire led to "a long process of continued domination of the West over the rest of the world." This domination—"cultural, economic, and political"—as Nair notes, continues to "characterize global politics." Consequently, rather than the mainstream IR's focus on the great powers and the anarchic international system, postcolonial IR scholars, whose work began in the 1990s, consider the international system as one of hierarchy.[84]

Relatedly, postcolonialism examines power, one of the key concepts in IR (along with states and security), in terms of how power "serve[s] to reproduce the status quo." In so doing, postcolonial IR scholars analyze how power operates in international relations, and the discourses and narratives about hierarchy.[85] For example, during the Cold War, states that were aligned with neither the United States nor the Soviet Union were described as "backward" or "primitive." These narratives and discourse are often racialized.[86] In another example, humanitarian intervention is often framed as one in which those living in the Global South "are in dire need of protection" by those in the states of the "civilized" Global North.[87] In effect, postcolonial IR scholars argue the importance of studying the "non-core actors" and their "ideas, perspectives, experiences, and practices." As Mine Nur Küçük makes clear, non-core actors have agency "in shaping world politics."[88]

Postcolonial feminist theory emerged in response to the recognition that a gender analysis was missing in most postcolonial studies. And postcolonial analyses were missing in much of Western feminist scholarship. As Nyland et al. argue, "Women's racialized experiences during colonial and postcolonial periods was, and still is, largely absent from postcolonial studies."[89] They further assert that accounting for differences among women is not sufficient in any analysis of IR issues. Instead, it is important to take into account the "intersections of privilege and subordination within the group of men. . . . Gendered and postcolonial structures affect other genders in an equally diverse way as they affect women in different conditions and contexts."[90] In essence, "postcolonial critiques of Western feminism are strongly related to intersectional theory."[91]

We can see these tensions at play at UN conferences and Western development agencies in terms of strategies and programs to integrate women in developing countries into these programs. The result was that critiques emerged by women in the Global South regarding the Women in Development (WID) agenda (and later, the Gender and Development [GAD] agenda) and the underrepresentation and marginalization of women (see chapter 4 on WID and GAD). Additionally, narratives of women in the Global South were stereotypical: "as powerless, ignorant and trapped in inferior roles . . . women in need of help and with little to contribute to development planning."[92] These depictions reflected that much of the agenda was developed from a Western perspective and values.[93]

Postcolonial feminist theory helps to unpack the ways in which gender, race, class, sexuality, and so forth intersect. In so doing, such work "uncovers the deeper implications of how and why systemic violence evident in war, conflict, terror, poverty, social inequality and so forth have taken root"—the issues that are at the forefront of the field of international relations.[94]

CONCLUSION: OVERVIEW OF CHAPTERS 2–6

We began this chapter with a brief case study of the war between Ukraine and Russia in order to illustrate the complexities of studying this conflict, and as a reminder that as we continue to look at specific topics in IR, we need to look at a range of variables. The next four substantive chapters, 2 through 5, look at a number of important concepts in IR through an intersectional lens. Underlying much of the approach we take in these chapters is the need to move beyond the state-centric approach used in traditional IR theories to broaden our approach and, therefore, to arrive at better explanations for and understandings of these issues. We do so by applying an intersectional analysis to historical examples and case studies, as we did with the case of Ukraine.

Chapter 2 focuses on intersectionality and issues of war, peace, and security, with special emphasis on understanding what is meant by each of these concepts. War is often defined as organized violence between political actors.

And yet, as Cynthia Cockburn and other feminist scholars have noted, violence is much more than that. Instead, there is a "continuum of violence" in which there is gendered violence in the home, in the state, and in the international arena.[95] With regard to the concept of "peace," is this just the absence of violence, simply ending a conflict by signing a treaty or agreement? Or does peace mean something more broadly? And it is those varied definitions of peace that play an important role in what happens after the conflict ends—the post-conflict reconstruction. Relatedly, we look at the various understandings of "security," including what is meant by the term "human security": security in which people are the referent object rather than the state or global system. Here we owe a debt to the feminist scholars who ask us to broaden the definition of the concept so that it is considered in terms that go beyond just the traditional military definition of security. It would be impossible to engage in any discussion of security without bringing in the Women, Peace and Security agenda embodied in UN Security Council Resolution 1325 (and subsequent resolutions). This resolution raised to the top of the international agenda not only the impact that war has, and had, on women, but also the important role that women can and should play in ending conflicts if the peace that follows is to endure.

Chapter 2 includes a case study that illustrates the greater explanatory value that comes from an intersectional analysis: the conflict in Northern Ireland, known as the Troubles. While framed as a sectarian conflict between Catholics and Protestants, it is clear that the Troubles had a differential impact on members of the society, most notably factors including gender, age, and class, as well as religion. Moreover, the conflict in Northern Ireland is also an international relations issue, as it involves the Republic of Ireland and the UK, as well as the United States and the European Union. So, a seemingly intrastate conflict has an international dimension.

In chapter 3 we explore the relationship between intersectionality, human rights, and humanitarian intervention, starting with a definition of "human rights." Here too the definition is not as straightforward, because when we mention human rights, we need to ask "whose rights?" and who makes that determination? Are human rights universal? How does the concept of "human rights" relate to racial justice? To explore this in more detail, we use CEDAW (the Convention on the Elimination of All Forms of Discrimination Against Women) as a case study of women's rights. While the convention was an important step, it raises questions about the rights of nonbinary people, LGBTQ+ rights, and how it applies to women beyond those who are economically and socially privileged and White. In many ways, chapter 3 builds directly on the ideas raised in chapter 2, with the broader definition of the concept of "security." Ensuring human rights is essential to ensuring security, but for whom?

Chapter 4 examines the global economy, development, and economic globalization. The end of World War II and the emergence of the international economic order, as defined by the United States and the other liberal capitalist democracies, necessitates an understanding of the international political economy (IPE). As was the case with traditional approaches to security studies, the field of IPE within the IR discipline was generally premised on the dominance of the nation-state, and neorealist and neoliberal approaches to understanding issues of economic cooperation and conflict between states. Yet the liberal international order has experienced significant strains in the post–Cold War period, for example, with the rise of China as a challenge to the United States' dominance and power internationally. Focusing on the major powers, such as the United States and China, is insufficient to understand the connection between economic globalization, the global economy, and development. In this chapter we illustrate the differential impact of economic development and globalization across countries as well as on people and groups within countries, which varies according to race, ethnicity, class, and age, in addition to gender. We use a case study of the COVID-19 pandemic to illustrate the varied economic impact the disease has had on different groups, both within and across countries.

Chapter 5 completes the intersectional analysis of specific issues in IR by addressing the environment and how environmental issues transcend state borders. We examine the history of the global environmental movement as an example of the ways in which pressure at different levels—top down (governments, international governmental organizations) and bottom up (environmental activists)—had an impact on the emergence and outcomes of various international treaties and conventions. The environment is also an important social justice issue, in that many people call for environmental justice, given that those who are the poorest often suffer the most from the impacts of a depleted environment. We utilize the case study of climate change to explore the connection between intersectionality and climate justice. Considerations of factors such as race, gender, and socioeconomic status demonstrate that environmental problems are not experienced the same by everyone, and not everyone is able to participate in efforts to address environmental problems within states and across them.

In the concluding chapter, chapter 6, we return to the original goals of the book to summarize what we have learned from the substantive chapters, and the ways in which an intersectional analysis can help clarify and elucidate important issues in the field of IR. In turn, we offer some tentative suggestions about next steps for others in the field to use this approach in the study of IR.

Chapter 2

Intersectionality and Issues of War, Peace, and Security

Historically, the study of international relations has focused on interstate relations, and in particular the causes of war and "the prerequisites of peace" between states. Scholars also have analyzed "the conditions necessary for stability, order, and justice."[1] As we noted in chapter 1, the field of IR came about in order to understand interstate wars, especially the two World Wars. During the Cold War, IR scholars continued to study the interactions between states, namely the relationship between the United States and the Soviet Union. The development of nuclear weapons gave rise to the subfield of security studies, examining how states can ensure their security in a nuclear world.[2] Scholars also studied crisis decision-making, democratic peace, deterrence, and international regimes.[3] As Georg Sørensen asserts, "The core issues of world politics are the big questions of war and peace, conflict and cooperation, wealth and poverty" in a world of sovereign states, which are "the single most important macrostructure determining the lives that people live."[4]

In the post–Cold War period, the study of IR has continued to analyze states, international order, and sovereignty, as well as democracy and democratization and globalization. With the end of the conflict between the two superpowers, the United States and the USSR, given the collapse of the Soviet Union, and the increased number of intrastate (civil) wars, IR scholars began to focus on the causes of these wars.[5] Analyzing the causes of war, whether interstate or intrastate, also necessitates an analysis of peace and security.

In this chapter we begin by asking the question "What is war?" In so doing, we present the mainstream IR approaches to the study of war, and the limitations of those approaches, followed by a discussion of other IR approaches, namely feminist and postcolonial approaches, to the study of war. The section that follows then asks, "What is peace?" As in the question about war, the mainstream IR theories often define peace as the absence of war. Other critical theories offer a contrasting understanding of peace, noting that the end of conflict does not necessarily entail a durable peace. We then discuss security, as the connection between war and peace—what is meant by this is that often interstate and intrastate wars are about ensuring a state's (in the case of an interstate war) or a group's (in the case of a civil war) security. At the same time, a durable peace is one in which people and states are secure. But whose security and what kind of security? In this, we can explore the concept of human security—a much broader understanding of security—and its relationship to peace.

The next section applies an intersectional perspective on war, peace, and security through an examination of UN Security Council Resolution 1325 and the Women, Peace and Security (WPS) agenda. While a landmark shift in the international community's recognition of the impact of war on women and girls, UNSCR 1325 and the broader WPS agenda have been criticized for their lack of an intersectional perspective. In a further look at an intersectional approach to war, peace, and security, the section that follows discusses the conflict in Northern Ireland (the Troubles) as a case study. We conclude with a recap of the main points of the chapter.

WHAT IS WAR?

War generally refers to a condition of organized violence that takes place between or among states (interstate war) or within a given state or society (civil or intrastate war). British historian Margaret MacMillan uses a range of examples to illustrate the role that war has played in different societies and how they, in turn, have engaged with war. And she makes an important point that echoes what others have said about the relationship between war and the nation-state: "The strong nation-states of today with their centralized governments and organized bureaucracies are the products of centuries of war."[6] Charles Tilly asserts that the modern nation-state was born from war, and that the military was integral to the existence of and continued success of the state.[7]

When we consider mainstream IR theories, realism, particularly its neo-realist/structural realist variant, argues that in an anarchic international system in which there is no world government, states take measures to ensure their survival. They balance against threats from other states, including building weapons and forming alliances. Sometimes states engage in the use of force—going to war to protect themselves.[8] In the case of interstate war, according to the UN Charter's Article 51, states can use armed force in self-defense in response to an armed attack by another state.[9] Further, the international system has developed guidelines as to when a war between states is justified (*jus ad bellum*), how it is to be fought (*jus in bello*), and what happens after war ends (*jus post bellum*). Developed as the basic elements of Just War Doctrine, if adhered to, these precepts would ensure that civilians are protected (civilian immunity principle), war would only be waged under a limited set of circumstances, and the sovereignty of another state would not be violated without just cause (self-defense).[10] Yet, as we saw in chapter 1 in the case study of Russia's invasion of Ukraine and the war that followed, these precepts are often violated, and the international system has few options to deal with the aggressor state.

While much of the study of IR is focused on interstate wars, data show that the number of intrastate conflicts has grown considerably since World War II in general, but especially after the Cold War ended.[11] Without the constraints of the Cold War, there was little that seemed to hold countries in check, along with the emergence of nationalist leaders who fomented dissent and ultimately conflict and war within their own country, secure in the belief that the international system would do little to stop them. Generally, that assumption proved to be correct. Coupled with the growth in virulent nationalism and nationalist leaders, a proliferation of militant groups of various kinds also fomented civil war that could drag on for years, as is the case with Syria today. MacMillan explains why it is often so difficult to end these wars and arrive at a situation of peace: "Each side in a civil war is struggling for legitimacy and dominance within a space that was once shared."[12] As we will see in the case study of Northern Ireland, the lines between civilian and combatant and private and public spheres are often blurred.

In challenging the traditional IR theories, utilizing a gender analysis, feminist IR scholars encourage us to think about questions such as: Where are the women? Where are the men? Where is gender? In asking these questions, such scholars demonstrate the connection between power and gender, and how this connection relates to war (and peace). As Elisabeth Prügl notes, "The question of the relationship of war and gender has animated feminist IR from its beginnings."[13] The gendered hierarchy, in which men and masculinity(ies) are dominant relative to women and femininity(ies), manifests in war. Men are deemed the citizen-warriors and protectors (public sphere), while women are considered the victims and in need of protection (domestic or private sphere). In essence, women and men are positioned differently in any given society.[14] That differentiated positioning gets reflected and reinforced in times of war, particularly in the context of militarized masculinity. As Cynthia Cockburn argues, "War deepens already deep sexual divisions, emphasizing the male as perpetrator of violence, women as victim. In particular, it legitimates male sexual violence, enabling mass rape of women."[15]

Additionally, while mainstream IR focuses on organized violence between warring parties, feminist scholars broaden the definition of war and violence to include the notion of a "continuum of violence." Violence includes domestic violence, sexual violence, state violence, and interstate violence. The evidence shows, for example, that sexual and gender-based violence that occurs during wartime does not necessarily end when the war ends.[16]

Feminist scholars have also shown that while women engage in peace activism (which we discuss in the next section) in times of war, they are also supporters, including engaging in political violence. As we write in a different volume, women serve as combatants, "participating in state-sanctioned violence (as members of militaries) as well as non-state-sanctioned violence (members of rebel groups, paramilitary organizations, and militias, and as suicide bombers). This form of political activism—as combatants rather than as peacemakers—challenges gender norms about women's 'proper' roles and behavior."[17]

As discussed in chapter 1, feminist scholars have incorporated intersectionality in their analysis, including analysis of war and conflict. In the case of civil wars, for example, as Prügl asserts, "A less static understanding of ethnicity, race, nationality and other markers of difference make it possible to think of them as entangled with gender, interacting to become drivers of violent conflict."[18] By way of example, following the terrorist attacks on the United States in 2001 and the subsequent "war on terror," "masculinist protection in the US emerged as gendered and racialized" in which US forces were protecting Afghan women from Afghan men.[19]

An intersectional analysis, one that incorporates findings from critical IR, such as feminist and postcolonial approaches, broadens our definition and understanding of war and violence beyond warring states in interstate wars and warring groups in intrastate wars. War is more than military strategy and doctrine, battlefield deaths and casualties of soldiers, and the threat of force to deter others. War is also about gender, race, and class, as well as ethnicity, and the intersections of these; it is also about violence in the home and violence in and across the state.

WHAT IS PEACE?

Peace is often defined as the absence of war, namely between sovereign states in the international system. Liberal IR approaches support the democratic peace theory, in that democracies do not go to war with each other (see chapter 1). This is a liberal peace, the condition of peace (absence of war) between liberal democracies. Moreover, international institutions are mechanisms by which states can cooperate (rather than engaging in conflict) and thus contribute to peace. For realists, peace emerges as a result of the balance of power between great powers or domination by a hegemon (preponderance of power).[20] And for constructivists, as Oliver Richmond observes, "state behavior is determined by their interests and their identities, this implies that their construction of peace is also determined by their interests and identities."[21] With regard to orthodox (traditional) IR theory, "peace is seen to be something to aspire to although it is perhaps not achievable. This failure rests on human nature for realists, or the failure of institutions for liberals and idealists."[22]

Given these traditional theories, what would such peace look like? When the formal hostilities end in any given conflict (both interstate and intrastate conflicts), the opportunity arises to construct a stable and durable peace. The post-conflict transformation processes involve more than negotiating a formal peace agreement. Such transformations can include legal and political reforms, transitional justice mechanisms, and disarmament, demobilization, and reintegration (DDR) programs.[23] That said, according to Elena B. Stavrevska and Sarah Smith, "both peacebuilding practice and mainstream peace studies literature have predominantly approached the examination of post-war societies in a static and unidimensional manner, portraying events, practices, and actors as fixed in space, time, and identity."[24] In other words, such "a static and unidimensional manner" in ethnic conflicts within states, for example, does not take into account "differences within ethnic groups, be they along class, gender, sexuality, age, geographical, war experiences, political views, or any other lines."[25]

Feminist scholars have had an important impact on our understanding of the concept of "peace" as a condition that is more than simply the absence of armed conflict or war. It is this larger understanding of peace that is especially relevant when we look at the case of Northern Ireland later in this chapter. The more expansive understanding of peace is indicated in the UN-sponsored Third World Conference on Women, held in Nairobi in 1985. At that conference, the definition of peace is "not only the absence of war, violence and hostilities at the national and international levels but also the enjoyment of economic and social justice, equality and the entire range of human rights and fundamental freedoms within society."[26] And a range of feminist authors "define peace as the elimination of insecurity and danger" and as "relations between people based on 'trust, cooperation and recognition of the interdependence and importance of the common good and mutual interests of all peoples.'"[27]

Feminist scholars also make clear that the peace that often emerges after a war has ended is a gendered peace. According to Donna Pankhurst, a gendered peace is one in which women "suffer a *backlash* against any new-found freedoms, and they are forced 'back' into kitchens and fields" (emphasis in original).[28] Here the work of Jane Parpart is also useful when she writes about "the gap between promises of a more gender-equal future and realities on the ground during and after conflicts."[29] The example of women and the Afghan peace process in the decade following the US invasion of Afghanistan and the ouster of the ruling Taliban in 2001 is instructive of intersectionality and peace. Althea-Maria Rivas and Mariam Safi show how calls for Afghan women's participation in the peace talks in the period 2010–2014 "offered little consideration of the hopes and concerns of Afghan women themselves, or of the structural and intersectional dynamics of the local context that influenced their engagement with the peace process."[30] More than sixteen hundred delegates participated in the peace talks ("Peace Jirga") held in June 2010. Only as a result of advocacy by women's groups based in Kabul were women included as delegates. And even then, Rivas and Safi argue that while women were represented at the Peace Jirga, it "was more symbolic than substantive."[31] Whether at the "national or subnational levels . . . women were regularly marginalized and excluded."[32] As a result, the subsequent peace framework focused on a series of activities, such as "encouraging insurgents to renounce violence, increasing security in districts and provinces (as the threat and presence of insecurity were most evident at the subnational level), initiating a countrywide debate on the political approaches to peace and promoting regional cooperation for peaceful coexistence."[33] Women had limited, if any, participation in these efforts. For example, they "were often excluded from decisions regarding the acceptance or rejection of the reintegration of insurgents at the local level." This stemmed in large part from restrictions placed on their travel, "and shame and honour factors prevented women working in the PPCs [provincial peace committees] from participating in negotiation and grievance resolution efforts."[34] It is also important to note that not all Afghan women supported the women involved in the formal peace process.[35] Interviews with Afghan women revealed "that the diversity of women from all sectors was not adequately represented. . . . The women in the security sector noted frustration at the omission of their perspectives from the process." Moreover, in the discussions with the Afghan women, those in the security sector noted that they "were excluded not only by the peace process and its female leadership, but also from the wider gender discourse promoted by women outside the process."[36] This example shows how important it is to unpack what is meant by peace, who participates and how in peace processes, and what peacebuilding entails using an intersectional lens.

In studying peace, it is also important to move beyond the essentialist notion that "peace is a woman's issue." What is important here is the fact that a situation of peace means different things to different people. Not all groups, and not all women, envision peace the same way, although there are certain commonalities, such as the need for trust, feeling of security, need to move forward after conflict, etc. Again, this is where moving beyond just looking at women (or men) as a single category becomes important. As we will see in the case of Northern Ireland, to working-class women who were most affected by the violence of the Troubles, "peace" meant something different than it did for middle-class women, many of whom could escape the worst of the violence. Different ages/generations understood the notion of peace to mean different things because of their own history and experiences. Even different ethnicities, within a largely homogeneous population, experienced the conflict and therefore peace in different ways. And of course, peace meant something different if you were Catholic/Republican or Protestant/Loyalist.

WAR AND PEACE FROM AN INTERSECTIONAL PERSPECTIVE: HUMAN SECURITY

Understanding "security" is an important part in addressing the critical concepts of war and peace. In traditional IR terms, one of the core values of any country is ensuring the safety and protection of the population, or ensuring its security. Generally, as noted earlier, this is thought of in military terms—that is, having enough weapons and the capability to use those weapons to deter any country from attacking or, should an attack occur, ensuring that it will be met and repelled.

According to the United Nations, "For many people, today's world is an insecure place, full of threats on many fronts. Protracted crises, violent conflicts, natural disasters, persistent poverty, epidemics and economic downturns impose hardships and undercut prospects for peace, stability, and sustainable development. Such crises are complex, entailing multiple forms of human insecurity. When they overlap, they can grow exponentially, spilling into all aspects of people's lives, destroying entire communities and crossing national borders."[37] This broader definition of security, human security (and human insecurity, as highlighted by the UN quote above), encourages us to think about what "security" means in a different and more capacious way, that is, an "inclusive definition of security."[38] As Jill Steans proffers, "The security of all people is deemed to be equally important, regardless of nationality and/or citizenship."[39]

Anne Runyan and V. Spike Peterson highlight two factors to account for the redefinition of security in the IR field with the end of the Cold War. One factor is that states were encountering new "threats" to their security, for example, from the impact of globalization and a warming climate. The other factor they point to involves "recognized notions of security arising from critical perspectives (including feminist ones) entering the field, which pointed out that state security often compromised the welfare of people and the planet."[40] There is little doubt that feminist scholars, as Runyan and Peterson point out, increased our understanding of security by encouraging us to ask "Where are the women?" Yet, as noted in chapter 1, women are not a monolithic group. As Laura Shepherd notes in her discussion of feminist security studies, gender is one identity category, but it is only one and it is far from fixed. For example, in her discussion of sexualized violence, Shepherd further claims, "We cannot simply take the subject of 'victim' and assume homogeneity across contexts. These subjects will be differently gendered and racialized, situated differently within operative power structures in the local context and mobilized differently within the policy contexts that aim to ameliorate suffering."[41] Steans enumerates sources of security and insecurity: "The security of all people matters, regardless of race, class, gender or citizenship status. There are multiple sources of insecurity; 'threats' to security vary according to the gender, class, race or nationality of the individual."[42]

In her work on the securitization of human rights, for example, Katherine Brown makes an important point about security: "Security therefore is not an objective condition, but a sustained strategic practice aimed at convincing others that a specific development is threatening and risky, requiring immediate action. The process by which this occurs, and how issues and groups are absorbed into the 'security drama,' is referred to as 'securitization.'"[43] What is especially important, though, is her assertion that "feminists who theorize this area note that *securitization measures are constituted and experienced differentially by class, location, race, religion and gender*" (emphasis added).[44] Once again, this argues for the importance of an intersectional analysis, incorporating a range of variables and the interaction among them for elucidating the concept of "security," especially human security, and how different groups might perceive the term differently. Or, as articulated by Runyan and Peterson, "Thus, gendering, racialization, classing, and sexualizing go on unabated (and become even more pronounced) in order to affix blame and control, contain, and quarantine these new 'threats.'"[45] An example they give that supports this point is how "racial profiling becomes a weapon in the 'war on terror'"[46] or, in a more recent example, the ways in which the US government under former president Trump equated the COVID-19 pandemic with the "China flu," thereby prompting attacks against Americans who appeared to be Asian.

What all this tells us is that we need to rethink and reexamine the concepts of war, peace, and security from a broader perspective than the ones advanced in traditional IR and even beyond that advocated by scholars of feminist security studies for a more complete understanding of these concepts. It also suggests the importance of going beyond stereotypes and myths to examine questions of war, peace, and security as they fit within the canon of IR theory.

In the next section we examine the Women, Peace and Security (WPS) agenda as it emerged from UN Security Council Resolution 1325 (UNSCR 1325). By labeling it as the *Women*, Peace and Security agenda, the focus shifts to women, and presumes that women are a homogeneous group. While this resolution did promote the role of women regarding peace and war, it minimized differences among women, as well as other groups affected by war, and the need to participate in the peace process.

THE WOMEN, PEACE AND SECURITY AGENDA
AND UNSCR 1325

When the Beijing Conference (Fourth World Conference on Women) was held in 1995, growing international attention was being given to the civil conflicts that had emerged in the wake of the end of the Cold War. For example, the war in the Balkans, with its ethnic cleansing and public attention given to women as refugees and rape as a weapon of war, made apparent the concerns regarding the impact of conflict on women and children. The UN Security Council, in passing Resolution 1325 unanimously in 2000, recognized both the impact of war on women and also the contributions that women could make in conflict prevention and resolution and in building sustainable peace. As a result, the Security Council affirmed

> the important role of women in the prevention and resolution of conflicts and in peace-building and *stressing* the importance of their equal participation and full involvement in all efforts for the maintenance and promotion of peace and security, and the need to increase their role in decision-making with regard to conflict prevention and resolution. (emphasis in original)[47]

TEXTBOX 2.1

SELECTED UN SECURITY COUNCIL RESOLUTIONS
GROWING FROM UNSCR 1325

There are two groups of UN Security Council resolutions that encompass the Women, Peace and Security (WPS) agenda. According to the UN, the first group focuses on "women's active and effective participation in peacemaking and peacebuilding." These resolutions begin with 1325 (2000) and include SCR 1889 (2013), SCR 2122 (2013), SCR 2242 (2015), and SCR 2483 (2019). The second group of resolutions "aims to prevent and address conflict-related sexual violence (CRSV)." Beginning with S/RES/1820 (2008), four other resolutions are in this second group: S/RES/1888 (2009), S/RES/1960 (2010), S/RES/2106 (2013), and S/RES/2467 (2019).[48] Below are highlights from some of those resolutions.

1325 (2000): *Urges* Member States to ensure increased representation of women at all decision-making levels of national, regional and international institutions and mechanisms for the prevention, management, and resolution of conflict.[49]

1820 (2008): *Urges* appropriate regional and sub-regional bodies in particular to consider developing and implementing policies, activities, and advocacy for the benefit of women and girls affected by sexual violence in armed conflict.[50]

1888 (2009): *Reaffirms* the role of the Peacebuilding Commission in promoting inclusive gender-based approaches to reducing instability in post-conflict situations, noting the important role of women in rebuilding society, and urges the Peacebuilding Commission to encourage all parties in the countries on its agenda to incorporate and implement measures to reduce sexual violence in post-conflict strategies.[51]

2122 (2013): *Recognizes* the need for timely information and analysis on the impact of armed conflict on women and girls, the role of women in peacebuilding and the gender dimensions of peace processes and conflict resolution for situations on the Council's agenda.[52]

2493 (2019): *Urges* Member States to commit to implementing the Women, Peace and Security agenda and its priorities by ensuring and promoting the full, equal and meaningful participation of women in all stages of peace processes, including through mainstreaming a gender perspective, and remain committed to increasing the number of civilian and uniformed women in peacekeeping at all levels and in key positions.[53]

The WPS agenda "focuses on changing the culture and values that have historically precluded women and women-inclusive policies from broader acceptance within the national security apparatus" of individual states.[54] Or, put another way, it makes women an integral part of a state's national security, broadly defined. Specifically, UNSCR 1325 rests on four pillars: Participation, Conflict Prevention, Protection and Relief, and Recovery. Important research findings regarding the conflict prevention pillar show "that states that have higher levels of gender equality (political, social and economic) are less likely to resort to the use of force in relation to engagement with other states."[55] Research also shows "that the security of women is one of the most reliable indicators of the peacefulness of the state. Where peace is understood as being more than simply the absence of armed conflict."[56] Addressing these four pillars is essential to ensuring that conflict can be avoided and that, if there is a conflict or war, a lasting peace will be sustained—such a lasting peace includes guaranteeing gender equality for women.

This point argues for the importance of including women, especially in the peace processes that will determine the direction of the society after the conflict ends and whether there will indeed be "peace" as well as a sense of security. Research from the Geneva Graduate Institute's Broadening Participation Project is telling, as it "shows that when women's groups were able to effectively influence the process, a peace agreement was almost always reached and the agreement was more likely to be implemented."[57] Studies further demonstrate that when women are included in peace processes, there is "a 20 percent increase in the probability of a peace agreement lasting at least two years. This percentage continues to increase over time, with a 35 percent increase in the probability of a peace agreement lasting fifteen years."[58] Since most decision-makers are men, women's involvement is often determined by men. Despite the often-institutionalized barriers to women's participation, models and strategies have been developed to increase the inclusion of women.[59] And, as a report from the International Peace Institute makes clear, one of the other important impacts of changing the approach in the political transition process to peace is that it can result in "major reforms that transform institutions, structures, and relationships in societies affected by conflict or crises."[60]

Here it is also important to note the difference between the representation of women in formal peace negotiations and the work that women do, and have been doing, at the grassroots level. While barriers exist that limit women's involvement in formal negotiations, women have long been involved in working for peace at the community level, allowing women to "dialogue across difference" that helps build a sense of trust among women. According to Elisabeth Porter, "Women constantly share each other's life stories and the myriad details that make up mundane ordinary lives, shared over the telephone, when walking the children to school, over coffee when borrowing a household item or clothes. Talking through our narratives with those who come from different traditions, communities and regions is crucial to break through the barriers of distrust that too often are based on fear cultivated through ignorance."[61] Women share common concerns and issues that can transcend political differences, thereby allowing them to build bonds of trust that contribute to the sense of security so essential to peace that follows conflict.

At the same time, it is important to recognize that "women" are not a monolithic category, and even when women are included in formal peace negotiations, it generally is up to the (male) decision-makers to determine which women should be included. When they are, which women are selected to participate? Women often do not have the training and background necessary to be active participants in any peace negotiations. Those that do are often educated women who do not necessarily represent the women of the country by ethnicity, race, class, age, etc. If and/or when they are included, their participation is often minimized, as was the case with the Northern Ireland Women's Coalition. Part of the reason for the minimized participation ties to stereotypical attitudes and beliefs, which are deep-seated and difficult to change or address. This is especially true in patriarchal societies where not only gender but also class, ethnicity, and race can be factors.

One of the tenets of UNSCR 1325 was that countries develop National Action Plans (NAPs) to serve as guidelines for the implementation of the resolution. But more than just serving as guidelines, as noted by Laura McLeod, "the goals established within these NAPs are reflective of how the state configures its relationship to conflict and post-conflict." And in her example of Serbia, "the NAP is utilized as a way of demonstrating to the world 'that Serbia is a progressive and forward-thinking state that has dealt with the bulk of the problems caused by the wars of the 1990s.'"[62] Following Serbia's role in the wars in Yugoslavia from 1991 to 1995 and then Kosovo in 1999, this was important symbolically.

UNSCR 1325 played an important role in rethinking what is meant by "security" and was seen as the "document where 'gender' and 'security' intersect," not an insignificant accomplishment.[63]

CRITIQUES OF UNSCR 1325: INTERSECTIONALITY MATTERS

UNSCR 1325 (and the numerous resolutions that followed) has been hailed as critically important for the ways in which it drew attention to the plight of women and girls in times of conflict, but also for its recognition of the important role that women can and do play in preventing conflict and then working toward peace in the event of conflict or war. Few would disagree with the importance of UNSCR 1325 and the points it raises. Nonetheless, there are a number of issues or critiques that can be raised about the resolution more than two decades after it was passed. These are especially salient from an intersectional perspective.

According to a report from the International Peace Institute, in the two decades between 1992 and 2011 "just 2 percent of chief mediators and 9 percent of negotiators in peace processes were women." That period starts eight years before UNSCR 1325 and continues more than a decade after the resolution was adopted. And the report explains that the barriers to women's participation in high-level peacemaking start with a basic dilemma: "If the goal of a peace process is only to end violence, then women—who are rarely the belligerents—are unlikely to be considered legitimate participants. If the goal is to build peace, however, it makes sense to gain more diverse inputs from the rest of society—women and others who will be affected by these decisions."[64]

When looking at the role of women, especially in formal negotiations, there is another important point that must be considered: "Most efforts to advance women's participation in peace processes have been 'from the top down'—directed by governments and elites. The inclusion of women as official signatories or delegates in peace negotiations often has been temporary or their roles have been more symbolic than substantive."[65] Furthermore, as noted previously, the women who are represented at the peace negotiations are not necessarily representative of women within the society as a whole in terms of race, ethnicity, class, and education. That raises questions about who the women in the peace negotiations are and whom they represent. While having women as part of the negotiations certainly seems to have a positive impact on the success as well as endurance of any peace agreement, it can be argued that working from the bottom up, instead of the top down, can have an even greater impact on more women in the society. Perhaps even more important, working from the bottom up might mean including not only women but also other groups within the society who were affected and marginalized by conflict.

Monica McWilliams, one of the women in Northern Ireland who was critical to the creation of the Northern Ireland Women's Coalition (discussed later in the chapter), makes an important point when she notes that existing structures and systems have to change if women are to be included in the decision-making process. Simply saying that women *should* be included is not enough if the existing structures of the society make it impossible for women to participate because of barriers imposed—for example, lack of childcare, access to a political system controlled by men, or their positions are not taken seriously.[66] And the structures will not change unless or until there is enough pressure on the existing decision-makers to make that happen. This can be critical to the reconstruction process necessary to rebuild a society after the conflict ends. Reconstructing a society after conflict and getting to a condition of peace built on trust (as noted above) means recognizing the ways in which *all* groups were affected by the conflict and need to be part of the post-conflict peace process. While the focus on women, as in UNSCR 1325, is important, it is not enough.

One of the other major critiques of UNSCR 1325 is the ways in which the discussions about it tend to ignore or minimize the contributions made by the Global South to the WPS agenda. As Soumita Basu notes, "The Global South is not a mere recipient of policies formulated elsewhere, but can claim 'ownership' of the WPS resolutions as well." Basu continues the argument: "The global narrative of UNSCR 1325 must take account of divergences from the canon—understood as differing interpretations, resistances and subversions—particularly, as these manifest in the Global South, which tends to be marginalized at the international level."[67] This critique also speaks to the argument about intersectionality, including voices from different geographic regions as an important part of assuring that *all* voices are heard and different perspectives represented. As Basu argues, "UNSCR 1325 appears to be a tool that is used by powerful countries, located in the Global North, to establish favorable policies in post-conflict countries, located primarily in the Global South, in the name of gender equality."[68] Nicola Pratt also makes an especially valid point when she notes that "1325 privileges gender above race, class, or other significant relations of power in understanding women's experiences and responses to conflict." She goes on to identify what is absent in 1325, "namely black/postcolonial feminist understandings of women, peace, and war."[69] These critiques once again bring us back to what is lost by looking at issues through a single lens or, put another way, what is gained in explanatory value when we bring in an intersectional perspective. By labeling it as the *Women*, Peace and Security agenda, the focus is on women, and presumes that women are a homogeneous group.

Smith and Stavrevska look at WPS through an intersectional lens and argue, "As intersectionality work shows, categorization based on sex-based difference does not provide a sufficient platform, or sufficient protection, for all women, or all men. Intersectionality work has shown how categorization and subsequent policy based only on sex-based comparison/difference works in favor of those whose race/age/sexuality/ethnicity concerns are already appeased."[70] Part of their argument, then, is that the WPS agenda, as defined by UNSCR 1325 and subsequent resolutions, divides participants into two categories: men and women. The reality is far more complex. "In WPS, then, to categorize differently vulnerable women only in relation to 'women/gender' makes it difficult to account for their interests and needs that may fall outside gender concerns and makes visible that marginalization only where it intersects with 'gender.'" Or, as they succinctly note, "What becomes visible is not the presence of women of color, but their absence."[71] They further argue that "the resolutions fail to grasp or acknowledge the historical and political structures within which conflicts unfold and gendered violence (direct and structural) occurs."[72]

To be truly inclusive, a peace process must go beyond the categories of gender or the binary of men and women to include other groups within the society who have also been affected by the conflict, and who are critical in creating peace and the security needed to ensure that the peace will continue. This also means identifying and addressing the root causes of the violence, Johan Galtung's "structural violence," as part of any discussion of peace.[73] That, in turn, requires a broad range of participants to be included in the peace process, as different groups experience that structural, as well physical, violence of the conflict differently. Similarly, their understanding of what "peace" means will also be different. While UNSCR 1325 and the creation of a WPS agenda was important for the prominence it gave women, it minimizes or disregards not only a range of other variables and categories but also the intersection of them.

In their conclusion, these various authors bring together a number of points that grow from traditional IR, albeit with the feminist perspective injected, and that is the importance of power and power relationships which affect and are in turn affected by different groups in various ways. Hence, looking at WPS through an intersectional lens should include an analysis of who has the power and how that affects the relationships among groups. This same argument can be applied beyond UNSCR 1325 to all the UNSC resolutions that developed from that seminal resolution. While some, such as UNSCR 1889, mention gender as opposed to women, the understanding is that it addresses "women." And all are about the inclusion of women in some aspects of conflict prevention and resolution, as well as peacekeeping. But this minimizes the fact that access to these processes for women is limited, and that those limitations will be greater in some societies than others given issues of culture, race, ethnicity, and other determinants of power. Unless this larger set of conditions or variables are brought into play, understanding the WPS agenda will be confined only to some women.

To summarize, the WPS agenda made great strides toward identifying the critical role that women play in many aspects pertaining to conflict and also peace. Research shows that the presence of women in peace negotiations can not only ensure the success of an agreement but also that it will endure. On the other hand, WPS also essentializes women and the need for them to be protected, rather than seeing them as active agents and participants in these various processes. Perhaps even more important for our purposes, both WPS and International Humanitarian Law, which we will look at more closely in chapter 3, seem to categorize people as a binary, men or women. As we mentioned above, neither women nor men are homogeneous categories, but rather are made up of various intersecting groups that affect who they are and the ways in which they see the world.

From this starting point, we turn to an intersectional analysis of the case of Northern Ireland and the Troubles to illustrate more clearly why and how it is important to bring in a range of variables and categories if we are to get a more complete understanding of the conflict, its causes, who was affected by it, and how "peace" came about.

CASE STUDY: NORTHERN IRELAND

While much of the study of IR focuses on interstate wars, as the example of Russia's invasion of Ukraine in February 2022 (chapter 1) demonstrates, the intrastate violence in Northern Ireland, known as the Troubles, is an example of a conflict within a country. Often described as a religious conflict between Catholics and Protestants, the reality illustrates a far more complex situation, as noted in the brief history below. However, another factor that needs to be considered in what might otherwise appear to be a civil or intrastate conflict is how it can quickly become internationalized. In the case of Northern Ireland, not only was the neighboring state, the Republic of Ireland, affected by the conflict, as were other parts of the United Kingdom, but one could argue that the 1998 Good Friday Agreement would not have been possible without the intervention of the United States and the EU. Looking at the conflict from that perspective, any number of countries were not only affected by the "internal" conflict, but all had a vested interest in seeing a peace agreement reached that would end that violence.

There is a great deal of information available about this conflict; however, there is little from an intersectional perspective explicitly. Understanding the Troubles, both its origins and attempts at peace, must be put within the political, social, and economic context of the time. Doing so illustrates clearly why an intersectional analysis, as opposed to a more traditional IR approach to understanding an intrastate conflict, is a more appropriate explanatory and analytical tool.

Brief Background of the Troubles

The conflict has its origins over the course of several centuries as Protestants migrated from the British Isles to Ireland.[74] Tensions early in the twentieth century in the struggle for Irish independence against the British resulted in 1921 in the division between the independent Republic of Ireland and the six provinces in the north of Ireland that remained under British rule. The subsequent conflict, the Troubles, was seen as a religious conflict between Protestants and Catholics. However, underpinning this division were the economic and civil rights of the Catholics, which were limited by the Protestants, backed by the British government. Thus, while the shorthand for the struggle was a religious fight, in actuality it was a political struggle for equality and civil rights, an economic struggle, and a social conflict. In short, it embodied what Johan Galtung referred to as "structural violence," in that it was a struggle to redress the inherent inequalities that existed between the two groups in Northern Ireland.[75]

In effect, each side saw the conflict differently: To the Catholics, this was a war of independence against the British occupiers for their civil rights; to the Protestants, the violence was a response to an uprising perpetrated against the Crown. That said, Cynthia Cockburn has a different understanding of the distinction between Catholic and Protestant identities, which, to some extent, were "politically manipulated." Constructing and promoting two distinct identities, British and Irish, effectively became utilized in such a way that further divided people.[76]

The modern period of the Troubles began in 1969 following civil rights protests modeled on the civil rights marches in the United States; they quickly became violent, especially in Belfast and Derry (Londonderry). What followed was a period of increasing violence, ultimately making 1972 "the worst year of the troubles," with the "death toll of almost five hundred far exceeding that of any other year."[77] The context is important to understanding the growing politicization of women, especially Republican (Catholic) women, during the period from 1969, when the violence of the Troubles accelerated, through the early 1980s. The British policy of "internment without trial," implemented in 1969, not only further inflamed the situation but also resulted in the imprisonment of more men, ultimately leading to the greater involvement of women, who stepped in to fill the void.[78]

Moreover, despite many attempts to negotiate ceasefires, if not actual peace agreements, this was not achieved until the signing of the Good Friday (Belfast) Agreement (GFA) on April 10, 1998. While "peace" is far from assured, and with the uncertainty that Brexit tensions could grow once again, the GFA did result in the cessation of most of the violence and provided a framework for the future of Northern Ireland.

Understanding the Troubles in Northern Ireland from an Intersectional Perspective

In this case study we ask the following broad question: How did gender, ethnicity, class, race, and even age, as well as religion, affect the conflict and the post-conflict periods in Northern Ireland? Looking beneath the religious identity of Catholic and Protestant, who was involved with perpetrating and supporting the acts of violence? What groups were involved with working for peace at the national level, but also at the community/grassroots level? And how did gender intersect with religion and economics to influence not only the course of the Troubles but also the society that emerged since the signing of the GFA and the advent of "peace"?

Eilish Rooney, writing about Northern Ireland specifically, makes the point about the need for an intersectional analysis: "The paradigm of intersectionality helps to reference how race and/or sect, class and gender work as integrated regimes of inequality in state formation." She then continues, the ways in which this "offers an approach that seeks to identify specific ways that gender and sect are integrated in economic class relations, what the consequences are, and how these may be made visible in order to be remedied. The application of such an analysis could make a difference to understanding conflicts more generally."[79] The point that Rooney makes, and it is an especially important one regarding Northern Ireland, is that we need to go beyond gender or even religion to understand this conflict and bring in other variables, such as race and age/generations, that are not usually associated with Northern Ireland in general and the Troubles in particular but that elucidate aspects of the conflict.

Gender and Class

Much has been written about the role that women played during the Troubles, working for peace especially across the religious and sectarian divide as well as some who were actively engaged with acts of political violence, especially on the Republican (Catholic) side. The former, women working for peace, is more consistent with the gender norms of woman as peaceful by nature, although the reality often belies this stereotype. Nonetheless, in the case of Northern Ireland, there are examples where that gendered assumption holds.

The intersection of gender and class is a common theme within the literature about women working across community lines in Northern Ireland. Hence, an intersectional analysis is helpful in that understanding women's roles in the Troubles cannot be removed from economics and class. This was especially true about working-class women, where Protestant and Catholic women had more in common with one another than each group had with middle- or upper-class women within their own religious community. "Working-class women, both Catholic and Protestant, tend to have the lowest-paid unskilled jobs. And it is the working class which has fewer opportunities, generally lives in segregated communities and has borne the brunt of the impact of the ongoing violence and that has contributed to their political activism."[80] Hence, women's activism at the community level tends to focus on issues of common concern that transcend religious or sectarian differences; examples include childcare, domestic violence, economics, and health care. Or, as summarized by Grainne McCoy, "Women have been described as the 'mainstay of community groups,'. . . whose activities have helped to hold the society together through years of great adversity."[81] It was "the health and well-being of their families" that motivated women to organize and engage in activism in order to improve "social, welfare and environmental policies."[82]

Cynthia Cockburn approaches the issue of commonality across the communities in a slightly different way when she addresses the working-class communities, and the ways in which economics were gendered. "There are, however, three things the two working class communities share: *poverty*, *violence*, and *political neglect*. And women of those communities experience all three in a distinctive, gendered, way" (emphasis in original).[83] The common experiences of poverty, violence, and political neglect shared by women in working-class communities created an environment that allowed them to work together at the community level transcending the sectarian divide.

Further, according to Carmel Roulston, "women in both Catholic and Protestant areas also mobilized against paramilitary violence on occasion. Poverty and poor housing also provoked campaigns in which women took initiatives. . . . Women became involved in such campaigns as the guardians of family life and in the interests of the community rather than as fighters for women's benefits."[84] Thus, although they did not work for peace per se, at least in the sense of working to end the Troubles at the national level, they did work across the communal divisions in order to build the trust that was necessary to ultimately bring peace or, at the very least, diminish the violence. Put another way, this grassroots activism allowed women to have some control and effect change even as they were excluded from "big-P" politics.

This is not to suggest that ending the violence of the Troubles was not a priority for women, but simply that, especially for working-class women, having access to the formal political system in a way in which they could actually have an impact seemed out of reach. Where they were involved at the community level, women generally were underrepresented in national-level politics for a host of reasons. Here context is important. Northern Ireland is a fairly conservative patriarchal society where women's roles were defined primarily in the private sphere, especially as wives and mothers. Relatedly, in examining women's roles in Northern Ireland, and more generally gender, it is important to consider sexuality. In this case, as well as many other ethnonationalist conflicts, women's roles as mothers and wives made clear the connection between heterosexuality and ethnonationalism.[85]

It is also important to remember that amidst the violence, there were pockets of relative peace and stability, which illustrate the importance of viewing the Troubles through a broader intersectional lens. For example, Eamon Collins identifies the town of Warrenpoint, which he describes as "cocooned and relatively prosperous. Middle-class Catholics and Protestants lived in harmony united . . . by their class interests in maintaining their high standard of living. The Catholics were in a majority, yet the IRA hardly ever attracted recruits from the town."[86] In this case, we see the role that economics and class played through the protection of these groups' interests. In effect, class explains why some groups were relatively protected from the violence or chose to not become directly involved because of self-interest.

While much of women's political activism centered on the community, as noted above, the area in which women could establish commonalities, there were also women who desired to do more specifically to work for peace and an end to the violence at the national level. This was extremely challenging for women, who not only had to break into the political (public) realm but who also had been systematically excluded from the formal peace process.

While some women and women's groups did play a role, it was the Northern Ireland Women's Coalition (NIWC) that was critical in negotiating the GFA and serves as an example of the importance of understanding an intersectional approach. The NIWC was created in 1996 "as a cross-community party, founded on human rights, inclusion and equality," and to "bring a voice of common sense and a new approach to traditional problems in Northern Ireland."[87] But perhaps of greater importance, they wanted to make sure that women had a seat at the table when the GFA was being negotiated, and therefore that women's voices were included in the discussion and the agreement that was reached.

What is especially instructive in the case of the NIWC and its approach to negotiating peace was its belief that solving the political problems that manifested in the violence of the Troubles required a deeper understanding of the underlying issues that caused that violence, and then finding ways to address them. They were also concerned about the exclusion of women from mainstream politics and firmly believed that there would not be a lasting peace unless or until women could bring their ideas to the table.

While the NIWC was a group of women working together for a common cause, it is also important to remember that they were by no means monolithic. As Kate Fearon and Monica McWilliams, two members of the NIWC, described it, "The members of the NIWC, coming from many religious, cultural and political backgrounds, were to find that they disagreed profoundly with each other over the ways to resolve social and political problems."[88] The women also had very different educational and economic backgrounds. But they sought to address those differences through discussion and an exchange of ideas consistent with the goals of the NIWC.

Despite the differences they had, the representatives to the GFA negotiations believed strongly that peace could not be achieved unless or until the underlying causes of the structural violence that plagued the country were addressed. This was not to happen, however; the men at the talks, the majority of the participants, focused instead on such issues as demobilizing and disarming the militias, which were seen as part of the problem. Their belief was that if you disband and disarm the militias, there would be peace, or at least the violence would recede. That stands in direct contrast to the approach taken by the women, which was that these were only symptoms of the underlying structural problems. While that larger issue was not addressed, the NIWC did achieve its goal of making sure that women were represented at the talks and that all voices could be heard. The two representatives from the NIWC were the only women at the negotiations table.

The "peace" that followed the signing of the GFA did not bring a complete absence of violence in Northern Ireland, although many of the most overt instances of violence did disappear. It did not address the larger underlying issues or how to knit a divided country back together to create the sense of trust and security so important to the concept of peace. As Colin Coulter et al. note, "A vast body of work documenting the many instances of violence against women in the aftermath of, and of course during, war challenges the conventional discourse of 'post-conflict' or a 'return to normal.' . . . While the GFA is lauded by many for ending decades of 'violence,' increased levels of domestic and sexual violence in the aftermath of the 1994 ceasefires and the [Good Friday] agreement serve to illustrate the androcentric and state-centric orthodoxies which underpin the partial peace. In Northern Ireland, violence specifically directed against women and girls—rape, trafficking, abuse in the home—appears to be growing rather than diminishing with the 'peace.'"[89] This further underscores the tenuous relationship between the signing of a peace agreement and stable peace, especially for women in general and women of lower economic status in particular.

Race and Ethnicity[90]

Northern Ireland is fairly homogeneous racially and ethnically; as of the 2021 census, nearly 97 percent of the population is Caucasian (White); ethnic minorities comprise slightly more than 3 percent of the population, with 0.6 percent Black, 0.5 percent Chinese, and 0.5 percent Indian.[91] This demographic means that when thinking about Northern Ireland, the onset of the Troubles, and the divides that explain the violence, generally the assumption is that the analysis will be on religion and/or gender, not ethnicity or race. And although the non-White population is quite small, what is meant by race and racism in this setting—an intersectional analysis—will provide a more comprehensive picture of the inequalities within Northern Ireland that go beyond just the religious divide and help explain the violence and post-conflict society.

In a review of some of the literature on race and ethnicity in Ireland—both Northern Ireland and the Republic of Ireland—scholars focus on race in several ways. First, race and ethnicity in the context of migration, starting in the nineteenth century. Here, examples cited include Jews settling in Belfast, Dublin, and Cork. In the twentieth century, immigrants from China and Poland settled in both parts of Ireland, with a "wave of Chinese immigration" into both the Republic and Northern Ireland in the 1960s. The removal of visa requirements for people from countries that joined the EU in 2004 effectively increased emigration from Poland and Lithuania so that "by 2011, there were 81,318 migrants in Northern Ireland not from elsewhere in the UK or the Republic." Nearly a quarter were from Poland (19,658).[92] As Bryan Fanning and Lucy Michael note, focusing specifically on Northern Ireland, there are the "legacies of colonial racism and the relationship between racism and sectarianism."[93] They continue that "the persistent pattern of organized racist violence in predominantly Unionist areas [Protestant] areas has made this politically difficult to address in the context of shared government."[94] This relationship is often ignored or simply overlooked in any study of Northern Ireland and the violence of the Troubles.

In Northern Ireland during this period, racism manifested in the emergence of far-right groups such as Combat 18, which was tied to the Local Ulster Volunteer Force (UVF), an extremist Protestant militia group that attacked immigrant communities, especially those of color. Hence, racism and sectarianism are directly linked.[95]

Thus, we can conclude that the sectarian divide impacts understandings of how race is addressed in the Republic of Ireland and Northern Ireland, if at all. As Fanning and Michael assert, "Understandings of and responses to racism in Northern Ireland have been influenced by political priorities of addressing sectarianism. . . . Sectarian politics make cross-community consensus on how to define racism almost impossible. Simply put, nationalist politicians support definitions of racism which include unionist sectarianism, a perspective that has been supported by the predominant literature on racism in Northern Ireland." What this means is that "the persistent hold of sectarianism in the region has meant that anti-racist campaigns have often been characterized by partisanship and failure to translate into cross-community engagement."[96]

In the context of the violence of the Troubles, which was the focus for the government and civil society, addressing racism was not a priority, if it was addressed at all. Fanning and Michael conclude, "An imbalance of power prevails in which black, ethnic minority and immigrant communities are politically marginalized and in both jurisdictions are dependent upon the goodwill of a civil society that is influenced by transnational anti-racist norms and which speaks on behalf of rather than represents those experiencing racism."[97]

The second way that race and ethnicity can be analyzed in the Northern Ireland context is in considering the link between sectarianism and racism. In their 2007 article (nine years after the signing of the Good Friday Agreement), Robbie McVeigh and Bill Rolston put forward an interesting claim about the relationship between sectarianism and race in Northern Ireland when they write that sectarianism is "a form of racism. Sectarianism is rooted firmly in the process of British imperialism in Ireland. The British conquest of Ireland led to a specific power structure linked to the imperialist project. . . . All of this [dispossession of land, subordination of Irish administration, etc.] was justified and advanced by a racial ideology that suppressed the indigenous population on account of their supposed moral, intellectual and other failings." But perhaps the most telling part of their analysis lies in this statement: "The main signifier of the racialization of the Irish was that of religion: the native Irish were Catholics and the colonizers Protestant."[98] To further support their argument, they note that "we know enough about racism now to realize that it is not a natural outcome of skin color differences, but a social process that selects skin color or some other real, exaggerated or imaginary characteristic as the mark of difference."[99]

According to their analysis, the 1998 Good Friday Agreement "institutionalized sectarianism" as the political parties identify, effectively, as nationalist or unionist.[100] As they note, "The GFA did not usher in an era of instant peace. It is not merely that sectarian divisions and practices live on; the apparent paradox is that both have been exacerbated in peacetime."[101] Where the Good Friday Agreement seemed to bring with it the *promise* of peace, or at least a halt if not an end to the violence, it again raises the issue of what does "peace" mean? And "whose peace?" And, as McVeigh and Rolston assert, "Racism has risen exponentially in Northern Ireland in the years since the GFA," and with that, has come awareness of racism, which had been obscured by the religious and sectarian violence of the Troubles.[102]

Additionally, Adele Lee makes an important point about race, ethnic minorities, and the sectarian violence that has plagued Northern Ireland, specifically in Belfast: "Sectarian tensions have overshadowed the plight of ethnic minorities in Belfast—a city which, unbeknown to many, has been home to substantial numbers of Chinese, Indian and Pakistani migrants since the 1960s."[103] These are the legacy of the British colonial empire. And with the signing of the Good Friday Agreement, coupled with the expansion of the EU in 2004, "Belfast has experienced a new influx of migrants, mostly in the form of Polish and Lithuanian workers."[104] Understanding this reinforces the important point that when we consider people's identity, it "is much more complex than a simple Catholic-Protestant dichotomy after all."[105] Hence the need for an intersectional analysis that goes far beyond a simple gender and/or religious analysis. But she makes another important point here: that migrants would choose to travel to Belfast may be a function of their recognition that the city is a destination given that the worst of the sectarian violence has ended.[106] Inherent in this is also the understanding that Belfast's growth and recognition as a "new capitalist city" is due, in no small measure, to its cultural diversity and "greater tolerance of difference."[107] In her conclusion, Lee notes, "While in many ways, the changing racial make-up of Belfast reinforces the common perception of the city as a place of violence and bigotry, the new ethnic diversity has the potential to destabilize entrenched sectarianism, provide an 'antidote' to dominant discourses, and reconfigure the city away from its association with the Troubles." Although, even with the changes, Lee notes that "Belfast is still a society marked/marred by sectarian bifurcation."[108]

Much of the literature on race and racism in the two Irelands does not explicitly use an intersectional analysis in the sense of linking race to gender or other critical variables. And yet we can see issues of race and ethnicity at play in this case study, which further explain what might otherwise be seen as simply a religious conflict.

Age/Generations

While age is not often seen as a critical variable to understand a conflict, it comes into play in the case of Northern Ireland. This intersection can be seen in a number of ways. First, members of a generation that came of age during the period of the Troubles were socialized by older members of their family. While this was true of men, where it is often demonstrated that the family had an impact on subsequent generations, it is also true of women. For example, this can be seen quite clearly in the case of sisters Marian and Dolours Price, who became known for the violent role they played on behalf of the IRA. They were raised in a staunch Republican household; their parents shared a strong commitment to the nationalist cause and "the belief that for hundreds of years the British had been an occupying force on the island of Ireland—and that the Irish had a duty to expel them by any means necessary."[109] The sisters grew up with a belief system they internalized. Marian and Dolours became known for their role in the London bombing of the Old Bailey, but also for their ongoing and often violent support of the nationalist movement. In this case, we see the role that age and also the transmission of values across generations played in perpetuating the violence of the Troubles. It also gives us another insight into the gender roles that these women defied, thereby increasing our understanding of who was perpetuating violence and why.

Second, just as the civil rights movement in Northern Ireland was influenced by the one in the United States, so a generation of women coming of age in the 1970s during the Troubles were part of the transnational feminist movement, and they started to demand a greater role in the struggle as a result. The women's movement in Ireland had its genesis in the Republic and quickly spread to the North and "should be seen in the wider context of the international climate of change and protest which witnessed the emergence of the civil rights movement, mass protests against the Vietnam War in America, and student demonstrations in major American and European cities."[110] In a relatively traditional society, however, women's involvement in the struggle, especially among young women, was also met with derision in the press. One "exclusive" to the *Sunday World* newspaper starts: "Women's Lib in parts of the North is far removed from bra-burning females in New York and London. In Dublin, Women's Lib means pro-contraception legislation and demands for job equality. But, up North, liberation for some women means a pistol stuck in the waistbands of their skirts, or an Armalite carbine tucked down the leg of their jeans."[111] The main point, though, is that women, especially young women, were becoming more politicized and involved with the struggle publicly.

Myrtle Hill describes the ways in which women's politicization resulted in more active involvement. "Young women were recruited at street barricades and moved from stone-throwing to training in surveillance and the use of weapons. . . . However, many of this new generation, highly politicized by current events, demanded a more central involvement, and responded quickly when the IRA itself began to recruit women."[112] As noted by Azrini Wahidin, "The increasing number of women involved in the IRA was resisted by some men but was driven by a number of factors: changing gender attitudes, pressure from the women, recognition by the leadership for the need to have some military-trained women as more young men were interned or died in combat, and there was a strategic need to have more fighters. This, and the fact that IRA male officers were providing women with military training, led to women becoming integrated into the IRA, particularly from the mid-1970s onwards."[113] This also meant that women were being arrested and interned along with men; between 1973, when women started to be interned, and 1975, thirty-three women were held at Armagh Prison, the only women's prison in Northern Ireland.[114] Women wanted and were given an increasing role in the violence and, like men, paid a price for their involvement.

According to Niall Gilmartin's interviews with Republican women combatants, when they spoke of the IRA, they depicted "an organization that strictly adhered to very patriarchal definitions of masculine and feminine roles within a militant movement . . . so the armed struggle represented a site of perpetual struggle for republican women to be acknowledged and accepted as equal participants."[115] In his interviews, Gilmartin found that although the women saw the struggle as a "fight for national independence and self-determination," they also saw the relationship between what they were fighting for and the society that would later emerge. The interviewees stressed that "peace and equality also means education, resisting austerity and challenging the subordinate position of women."[116] For young women especially, then, there was a direct relationship between the future of the country and their own future, both of which were worth fighting for.

A third way in which we see the impact of age/generations as an important variable is looking at the generation that has come of age since the Good Friday Agreement was signed. Unlike the Price sisters, brought up in a household in which the struggle against the British was a constant reality, or the "women's lib" generation that saw their own future tied to that of the country, this generation came of age at a time when the worst of the violence was over and "peace" was the norm. "Time series data on public attitudes . . . reveal a growing cohort of those who are non-aligned politically, those who are of no religion, those who have dual nationality, and those who were born outside Northern Ireland. They also show a fairly stark generational divide in terms of attitudes and political identities and engagement."[117] What is relevant here is that over a ten-year period, University of Liverpool Northern Ireland General Election Surveys "found that major attitudinal divides are not along traditional lines but between younger and older and voters and non-voters—younger people being less likely to vote." One conclusion is that "younger people are growing up in a society no longer afflicted by the levels and intensity of political violence that their parents experienced."[118] Younger respondents did not see the world in the same binary terms as their parents' generation, and they are more diverse in terms of their own identities and communities, leading to the conclusion that "Northern Ireland is a society not just of two communities but of many."[119] This too reinforces the importance of looking at the Troubles and questions about the peace that followed the signing of the Good Friday Agreement in intersectional terms that take age, among other variables, into account.

Northern Ireland Since the GFA

While the GFA resulted in the decommissioning of arms, the reality is that the threat of violence remains just below the surface, exacerbated by Brexit in 2016 and the sense that the Loyalist/Protestant community has "lost" while the Republicans/Catholics have "won."[120] At various times, that violence has become real, shocking those who had thought the country had moved on and was at relative peace. Northern Ireland struggles to deal with its past and with what peace really means. "While Northern Ireland is certainly no longer at war, it does not even now seem to be a society that is entirely at peace with itself."[121] Despite the creation of commissions and a number of initiatives designed to address aspects of the reconciliation process since 1998, recent history has shown that divisions remain just beneath the surface. The legacy of the thirty years of the Troubles supports the contention that "peace" is far more than just signing an agreement but, as noted earlier in the chapter, must be tied to a condition of trust and sense of security for all members of the society.

This case study illustrates clearly the increased explanatory value related to understanding an intrastate conflict when it is examined from an intersectional perspective. While much has been written about the role of women during the Troubles, both working for peace and supporting the violence, that minimizes or ignores the additional information that can be gleaned by also examining factors such as age/generations and even race and ethnicity (and how these relate to the legacy of colonialism and empire), as all factor into an understanding of the continuation of the violence and tensions to some extent.

CONCLUSION

We started this chapter by addressing some of the most important concepts in IR: war, peace, and security. In so doing, we discussed briefly how traditional IR theories approach these issues, and the limitations of those approaches. An intersectional perspective, as offered by feminist scholars, for example, provides a more nuanced analysis and understanding of war, peace, and security. The shift from narrow conceptions of state security and survival to human security illustrates the importance of intersectionality. The Women, Peace and Security (WPS) agenda that developed and evolved from UNSCR 1325 was an important step in broadening the conception of security and peace to include women's participation in peace negotiations and post-conflict reconstruction efforts. At the same time, as other postcolonial feminist scholars have pointed out, UNSCR 1325 and the WPS agenda were also flawed in many ways. The case study of the Troubles in Northern Ireland provided a way to illustrate clearly why an intersectional approach provides broader answers to some of the basic questions about conflicts and peace, why and how the members of society engage in political violence, and why it is then often so difficult to reconcile and create a true condition of peace.

The next chapter grows logically from the work in this chapter, as we move into a discussion of intersectionality, human rights, and humanitarian intervention, issues that are present in situations of war/conflict and the quest for peace.

Chapter 3

Intersectionality, Human Rights, and Humanitarian Intervention

It is virtually impossible to talk about the issues of war, security, and peace that were discussed in chapter 2 without also talking about human rights and the violations of human rights that all too often take place during war and conflict. This chapter focuses on human rights and humanitarian intervention, and the connection to international law. Human rights as a concept evolved over time, highlighted in the UN Charter and the 1948 Universal Declaration of Human Rights (UDHR). Other human rights agreements and conventions have followed, such as the International Covenant on Civil and Political Rights, which focuses on specific rights such as freedom of assembly. With regard to women's rights, the 1979 Convention on the Elimination of All Forms of Discrimination Against Women (CEDAW) is presented in this chapter as a case study of an international agreement analyzed from an intersectional perspective. Moreover, as a result of the human rights violations that occurred during the civil wars in Bosnia and Rwanda in the 1990s, the international community responded with the establishment of the Responsibility to Protect (R2P) doctrine in 2005. Both CEDAW and R2P have laudable goals, and yet both are limited, as this chapter will show.

In considering human rights, international humanitarian law, and humanitarian intervention, IR theories differ in their assumptions and conclusions. For realists, given the anarchic international system in which states are sovereign, those governments that engage in human rights violations against their own populations can look to international law to protect them, essentially ensuring that other states cannot intervene in their domestic affairs. Moreover, international law is only as effective as its enforcement, and that relies on the states themselves, as there is no greater political authority to enforce international law. In contrast, liberal institutionalists can point to various international treaties and conventions that states have ratified and thus promote and protect human rights. Constructivist IR can tell us about how international human rights norms have emerged and become institutionalized in both domestic and international law.[1] As we show in this chapter, feminist and postcolonial scholars encourage us to analyze human rights, international humanitarian law, and humanitarian intervention using an intersectional lens.

HUMAN RIGHTS AS A CONCEPT AND A NORM

The concept of human rights—that individuals have inherent rights and freedoms—is not new, as evidenced by England's Magna Carta in the thirteenth century, the American Declaration of Independence in 1776, and the 1789 French Declaration of the Rights of Man and Citizen. Rights such as free speech, free association, and the right to vote, as well as socioeconomic rights within countries, emerged over time.[2] The movement to abolish slavery in the nineteenth century can be considered "the first successful human rights campaign" and led to the abolition of the slave trade.[3] The League of Nations established the International Labor Organization (ILO) in 1919 to protect workers' rights.[4] While these are all clearly examples of measures to protect human rights, they addressed specific states (United States, France) or issues (slavery). It was only with the horrors of the Second World War, namely the abuses that the international system witnessed from Hitler's Germany and the extermination of Jews, Roma, homosexuals, and others, that an international consensus emerged with the establishment of the United Nations in 1945.[5] As Frans Viljoen asserts, "The core system of human rights promotion and protection under the United Nations has a dual basis: the UN Charter, adopted in 1945, and a network of treaties subsequently adopted by UN members."[6] The Commission on Human Rights, which was mandated by the UN Charter, led to "the elaboration and near-universal acceptance of the three major international human rights instruments: the Universal Declaration of Human Rights, [and] the International Covenant on Civil and Political Rights (ICCPR) and the International Covenant on Economic, Social and Cultural Rights (ICESCR)."[7]

In 1948 the UN General Assembly approved the Universal Declaration of Human Rights (UDHR). This document not only set forth the idea that there are basic rights and freedoms to which everyone is entitled but also became the basis for international humanitarian law and human rights law. This built on generations of theories and beliefs about human rights as those that are given to all individuals and that the government cannot take away. These human rights norms fit within the liberal theoretical tradition, although the basic premises are generally universally accepted. The understanding of these rights has been expanded over time to include not only the rights of individuals but also the rights of groups, especially ethnic and/or Indigenous minorities, with the Declaration on the Rights of Persons Belonging to Ethnic, Religious and Linguistic Minorities (1992) and the Declaration on the Rights of Indigenous Peoples (2007), respectively.[8] According to Karen Mingst, those rights include "the right to a safe environment, the right to peace and human security, the right to live in a democracy."[9] It should be self-evident that not all countries and/or governments agree with these aspirational rights, nor do they adhere to them.

TEXTBOX 3.1

UNIVERSAL DECLARATION OF HUMAN RIGHTS PREAMBLE

The Universal Declaration of Human Rights, passed in 1948, was an attempt to set standards for human rights internationally and prevent their systematic violation. The document "represents the universal recognition that basic rights and fundamental freedoms are inherent to all human beings, inalienable and equally applicable to everyone, and that every one of us is born free and equal in dignity and rights. Whatever our nationality, place of residence, gender, national or ethnic origin, color, religion, or any other statism, the international community on December 10, 1948, made a commitment to upholding dignity and justice of all of us."[10]

Preamble: Whereas recognition of the inherent dignity and of the equal and inalienable rights of all members of the human family is the foundation of freedom, justice and peace in the world,

Whereas disregard and contempt for human rights have resulted in barbarous acts which have outraged the conscience of mankind, and the advent of a world in which human beings shall enjoy freedom of speech and belief and freedom from fear and want has been proclaimed as the highest aspiration of the common people,

Whereas it is essential, if man is not to be compelled to have recourse, as a last resort, to rebellion against tyranny and oppression, that human rights should be protected by the rule of law,

Whereas it is essential to promote the development of friendly relations between nations,

Whereas the peoples of the United Nations have in the Charter reaffirmed their faith in fundamental human rights, in the dignity and

worth of the human person and in the equal rights of men and women
and have determined to promote social progress and better standards
of life in larger freedom,
Whereas Member States have pledged themselves to achieve, in cooperation with the United Nations, the promotion of universal respect for
and observance of human rights and fundamental freedoms,
Whereas a common understanding of these rights and freedoms is of the
greatest importance for the full realization of this pledge,
Now, therefore,
The General Assembly
Proclaims this Universal Declaration of Human Rights as a common
standard of achievement for all peoples and all nations, to the end that
every individual and every organ of society, keeping this Declaration
constantly in mind, shall strive by teaching and education to promote
respect for these rights and freedoms and by progressive measures,
national and international, to secure their universal and effective
recognition and observance, both among the peoples of Member
States themselves and among the peoples of territories under their
jurisdiction.[11]

That said, the UDHR is notable for a number of reasons. It was an attempt
to codify basic rights that could not be abridged, thereby potentially precluding the possibility of another Holocaust. It has led to the creation of more than
eighty international treaties, declarations, and conventions on human rights,
as well as individual states' domestic laws and constitutional provisions
guaranteeing human rights. These include, for example, the 1948 Convention
on the Prevention and Punishment of the Crime of Genocide and the 1965
International Convention on the Elimination of All Forms of Racial Discrimination. These various laws and conventions "constitute a comprehensive
legally binding system for the promotion and protection of human rights."[12] It
also lays out international law and obligations which, by signing the UDHR,
states must respect, as noted by the UN: "The obligation to respect means
that States must refrain from interfering with or curtailing the enjoyment of
human rights. The obligation to protect requires States to protect individuals
and groups against human rights abuses. The obligation to fulfill means that
States must take positive action to facilitate the enjoyment of basic human
rights."[13] Of course the fact that these human rights and the obligations of
states to protect those rights are embodied in a document does not mean that
countries will comply. In fact, there are numerous examples of cases where
that has not been the case.

WOMEN AND THEIR IMPACT ON THE UN CHARTER AND UDHR

The preamble to the UN Charter explicitly states that women and men have equal rights:

> We the peoples of the United Nations determined to save succeeding genera-
> tions from the scourge of war, which twice in our lifetime has brought untold
> sorrow to mankind, and to reaffirm faith in fundamental human rights, in the
> dignity and worth of the human person, in the *equal rights of men and women*
> and of nations large and small, and to establish conditions under which jus-
> tice and respect for the obligations arising from treaties and other sources of
> international law can be maintained, and to promote social progress and better
> standards of life in larger freedom (emphasis added).[14]

The inclusion of the language of equal rights in the preamble and various articles in the charter is a result of the efforts of non-Western feminists, such as
Bertha Lutz of Brazil and Minerva Bernardino of the Dominican Republic.[15]
Lutz was also instrumental in including Article 8 of the charter: "The United
Nations shall place no restrictions on the eligibility of men and women to participate in any capacity and under conditions of equality in its principal and
subsidiary organs."[16] Moreover, the language of "non-discrimination based
on sex was repeated in several articles of the Charter."[17]

A year later, in February 1946, Eleanor Roosevelt, widow of former US
president Franklin Delano Roosevelt, spoke at the inaugural session of the
UN General Assembly. Her "Open Letter to the Women of the World"
begins: "An Open Letter to the women of the world from the women delegates and advisers at the first Assembly of the United Nations: . . .This
new chance for peace was won through the joint efforts of men and women
working for common ideals of human freedom at a time when the need for
united effort broke down barriers of race, creed and sex."[18] It is also notable
that the letter was effectively intersectional: "We recognize that women in
various parts of the world are at different stages of participation in the life
of their community, that some of them are prevented by law from assuming
full rights of citizenship, and that they therefore may see their immediate
problems somewhat differently."[19] Bernardino followed Roosevelt's address,
supporting the Open Letter, and remarked on the role of women not just in
national delegations or other "high ranking positions," but also "to the wife;
the mother in the home; the teacher in the school; the church-worker; the
missionary; the social service worker." She continued: "The work which is
ours . . . must have the benefit of every effort of experience on the part of
women; but we cannot forget that women in many parts of the world are still

handicapped by the lack of right to play any role in the discussions of peace
and international affairs."[20]

Women's equality was further enshrined in the UN's Universal Declaration of Human Rights, adopted three years after the UN Charter, again
because of the work of feminists such as Bernardino and Hansa Mehta of
India. In fact, it was Mehta, one of two women delegates on the UN Commission of Human Rights (Eleanor Roosevelt was the chairperson of the commission), who "changed the wording in the UDHR from 'the rights of man' to
'human rights' and from 'all men' to 'everyone,' and 'all human beings.'"[21]
The changed wording of Article 1, from "All men are born free and equal" to
"All human beings are born free and equal" is because of Mehta.[22] Bernadino,
a signer of the UDHR, "pushed for the phrase 'equality of men and women'
in the preamble," and Begum Shaista Ikramullah of Pakistan "pushed for
articles and language in the UDHR that emphasized freedom, equality and
choice. For example, she championed the inclusion of Article 16 on equal
rights in marriage." For Ikramullah, such rights would "combat child marriage and forced marriage."[23]

In addition to Bernardino, Ikramullah, Mehta, and Roosevelt, other
notable feminists from around the world impacted the UDHR and contributed to the acknowledgment of women's rights "as part of the broader UN
commitment to human rights."[24] In 1946 Bodil Begtrup of Denmark served
as the chair of the UN Sub-Commission on the Status of Women. A year
later she was the chair of the Commission on the Status of Women. Her
advocacy in the UDHR led to the change from "men" to "'all' or 'everyone' as the holders of the rights." Begtrup also advocated for the inclusion
of minority rights in the document, but this was seen as too contentious.
While the document guarantees equal rights to all people, minority groups
are not mentioned explicitly.[25] From France, Marie-Hélène Lefaucheux
served as chair of the Commission on the Status of Women in 1948 and
succeeded in getting "nondiscrimination based on sex" integrated into
Article 2 of the UDHR. Because of her work, Article 2 of the document
reads: "Everyone is entitled to all the rights and freedoms set forth in
this Declaration, without distinction of any kind, such as race, color, sex,
language, religion, political or other opinion, national or social origin,
property, birth or other status."[26] Lakshmi Menon served as one of India's
delegates to the General Assembly in 1948. She supported the concept of
the "'universality' of human rights." Menon did not subscribe to "the concept of 'colonial relativism' that sought to deny human rights to people in
countries under colonial rule." For her, women and "people under colonial
rule" must be included in the UDHR. Otherwise, "they would not be considered included in 'everyone.'"[27]

TEXTBOX 3.2

BANDUNG CONFERENCE AND HUMAN RIGHTS

In April 1955 delegates from twenty-nine newly independent countries in Africa, Asia, and the Middle East attended the Afro-Asian Conference in Bandung, Indonesia (Bandung Conference). The countries of Burma, India, Indonesia, Pakistan, and Sri Lanka were the co-sponsors of the conference. As not all parts of the world had been decolonized following World War II, "the delegates at the conference took it upon themselves to speak for other colonized peoples (especially in Africa) that had not yet established independent governments."[28] In coming together for the first time, these newly independent countries sought to address problems that all faced.[29] The conference became the basis for the Non-Aligned Movement (NAM), in which developing states would neither side with the United States or the Soviet Union (USSR) in the Cold War.[30]

The final communiqué "declared its full support of the principle of self-determination of peoples and nations as set forth in the Charter of the United Nations" as well as the Universal Declaration of Human Rights, thus signaling their support for international human rights. The delegates highlighted several areas, including economic and cultural cooperation.[31] While the communiqué addressed human rights (such as racial discrimination, self-determination), there was no explicit reference to women, women's rights, or gender. And yet, as Aziza Ahmed remarks, "the spirit of the Conference has shaped feminist activism in the last sixty years." Global South feminists, with their Global North feminist allies, took "a broader structural approach to addressing issues facing women and girls. This included acknowledging the centrality of race, colonialism, and economic inequality in struggles for women's rights."[32] Moreover, this transnational feminist movement was explicitly intersectional as "gender was simply one category in a broader analysis of inequalities perpetrated by the legacy of colonialism and the international development agenda."[33] In the decades after the Bandung Conference, women's rights groups in the Global South would continue to focus on human rights issues such as reproductive rights and violence against women in the context of economic development.[34]

As this section demonstrates, the advocacy for the inclusion of women, people under colonial rule, and minority rights in the UDHR came about because of feminists from various states, in both the developed and developing world, participating in discussions about international human rights law.

From there, additional treaties and conventions on human rights were adopted that further solidified international human rights law. For example, in the 1950s the international community adopted the Convention on Consent, Minimum Age, and Registration for Marriage and the Convention on the Political Rights of Women (CPW). These conventions promoted gender equality for all women, thereby institutionalizing "the universality" of this human rights norm.[35] In the decades that followed, the global struggle for women's rights as human rights continued, as evidenced by various UN World Conferences on Women starting in 1975, culminating in the 1995 Fourth World Conference on Women, held in Beijing. It was at this conference that US First Lady Hillary Clinton addressed the representatives from 189 countries and declared: "If there is one message that echoes forth from this conference, let it be that human rights are women's rights and women's rights are human rights, once and for all."[36] This was "a rallying cry first circulated by grassroots women's rights groups and taken up by non-governmental organization (NGO) coalitions in the early 1990s."[37] This conference, according to the UN, "marked a significant turning point for the global agenda for gender equality"—the Beijing Declaration and the Platform for Action (see chapter 4) "was an agenda for women's empowerment and is now considered the key global policy document on gender equality."[38]

UDHR AND HUMAN RIGHTS FROM AN
INTERSECTIONAL PERSPECTIVE

In November 2000 the UN Division for the Advancement of Women, in conjunction with both the UN Office of the High Commissioner for Human Rights (OHCHR) and the United Nations Development Fund for Women (UNIFEM), organized an Expert Group Meeting on the topic of gender and racial discrimination. This conference was precipitated in part by the forty-fifth session of the Commission on the Status of Women, which was scheduled to meet in March 2001. On the agenda for that meeting was "the thematic issue of gender and all forms of discrimination, in particular racism, racial discrimination, xenophobia and related intolerance. It is also anticipated that the recommendations of the expert group meeting will be integrated into the preparations for the World Conference against Racism, Racial Discrimination, Xenophobia and Related Intolerance, as well as the World Conference itself which will be convened in Durban, South Africa from 31 August to 7 September 2001."[39]

Kimberlé Crenshaw, one of the most important thinkers associated with intersectionality (see chapter 1), served as the rapporteur and was also one of the speakers. The report issued about the meeting made it clear that there was a need for a more comprehensive analysis of issues about discrimination against women that went beyond CEDAW, discussed below. The introduction to the report states explicitly, "Historically, gender and other forms of discrimination, including racial discrimination, have been considered in parallel. However, interlinked and mutually reinforcing trends, including recommendations of United Nations conferences and summits, have increased the demand for a more comprehensive analysis of the dynamics of discrimination against women, *including the intersection of the various different forms of such discrimination*" (emphasis added).[40] This meeting considered not only the intersection of gender and racial discrimination directed toward women and girls but also "the disadvantages, obstacles and difficulties women face in the enjoyment of economic, social, cultural, political and civil rights as a result of the intersection of racial and sex discrimination both in public and private domain." It also claimed that it would address measures "to eradicate racism, racial discrimination, xenophobia and related intolerance and their specific effects on women and girls and provision of remedies and redress."[41]

While much of the emphasis of the meeting was on gender (note that this specifically refers to women and girls) and racial discrimination, the report also recognizes that "while it is true that all women are in some way subject to gender discrimination, it is also true that other factors relating to women's social identities such as class, caste, race, color, ethnicity, religion, national origin are 'differences that make a difference' in the ways in which various groups of women experience discrimination." It makes clear that "these factors can create problems and vulnerabilities that are unique to particular groups of women or that disproportionately affect some women relative to others."[42]

Perhaps of greater relevance here, the report states explicitly: "The idea of 'intersectionality' seeks to capture both the structural and dynamic consequences of the interaction between two or more forms of discrimination or systems of subordination."[43] The report further acknowledges that "intersectional discrimination which results in subordination creates consequences for those affected in ways which are different from consequences suffered by those who are subject to one form of discrimination only, be it based on race, gender, or some other form of discrimination, such as sexual orientation, age and class."[44]

The report shows that the discussion focused a lot on the notion of "intersectional subordination" of women, which is often the result of discrimination based on both gender *and* race. After enumerating various forms of discrimination and the impact they have on women, the recommendations were put forward by the Expert Group, starting with the assertion that existing international treaties, such as CEDAW, exist and "are designed to provide extensive protection against all forms of discrimination" against women. That said, the report also noted that "the United Nations approach to discrimination addressed specific categories of discrimination, rather than taking a holistic approach. At the national level the interpretation of discrimination has also been narrow, capturing only one form of discrimination, and avoiding its intersection with other forms."[45] Those recommendations indicate clearly some of the flaws in the international, and often national, approach to human rights, and why a broader, more intersectional approach is necessary.

To address these flaws, the Expert Group arrived at their recommendations, although they also state clearly the "the ultimate responsibility for the respect, protection, promotion and fulfillment of the human rights of all individuals and groups lies with the State."[46] That, of course, perpetuates one of the main issues associated with aspects of international law: the reliance on the state to do what is right. That said, the group put forward a number of recommendations, including "the need to develop an intersectional methodology" specifically "to identify intersectional discrimination and its effect on women and girls," and that "should be designed to uncover ways in which various structures of subordination converge to the disadvantage of women and girls in both public and private life, and should establish legal instruments for remedies and redress."[47] The Expert Group adopted a number of specific recommendations directed at both states and the various bodies in the international system, such as the Office of the UN High Commissioner for Refugees, the UN Security Council, and the Commission on the Status of Women. For example, the recommendations included admonishing governments to review all existing policies and develop new ones aimed at eliminating gender-based discrimination; reviewing and "rethinking" laws pertaining to immigration and refugees at all levels (state, regional, and international); increasing resources specifically for incarcerated women; and addressing the myriad issues pertaining to the feminization of migration.[48] While many of these recommendations were aspirational, they put forward an agenda that could improve the lives of many women substantially.

Of special note was the admonition that these issues needed to be addressed holistically. Johanne Bouchard and Patrice Meyer-Bisch have a slightly different take on what "intersectionality" means as it pertains to human rights, building on some of the themes raised in the UN Expert Group Meeting Report. In their discussion of discrimination, they allow as how "each person's identity is constructed by relying more or less strongly on gender, age, religion, ethnic, social and national origin, language, etc.; everyone defines one's self against or in accordance with what each of these elements means in the context in which they live."[49] This is very consistent with the accepted definitions of "intersectionality," and in this case they tie these various and interlocking markers of identity with discrimination. But they take these ideas one step further when they examine eight case studies of human rights violations, each of which "took place in different social, geographic, political, cultural and economic contexts," and arrive at an "intersectional nexus," or the "intersection of human rights violations *and* discrimination," which makes analysis of the situation even more complex (emphasis added).[50] Among the violations they cite are the case of a journalist covering the conflict in Sri Lanka whose right to freedom of expression and opinion were denied, the "sexual violence against women as a strategy of war" in the conflict in the Democratic Republic of Congo, and "the violations of the right to education" as well as discrimination in rural areas of Burkina Faso. Each of their eight cases documented various intersectional violations.[51]

In their analysis of these cases, therefore, the authors conclude that "intersectional" can refer to the intersection of multiple human rights violations as well as the intersection of identities. In fact, as they review the cases, what becomes apparent is that the intersection of these violations, attributed to some form of discrimination against the individual, had a far greater effect than if each violation were seen as discrete.[52] Hence their case studies led to a conclusion of "chain reactions of violations" which, in turn, "confirmed the relevance and applicability of the concept of intersectionality to the analysis of violations of human right more broadly (and not solely to discrimination)."[53] While they do not argue that their conclusions lead to the need to alter the existing UN human rights regime, they do suggest that understanding violations, both the causes and remedies, must be approached holistically and with the need to address not only the identities of the individuals that have contributed to the discrimination and human rights violations but also the range of violations.[54]

Twenty years after the Expert Group Meeting, in 2021 UN Women published an "Intersectionality resource guide and toolkit" specifically as a way to recognize structural barriers that contribute to inequality. These barriers serve as an impediment to achieving the Sustainable Development Goals that were developed in 2015 to make sure no one was "left behind." (See chapter 4 for more discussion of the Sustainable Development Goals.) As the publication notes: "With growing recognition that failure to address complex social systems and identities can obscure or deny the human rights protections due to all, it is crucial to design programmes and policies that effectively address not only discrimination based on disability but the situation of those affected by all forms of compounded and intersecting forms of discrimination."[55] The introduction to this document begins by stating, "Since their beginnings, human rights frameworks have formed the bedrock of the United Nations system; however, structural forms of inequality continue to pervade and prevent equality for all." It continues, "Applying an intersectional lens helps connect human rights to the multiple forms of discrimination that people experience.

It is essential to achieve equal outcomes for all in global efforts to fulfil the pledge to leave no one behind."[56]

The document begins by asking, "What is intersectionality?" and explains that the concept "recognizes that people's lives are shaped by their identities, relationships and social factors. These combine to create intersecting forms of privilege and oppression depending on a person's context and existing power structures such as patriarchy, ableism, colonialism, imperialism, homophobia and racism."[57] And then it asks and answers a critical question: Why does it matter? "Without an intersectional approach, the global pledge to leave no one behind will remain aspirational. Understanding the importance of inter-sectionality will lead us to ask ourselves who is left behind, why and under what circumstances."[58]

There are many aspects of this document that are important and relevant to our topic here, as it is specifically designed to help advise those who work in the field about the complexity of the topic. As discussed in chapter 1, while "intersectionality" as an approach or methodology has been integrated into a wide range of disciplines, it has also been politicized and dismissed by some politicians.[59] Nonetheless, the issue of protecting the human rights of all people, what that means, and how to do so remains an important component of the United Nations' approach to the topic of human rights.

CASE STUDY: CEDAW

While seen as an important step forward in ensuring human rights for women, examining CEDAW, the Convention on the Elimination of All Forms of Discrimination Against Women, through an intersectional lens also illuminates some of its flaws. The point here is that while it was important for women in general in and of itself, through its omissions it discriminates against some women, something that would not be apparent without an intersectional lens.

While the UDHR explicitly included women's rights as an essential human rights issue, it was negotiated at a time when political and civil rights for women were limited in many parts of the world. For example, while women in the UK were granted the right to vote in 1918, in the United States in 1920, and in Latin American countries beginning in the 1930s, women in many other countries were not given that right until after World War II, with Saudi Arabia among the last countries to allow women to vote; they voted for the first time in municipal elections in 2015.[60] Further, although the concept of basic human rights was written into the UDHR, that did not in any way guarantee that states would give women those rights. This led to a push to ensure that women's rights were enshrined in international human rights law, and that discrimination was outlawed universally.

CEDAW was adopted in 1979 and entered into force in 1981 after the twentieth country ratified it. CEDAW is often referred to as an international bill of rights for women. It grew out of UN efforts to address sex discrimination or discrimination on the basis of gender. It builds on the UDHR as well as the International Covenants on Civil and Political Rights (ICCPR) and Economic, Social and Cultural Rights (ICESCR), both adopted in 1966, as noted earlier. However, as Christine Chinkin elucidates, "these first UN human rights instruments provided minimal guarantees for women; in particular, with the exception of ICCPR, Article 26, there was no free-standing provision requiring equality before the law."[61] This led to a process that culminated in the adoption of CEDAW by the General Assembly in 1979.

Four years earlier, in 1975, at the first international conference on women held in Mexico City, delegates developed the World Plan of Action for the Implementation of the Objectives of the International Women's Year (1975 was International Women's Year). The Action Plan called for resolutions on topics such as "Research and training for the advancement of women in Africa," "Women and health," "Prevention of the exploitation of women and girls," "Research on population and the integration of women in development," "Political and social participation," "Women's participation in the strengthening of international peace and security and in the struggle against colonialism, racism, racial discrimination and foreign domination," and "Equality between men and women and elimination of discrimination against women."[62] Importantly, the Action Plan "called for a convention on the elimination of discrimination against women, with effective procedures for implementation," which became CEDAW.[63]

Unlike the UDHR, CEDAW is woman (as opposed to gender) specific. Discrimination against women is defined as "any distinction, exclusion or restriction made on the basis of sex which has the effect or purpose of impairing or nullifying the recognition, enjoyment or exercise by women, irrespective of their marital status, on a basis of equality of men and women, of human rights and fundamental freedoms in the political, economic, social, cultural, civil or any other field."[64] Further, "by accepting the Convention, States commit themselves to undertake a series of measures to end discrimination against women in all forms, including . . . the principle of equality of men and women in their legal system; abolish all discriminatory laws and adopt appropriate ones prohibiting discrimination against women; establish tribunals . . . to ensure the effective protection of women against discrimination; and to ensure elimination of all acts of discrimination against women by persons, organizations or enterprises."[65]

According to UN Women, "The Convention provides the basis for realizing equality between women and men through ensuring women's equal access to, and equal opportunities in, political and public life—including the right to vote and to stand for election—as well as education, health and employment." By signing on to it, states "agree to take all appropriate measures, including legislation and temporary special measures, so that women can enjoy all their human rights and fundamental freedoms."[66]

More than three decades of efforts by the UN Commission on the Status of Women led to CEDAW. The introduction notes that "the Convention takes an important place in bringing the female half of humanity into the focus of human rights concerns. The spirit of the Convention is rooted in the goals of the United Nations: to reaffirm faith in fundamental human rights, in the dignity and worth of the human person, in the equal rights of men and women. The present document spells out the meaning of equality and how it can be achieved. In so doing, the Convention establishes not only an international bill of rights for women, but also an agenda for action by countries to guarantee the enjoyment of those rights."[67] The body of the convention offers the assurance of civil rights, including basic political rights, reproductive rights (including the assurance of a right to family planning), and the right of "gender relations."[68] In fact, it "is the only human rights treaty which affirms the reproductive rights of women and targets culture and tradition as influential forces shaping gender roles and family relations."[69]

Currently, of 194 member states of the United Nations, seven have not ratified CEDAW: Iran, Niue, Palau, Somalia, Sudan, Tonga, and the United States. US president Jimmy Carter signed the convention in 1980; since then, it has been submitted to the Senate for ratification and the Senate has held hearings. To date, however, the convention has not been brought to the full Senate for a ratification vote, in large part due to opposition by conservative politicians, who oppose reproductive rights, including contraception and abortion.[70]

Flaws of CEDAW from an Intersectional Perspective

In spite of the important role it played in advancing the human rights of women internationally, CEDAW has a number of limitations that need to be addressed. As Chinkin explains, "Reservations have been made to CEDAW articles 1–5 which are critical to the fulfilment of its objectives."[71] Articles 1 through 5 define what is meant by "discrimination against women" (Article 1); condemn and agree to pursue policies against discrimination (Article 2); admonish countries to do all they can "to ensure the full development and advancement of women" in "political, social, economic and cultural fields" (Article 3); encourage countries to take all measures necessary to ensure equality between men and women (Article 4); and, in what is probably the most controversial part, ask states "to modify the social and cultural patterns of conduct of men and women, with a view to achieving the elimination of prejudices and customary and all other practices which are based on the idea of the inferiority or the superiority of either of the sexes or on stereotyped roles for men and women."[72] The extent of and reasons for the reservations vary but, as Chinkin points out, some states "claim that the Convention is not binding in so far as its provisions conflict with Islamic *Shariah* law or with the State's Constitution, or that the State is willing to comply with the Convention in so far as such compliance is not contrary to these other normative codes."[73] Thus, while the convention is accepted international law to protect the human rights of women, it again remains up to the individual countries to determine the interpretation and application of its components. As is the case with much of international law, there are no enforcement mechanisms.

Examining CEDAW from an intersectional perspective highlights many of its other flaws. One of the most prominent is "projecting a particular image of women," and the enumerated violations against them, based on sex (that is, "the biological difference between men and women") as well as "the measure of equality is by comparison with men."[74] It presumes that women will be married to a man, thereby precluding the guarantee of rights of lesbian women.

Additionally, Article 14 of the convention specifically acknowledges "the particular problems faced by rural women and the significant roles which rural women play in the economic survival of their families."[75] While this is important, the article privileges rural women over urban women, who also are the primary support of their own family, for example. While it acknowledges that women in general face discrimination, it does not differentiate the discrimination faced by women of color, by women who are poor and/or uneducated, by age, etc. In other words, with the exception of rural women, who are specifically identified, women are lumped together as if they were a single homogeneous group.

General Recommendations (GR) have subsequently been put forward by the Committee on the Elimination of Discrimination Against Women (the independent experts monitoring implementation of CEDAW), empowered "to make suggestions and general recommendations based on the examination of reports and information received from States parties."[76] This provision allowed for the convention to be updated as needed and, as noted in Article 21 of the treaty, allows states to "make suggestions and general recommendations based on the examination of reports and information received from the States Parties," which ensures that the convention can be a living document.[77] For example, GR 14, adopted in 1990, deals explicitly with "continuation of the practice of female circumcision and other traditional practices harmful to the health of women." While acknowledging that women's groups have been working to end this practice, which often confronts cultural pressures, the recommendation comes down heavily in support of countries working to eliminate this practice for health reasons and to protect women and children.[78]

GR 28, "on the core obligations of States parties under article 2 of the Convention on the Elimination of All Forms of Discrimination against Women," dated December 2010, "aims to clarify the scope and meaning of article 2 of the Convention on the Elimination of All Forms of Discrimination against Women ('the Convention'), which provides ways for States parties to implement domestically the substantive provisions of the Convention."[79] In recognizing the vast array of differences among women, according to Chinkin, "GR 28 recognizes the diversity in women's lives and the importance of addressing multiple and intersecting discriminations, for 'discrimination of women based on sex and gender is inextricably linked with other factors that affect women, such as race, ethnicity, . . . class, caste and sexual orientation and gender identity.'"[80] Thus this recommendation moves beyond the basic and monolithic approach to women initially outlined in the convention to recognize the intersecting categories that play a role in women's lives, and affect discrimination against them. However, it took nearly thirty years after the convention was signed to acknowledge that.

There is little doubt that CEDAW was an important document for women in that it enshrined many principles guaranteeing equality for women. However, we also contend that initially it was limited in scope. It omitted many groups of women and/or left it up to states to implement. Yet it was those same states that were allowing discrimination or violence against women to take place. It has taken years of review and modification through the General Recommendations to remedy many of these failings, and even with those changes, as is true with so many international agreements, it is up to each country and its government to determine whether the precepts embodied in this agreement will be honored.

HUMANITARIAN INTERVENTION AND THE RESPONSIBILITY TO PROTECT (R2P)

So far, this chapter has discussed the development and evolution of international human rights and the myriad treaties and conventions that address such rights in general (UDHR) and, in some cases, more specifically, such as CEDAW. As explained by the ICRC, these treaties and conventions are understood as human rights law, "a set of international rules . . . on the basis of which individuals and groups can expect and/or claim certain rights that must be respected and protected by their States."[81]

While complementary in terms of protecting lives, International Humanitarian Law (IHL) differs from international human rights law in that IHL "is a set of rules which seek, for humanitarian reasons, *to limit the effects of armed conflict*" (emphasis in original).[82] Human rights law, with its focus on human rights in peacetime, "was conceived to protect persons from abuse by the State," and "applies to all persons within the jurisdiction of a State. Unlike IHL, it does not distinguish between combatants and civilians or provide for categories of 'protected persons.'"[83]

IHL was codified in the nineteenth century, but it was the reaction to the atrocities perpetrated during World War II and especially the Holocaust that led to the Nuremburg trials, in which those individuals who committed such acts could and should be brought to justice. The Geneva Conventions of 1949 (and their additional protocols) embodied the principles of Just War Doctrine, discussed in chapter 2, and "are at the core of international humanitarian law."[84] IHL defines the legal bounds in which conflicts are to be fought in order to protect both civilians and even combatants from the worst of the violence. Helen Kinsella explains international humanitarian law in the context of the use of force in armed conflict: "It regulates the means (arms, for example chemical weapons) and methods (attacks on enemies, for example bombings) of war. And . . . it protects individuals who are not participating in armed conflict (for example civilians) and individuals who are no longer participating in conflict (for example prisoners of war)."[85]

Jeni Klugman et al. underscore the connection between international humanitarian law and gender: "Despite the law being couched in gender-neutral terms, IHL is a deeply gendered body of law . . . [that considers] men being fighters and women being victims of war."[86] These gendered assumptions were enshrined in many of the most critical tenets of international law, such as the Geneva Conventions. In effect, "a gendered analysis of IHL reveals that most of the provisions pertaining to women provide for special *protections* for women. Even the rules that prohibit sexual violence focus on the *protection* of women from sexual violence, rather than on the *prohibition* of such acts" (emphasis in original). However, as Klugman et al. also note, "This reinforces the gendered dichotomy in the law, of women as victims and men as perpetrators. IHL also fails to acknowledge that men also experience sexual violence in war."[87] In short, while IHL was designed to protect civilians and especially women, the reality is that the precepts of this body of law do not adequately address the realities of wars, especially intrastate wars, that emerged with greater frequency and with more extreme levels of violence in the post–Cold War period.

Again, returning to an important point made by Kinsella, under IHL, "technically all individuals are guaranteed equal protection . . . [but] women are granted special protections owing to their special needs which are held to be a consequence of their biological sex."[88] As a result, women are supposed to be treated differently and should be offered special protections, especially against sexual violence during conflict. In many ways, this diminishes the potential violations inflicted on men, who could also be violated but do not seem to need these extra protections, but it also essentializes women based on the perception that they need to be protected, and also elevates their reproductive roles.[89] It is that undercurrent of "protection," making sure the vulnerable (generally women and children) are protected in some way rather than prohibiting this behavior that undergirds another important principle of IHL, the responsibility to protect.

The Responsibility to Protect (R2P)

Viljoen asserts that "greater concern for human rights has also been accompanied with greater emphasis on the individual liability of those responsible for gross human rights violations in the form of genocide, crimes against humanity and war crimes."[90] The breakup of Yugoslavia (1991–1995) and the genocide in Rwanda (1994) witnessed gross human rights violations. In response, the international community created the International Criminal Tribunal for the former Yugoslavia (ICTY) in 1993 in the midst of the Bosnian War and the International Criminal Tribunal for Rwanda (ICTR) in 1994. These two tribunals were created to prosecute individuals for war crimes, rape, and genocide, for example. As these tribunals addressed two specific conflicts (breakup of Yugoslavia, Rwandan genocide), they were temporary. In response, in 1998 "a conference of 160 States established the first treaty-based permanent international criminal court [ICC]." The Rome Statute entered into force in 2002, with more than 120 states being party to the treaty.[91] The establishment of the two international criminal tribunals and the ICC "constitutes a trend towards the humanization of international law."[92]

The international community's response to investigate and prosecute individuals committing serious crimes—and the overlap between IHL and international human rights law—can be examined from an intersectional lens. For example, in cases such as Bosnia and Rwanda, the violations, including gender-based sexual violence, that occurred against women were also about ethnicity and national identity. During the war in Bosnia, ethnic cleansing combined with violence against women: Serbs (Orthodox Christians) raped Muslim Bosnian women, thereby perpetrating a number of violations against the women and their religion; but in the ultimate indignity, any child born of the rape was said to take on the identity of the Christian Serb father rather than the Muslim mother. The human rights NGO, Human Rights Watch, reported a Bosnian rape victim stating that "[it] was their aim to make a baby. They wanted to humiliate us. They would say directly, looking into your eyes, that they wanted to make a baby."[93] As Jennifer Turpin describes it, "because women are viewed as symbols of the family, and the family is the basis of society, the humiliation for women giving birth to the enemy's children symbolizes the destruction of the community."[94] This example underscores the intersection of gender (in this case, women), ethnicity, national identity, and, to some extent, even age, as women of childbearing age were especially vulnerable.

It was the cases of Bosnia and Rwanda, plus countless other conflicts during this period (such as the civil wars in Liberia and Sierra Leone), that finally motivated the international community to codify those situations where it is not only possible but necessary for international action to be taken, even if that meant defying the prohibition against intervening, including militarily, within a sovereign state. Thus the Responsibility to Protect (R2P) was born: "an international norm that seeks to ensure that the international community never again fails to halt the mass atrocity crimes of genocide, war crimes, ethnic cleansing and crimes against humanity."[95] As codified in the Outcome Document, adopted unanimously at the 2005 UN World Summit, if one's own state does not provide protection against mass violations of human rights, then it is the obligation of other states to interfere. Paragraphs 138 and 139 are the operative ones:

138. Each individual State has the responsibility to protect its populations from genocide, war crimes, ethnic cleansing and crimes against humanity.

139. The international community, through the United Nations, also has the responsibility to use appropriate diplomatic, humanitarian and other peaceful means, in accordance with Chapters VI and VIII of the Charter, to help protect populations from genocide, war crimes, ethnic cleansing and crimes against humanity. In this context, we are prepared to take collective action . . . should peaceful means be inadequate and national authorities are manifestly failing to protect their populations from genocide, war crimes, ethnic cleansing and crimes against humanity.[96]

The concept of the responsibility to protect "affirmed the notion that sovereignty is not just protection from outside interference—rather [it] is a matter of states having positive responsibilities for their population's welfare, and to assist each other. Consequently, the primary responsibility for the protection of its people rested first and foremost with the State itself." While this puts the burden on the individual states, the concept goes beyond that to include the roles and responsibilities of the international community: "However, a 'residual responsibility' also lies with the broader community of states, which was 'activated when a particular state is clearly either unwilling or unable to fulfil its responsibility to protect or is itself the actual perpetrator of crimes or atrocities.'"[97] In effect, it becomes the responsibility of the international community to protect people when the state abrogates that responsibility, even if that means violating international law and, specifically, the sanctity of state sovereignty.

The initial acceptance of R2P was not easy, as there was a division between those who advocated for the primacy of state sovereignty and those who insisted on the importance of humanitarian intervention. This can be seen in the debates leading up to the codification of R2P and what were perceived as the failures of the international system to respond to events such as the genocide in Rwanda and ethnic cleansing in Bosnia. According to the Global Centre for the Responsibility to Protect, an NGO based in New York, the violence seen in the wars in Rwanda, Somalia, and Yugoslavia in the 1990s illustrated that "the world was ill-prepared to act and was paralyzed by disagreements over the limits of international sovereignty." The result was a split within the international community, resulting in "a pair of unpalatable choices: either states could passively stand by and let mass killing happen in order to strictly preserve the letter of international law, or they could circumvent the UN Charter and unilaterally carry out an act of war on humanitarian grounds."[98] The R2P shifted the focus of the argument so that it became the responsibility of *all* countries to protect those at risk.

Four years after the adoption of the R2P doctrine, in 2009 the UN secretary general issued a report titled "Implementing the Responsibility to Protect," in which he outlined "three pillars of responsibility":

Pillar 1: Every state has the Responsibility to Protect its populations from the four mass atrocity crimes: genocide, war crimes, crimes against humanity and ethnic cleaning.

Pillar 2: The wider international community has the responsibility to encourage and assist individual states in meeting that responsibility.

Pillar 3: If a state is manifestly failing to protect its populations, the international community must be prepared to take appropriate collective action, in a timely and decisive manner and in accordance with the UN Charter.[99]

As of December 2023, according to the Global Centre for the Responsibility to Protect, R2P has been referenced in ninety-three UNSC resolutions and twenty-seven General Assembly resolutions. As of April 2024, R2P has been referenced in eighty Human Rights Council resolutions. These resolutions address crises in many states, including in the Central African Republic, Cote d'Ivoire (Ivory Coast), Libya, Mali, the Democratic Republic of Congo, Somalia, South Sudan, and Syria.[100] But the real question is whether R2P has made a difference in the conduct of international conflicts, and to whom? Has R2P really been able to protect those within a state who were most vulnerable or endangered? And how would we know?

Failures, Weaknesses, and Critiques of R2P: Importance of an Intersectional Analysis

The Global Centre for the Responsibility to Protect highlights three major challenges associated with implementing this concept: conceptual, institutional, and political. The first pertains to the need "to ensure that the norm is well understood in all parts of the world"; in effect, the need to have a "broad international consensus about how to respond in the context of R2P."[101] The second, the institutional challenge, requires that governments and other international organizations have the capacity needed to ensure action is taken if and/or when needed. "We need international institutions with a capacity to provide essential assistance to those countries who need it and to people desperately in need of protection."[102] This pertains to what we see in classical international relations theories as having not only the capability or capacity to take action but also the credibility to believe that action will be taken. The former (capability or capacity) without the latter (credibility) has no teeth.

The third challenge is the political one: specifically, the difference between cases of success and failure (as the civil war in Syria, for example, which began in 2011) "has depended upon political leadership and timely action by the UNSC, working with a committed regional organization." This is perhaps the most difficult of the three challenges identified by the Global Centre for the Responsibility to Protect, as success requires considerable commitments from international leaders.[103] Yet, many of these decision-makers may not accept an international norm if it runs counter to their own self-interest, such as staying in power (as realist IR theory would affirm).

The challenges identified by an organization that exists to support this doctrine are difficult enough, as all deal with some aspect of the institutionalized political structure that is required to take action if the R2P doctrine is to be successful. There are a range of other challenges they do not touch on, and yet are relevant to our understanding of this important international concept from an intersectional framework. Here the work of Jess Gifkins and Dean Cooper-Cunningham is instructive: "the many exclusions and silences built into the R2P framework, as well as the racialized and patriarchal power structures that R2P risks reifying and entrenching."[104] While the focus in their article is primarily on queer people's experiences,[105] the points they raise are important, as they pertain to aspects of power and also how minorities in general or any group that is relatively powerless can be subject to mass atrocities, such as those R2P is designed to protect. If the state fails to protect those individuals or groups, it is up to members of the international community to step in under R2P.

This also raises another set of issues, questions, and challenges. Given unequal power balances within a state, who makes the decision about when an abuse has been committed and when such alleged abuses become simply a pretext for illegal action against a state, for example, an invasion on the pretext of protecting individuals or groups. Here we see a conundrum that R2P can present. On one side, there is a need to defend especially those who are being abused and are often the most powerless group within a state when that government will not act (or the government itself is engaging in gross human rights violations). On the other, we can ask who makes that determination and can decide that it is appropriate to act within the borders of another state. Or, as Karen Mingst asks, "How massive do violations of human rights have to be to justify intervention? Who decides when to respond to the abuses? Can states be using the excuse of humanitarian intervention to achieve other goals? Is it an obligation to intervene militarily in these humanitarian emergencies?"[106]

Here too, context becomes especially important, and, given the colonial experiences of states in the Global South, postcolonial scholars argue, as Coralie Pison Hindawi asserts, that "in most of the critical literature, R2P is presented as a product from the West, whose liberal ideal relies on a perception of Southern states being potentially dysfunctional, which in turn justifies an interventionist discourse with neocolonial overtones."[107] Hindawi cautions, however, that such an interpretation is problematic because "it essentially ignores non-Western inputs on the concept."[108] Several individuals from African countries, such as Francis Deng (Sudanese scholar and diplomat) and Mohamed Sahnoun (diplomat from Algeria), contributed to understandings of sovereignty and responsibility.[109] Finally, it is worth noting that the R2P concept "was endorsed unanimously" in 2005 at the World Summit, including by countries initially skeptical of R2P.[110]

Another point needs to be made here under the broad category of R2P, and it is one that is often overlooked. One of the tenets of this aspect of IHL pertains not only to protecting people when crimes against humanity are occurring but also *preventing* such crimes from happening in the future. Section 138 of the World Summit Outcome Document, in addition to noting that governments have the responsibility to protect their population, also asserts, "This responsibility [to protect] entails the *prevention* of such crimes, including their incitement, through appropriate and necessary means. We accept that responsibility and will act in accordance with it. The international community should, as appropriate, encourage and help States to exercise this responsibility and support the United Nations in establishing an early warning capability" (emphasis added).[111] Hence, protecting is not enough. States and other members of the international system need to be aware of circumstances that could lead to such crimes, and act to prevent them. The essence of "prevention," however, requires knowledge of which groups are vulnerable, again a bedrock of intersectional analysis. Identifying the groups that are targeted for human rights violations means delving beneath any one category (i.e., women) and looking at the various intersecting variables or characteristics (e.g., race, class, sexual orientation, age) that could lead to violence and, in the event of violence, acknowledge that these groups are also the ones in greater danger.

Gifkins and Cooper-Cunningham provide an example of how that prevention aspect might work. They maintain that "the prevention aspect of R2P brings to the fore risk factors of the above crimes [genocide, war crimes, ethnic cleansing and crimes against humanity] and the need to act against escalating persecution of a minoritized group." They refer to a strategy originating with the UN Office on Genocide Prevention and the Responsibility to Protect specifically to combat hate speech, which "identified hate speech as a dangerous phenomenon that, by weaponizing public discourse and using 'incendiary rhetoric that stigmatizes and dehumanizes' for political gain, threatens 'democratic values, social stability and peace.'" The authors indicate the ways in which hate speech is "a risk factor" contributing to "armed conflict, atrocity crimes, and the violation of human rights."[112] Again referencing the strategy on combating hate speech, they underscore the ways in which it often "references women, migrants, people of color, Muslims and Jewish people as the main targets" and therefore as groups especially in need of protection.[113] In other words, there should be a priority not only to protect those who are the victims of various crimes including hate speech but also to prevent such things from happening in the first place. That too becomes an obligation or part of the responsibility to protect. If we can prevent such atrocities from being perpetrated, then protection will not be needed.

CONCLUSION

This chapter started by focusing on the issue of human rights as an international norm that has been contested but also institutionalized in various conventions and treaties, including international law, as evidenced by the attempts at ensuring the rights of women, minorities, Indigenous peoples, and so forth. The Universal Declaration of Human Rights enshrined human rights as part of international human rights law, as did CEDAW, another international agreement designed to promote women's rights and prevent discrimination based on sex. Yet an intersectional analysis of both agreements illustrates how, despite the good intentions underlying each, they are also flawed in their approaches by omitting groups the agreements should have protected.

We provided a review of the doctrine of Responsibility to Protect, born out of a need to confront the failures of the international system to address the violence perpetrated during internal conflicts in the 1990s. This is an example of international humanitarian law that calls for humanitarian intervention in cases of gross human rights violations in times of war—namely, intrastate war. As we note, one aspect of R2P that is often overlooked, and yet is essential to the doctrine, is the need to *prevent* such atrocities from occurring. While international humanitarian law, humanitarian intervention, and the R2P doctrine have all sought to promote and protect human rights around the world, as an intersectional lens shows, these remain gendered and racialized.

Chapter 4

Intersectionality, the Global Economy, and Issues of Development

This chapter addresses the connection between economic globalization, development, and the global economy. Today's liberal international economic order was created at the end of World War II, in no small part due to America's dominant position in the international system. During the interwar period, the Great Depression and protectionist economic policies were considered contributing factors to the outbreak of war in 1939. Thus, when the war ended, the United States and other Western liberal capitalist democracies set about creating several international financial institutions, namely the International Monetary Fund (IMF) and the World Bank, "and rules to govern an increasingly integrated global economy, based broadly on the principles of open markets and trade."[1] These institutions were seen as needed for "economic stabilization, trade, finance, and monetary relations."[2] The liberal international economic order calls for free trade for both developed and developing states, as international trade is intimately tied to economic globalization. Consequently, an understanding of the contemporary global political economy requires that we see the evolution of what has become an increasingly interconnected and globalized world, especially since the end of the Cold War. According to the World Bank, "From 1990 to 2017, developing countries increased their share of global exports from 16 percent to 30 percent; in the same period, the global poverty rate fell from 36 percent to 9 percent."[3] Data also shows that "the share of the world's population in *extreme poverty* has fallen from 42 percent in 1981 to just 8.6 percent in 2018" (emphasis added).[4] And "the past 40 years have also seen reduced global inequality."[5]

At the same time, data shows that many countries have also seen rising inequality.[6] According to Zia Qureshi, "Income inequality has risen in most advanced economies [such as the US] and major emerging economies [such as China, India, and Russia], which together account for about two-thirds of the world's population and 85 percent of global GDP."[7] For developing countries, there has been a mixed trend, with many experiencing increased inequality.[8] When we consider the impact of globalization on economic development and levels of income inequality, Qureshi further notes that globalization has contributed to "reducing inequality between economies by expanding export opportunities for emerging economies and spurring their economic growth." Yet new challenges have emerged, namely technological changes and automation, that have changed "production processes and trade patterns," thereby contributing to differing levels of development and economic growth around the world.[9]

What accounts for the unevenness of economic development within and across countries? Who benefits from globalization and international trade? Feminist political economic and postcolonial approaches—and hence intersectional analysis—can provide those answers. We illustrate the differential impact of economic development and globalization across countries as well as on people and groups within countries, which varies according to race, ethnicity, class, sexual orientation, and age, in addition to gender. We use a case study of the COVID-19 pandemic to highlight the varied economic impacts of diseases, as it has been estimated that in 2020, "70 million people [were] pushed into poverty . . . because of COVID-19."[10] Within the case, we look at two countries, South Africa and India, to demonstrate how different groups of people within those countries were impacted differently by the pandemic.

TEXTBOX 4.1

GLOBALIZATION

What is globalization? How do we define it? There are many definitions and understandings of the term "globalization." Sarah L. Henderson and Alana S. Jeydel define globalization as "the growing integration of economies and societies around the world." They continue: "Although early forms of globalization have existed since the Roman Empire, the current debates that swirl around Globalization refer to the massive changes in economic, social, and political interaction from the 1980s onward."[11] As Violet Bridget Lunga asserts, "There is general consensus that globalization points to a shrinking world, a world that is becoming more interrelated, interconnected, and interdependent—a totally interconnected marketplace, unhampered by time zones or national boundaries . . . widespread agreement that globalization is accelerated by improvement of information and communication technology."[12]

Economic globalization became especially prominent after the Cold War ended and with the disintegration of the Soviet Union. Rather than two major power blocs pitted against each other, the international economic system was becoming more integrated and interdependent. According to Michael Mandelbaum, the acceleration of the process of globalization was in part a result of the combination of technology and politics: "The advent of new technologies such as cheap satellite communication, cell phones, and the internet made possible the movement of goods and money (and people) across long distances even more rapidly and in ever greater volume." He continues: "At the same time, more and more countries that had had little or nothing to do with the globalized international order that the United States had taken the lead in reviving after World War II, notably India and China, made the political decision to join it."[13] The result was not only more economic interdependence but also the rise of two more economic powers, India and especially China, which have come to threaten the United States' dominant place in the international economic system.

While globalization certainly accelerated with the end of the Cold War, it is not new. Thomas Friedman describes three major periods of globalization: the first lasting from 1492 until around 1800; the second from around 1800 to 2000; and the third, which started in 2000 and continues into the 2020s. Each of these was made possible by new technologies that made the world smaller and more accessible, from the age of exploration to the growth of multinational corporations and non-state actors to the outside role individuals can now play because of technology. Or, as he describes it, "while the dynamic force in Globalization 1.0 was countries globalizing and the dynamic force in Globalization 2.0 was companies globalizing, the dynamic force in Globalization 3.0 [the present]—the force that gives it its unique character—is the newfound power for *individuals* to collaborate and compete globally" (emphasis added).[14] What Friedman omits here, and a point that feminist authors such as J. Ann Tickner and V. Spike Peterson stress, is that not all individuals gained that power and that, in fact, globalization made the world and the international economic system more unequal.

Historian Robert Marks, in his book *The Origins of the Modern World*, also identifies a number of cycles of globalization as they exist in a historical context based on systems of trade that can be traced back to the thirteenth century. However, in his analysis the modern interdependent world system can be traced to the evolution of the modern nation-state in the nineteenth and especially twentieth centuries and to the advent of industrialization that allowed states to grow and expand their territory. Along with that, however, came a growing gap between and across countries that differentiated not only the richest and the poorer countries but also a growing gap *within* countries as the rich became richer while the poorest—often the most powerless, especially women and minorities—stagnated at the bottom. Rather than globalization as a process where a "rising tide would lift all boats," globalization has exacerbated differences between and among nations rather than closing them, and he blames that on the unequal patterns of economic development that nations experienced.[15] He makes another important point that is relevant to our discussion: The differential patterns of trade and development across countries can be attributed in part to the fact that many of the countries in Asia and Africa were formerly colonies of the major Western countries, and therefore were dependent on them. While most have since gained their independence, that pattern of dependency has remained, leaving a legacy of inequality not only across countries but also within them, as individuals within a country did not similarly benefit equally from the country's economic growth, as postcolonial scholars would conclude.

IR APPROACHES TO THE GLOBAL ECONOMY

When we think of the global economy, we need to recognize that the global economy is intertwined with politics. Jill Steans describes economics and politics in the following way: "*Economics* is concerned with: systems of production; the operation of markets; the distribution of resources across the world; the distribution of wealth across national boundaries; the linkages between the global, national and local economies." In making the connection to politics, Steans continues: "*Politics* is understood largely in terms of governance: here, the institutions and rules by which economic interactions are regulated. . . . Global economic and political relations are regulated by states, inter-state forums such as the G8, the IMF, the WB [World Bank], the World Trade Organization, the International Labor Organization and international credit rating agencies" (emphasis added).[16]

International political economy (IPE) is an area of study in IR that focuses on the interrelationship between economics and politics as they affect relationships between and among states in the international system. Specifically, IPE explores "the intersection of politics and economics as goods, services, money, people, and ideas move across borders."[17] Recognizing the problems of development in particular parts of the world, namely the "Third World," IPE emerged as a scholarly area in the 1960s. IPE focused primarily on states as the primary unit of analysis, while global political economy (GPE) approaches examined other actors besides states that are part of the international system.[18] Within IPE works, liberals focused on the role of international institutions in the global economy that provided mechanisms for developing and developed states to cooperate in international trade and contribute to peace (see chapter 1).

Mainstream IR scholars studying the global economy tend to focus on the impact of globalization and international trade at the macro-level. Macro-level indicators include such things as states' exports and imports, balance of payments, and exchange rates.[19] Critical IR scholars have noted that such a focus does not sufficiently capture the impacts of globalization on development around the world. As we have argued throughout this book, feminist and postcolonial approaches provide the necessary intersectional lens to examine IR issues, and that includes globalization, the global economy, and development within and across countries. These approaches lend themselves to analysis of "how different systems of power, and access to power interact and impact on different groups in the society."[20]

Feminist political economy approaches argue that the mainstream global political economy (GPE) approaches do not take into account how the economy is gendered, given its focus on "productive (i.e., market-based) activities . . . that happen in society." The problem, as Renée Marlin-Bennett and David K. Johnson assert, is that given that the "reproductive activities"—"'unpaid work necessary to create a home life, provide leisure activities, and care for family members' . . . are almost universally associated with feminine characteristics," they are not usually studied by scholars in the mainstream GPE/ IPE.[21] As J. Ann Tickner points out, "Feminist perspectives on economic globalization are unanimous in pointing to continuities in various forms of patriarchy that have had detrimental effects on women's economic security through much of history. Given the increase in global inequality, the feminization of poverty, and the discriminations that women often face when they participate in the global market, some feminist scholarship is questioning the triumphalist story of a borderless world that is being told by supporters of economic globalization."[22]

Additionally, feminist political economy also links the economy to security, in that war impacts both "women's and men's ability to access decent work, health care, education, natural resources." Without access to economic and political decision-making, women and men face further insecurity.[23] In considering post-conflict situations, often investments are made in areas that promote the market rather than "investments into eradication of poverty, health and educational infrastructure (that would benefit wider society and support overcoming gender inequality)." In turn, without investment in gender equality in the context of economic investments, women will continue to remain in the "informal economy (as a means of survival) and unpaid care work."[24]

Postcolonial approaches to studying the global economy have criticized traditional IPE, noting its Eurocentrism, in which the North is considered "advanced and progressive" while the South is "backward, degenerative and primitive."[25] In a further critique, such works center "the structural impact that colonial histories continue to exert on economic life."[26] The colonial histories of capitalism are not divorced from the contemporary period in which power relations between the wealthy and poor states remain unequal. As Violet Bridget Lunga illustrates, "The inequitable distribution of resources and unfair labor laws that favor rich countries, the protectionism and Western systems of knowledge that sustain and maintain power weighted towards the West," continue long after former colonies gained independence.[27]

Bringing together feminist and postcolonial theories, as Sara Salem notes, "postcolonial feminists argue that colonial legacies across the Global South are central to the forms of gendered oppression or privilege women experience today. Central to this was their focus on capitalism as a key feature of colonialism—and therefore of postcolonial societies. . . . Gender inequality is about anti-capitalism and anti-colonialism, even in a world that seems to have 'decolonized.'"[28] She continues, "Part of the legacy of colonialism in the Global South is one of representation: women became understood monolithically as oppressed and therefore as the target of development."[29]

Division of Labor: Intersectionality and Disparities in the Global Economy

The division of labor found in many countries today, developed and developing alike, can be attributed to the growth of the nation-state and, with it, the division of labor needed to support the economic health of the state. As Robert Marks explains, the Industrial Revolution that started in Europe in the eighteenth century and then encompassed much of the rest of the world displaced what he calls "the biological old-regime," where women and children were critical contributors to the family and often the local and even regional economies. While different genders had specific tasks, both men and women contributed to sustaining the households.[30] Colonialization and industrialization, while seen as aspects of "development" or even modernization, "were key to constituting more rigid, less equal, and thus less complementary conceptions of how labor should be divided between and among sexes, classes, and nations,"[31] thereby putting into place a division of labor that privileged men at the expense of women, urban versus rural dwellers, and the able-bodied versus those who were disabled. In many ways, that division, and the hierarchy that went with it, remains in place today.

Anne Sisson Runyan and V. Spike Peterson reinforce this point in their analysis of colonialization and industrialization when they stress the ways in which what they call the "Western gendered division of labor" was imposed on countries and cultures with a result that "the economic status and well-being of women in diverse cultures were diminished by the patriarchal and political ideologies imposed by colonizers." An example they give is the way in which "farming in many African countries was almost exclusively women's work, and men were responsible for clearing fields, hunting and engaging in warfare."[32] In other words, there was a gendered division of labor that existed prior to colonization that empowered both men and women. With colonization, the assumption by the Western colonizers was that "land should be 'owned' and men should be 'heads of households' and hence the primary earners." The result was that land rights were transferred away from women to men, which also gave them access to training, cash, and credit.[33] Thus, we see the gendered impact of modernization/development. Another impact of this process of "development," however, with effects that continue to this day, was the emergence of a class system that divided landowners from those who worked the land, and the urban factory and business owners from those who were the laborers.

A further elaboration of this point is made by Tickner when she writes about the ways in which capital is rewarded relative to labor in the globalized world economy, which means that men are rewarded disproportionately compared to women. In part, this can be attributed to the fact that women's labor is often found outside the "formal" economy, where so-called "women's work" is less valued than men's, and women therefore earn less.[34]

This gendered economic disparity has often been exacerbated by free trade and export-led strategies of development. Structural adjustment programs (SAPs) imposed by international financial institutions, generally headed by Western developed countries, have also made the economic situation more unequal.[35] The SAPs were supposed to help a country develop by offering lower interest rates on loans, but these can actually have the opposite effect of putting a country further into debt, which can undermine its economic development rather than boost it. As countries try to rein in debt, under the terms of the SAP policies, they generally cut social welfare programs and services, which are often provided by women and support women. As Tickner makes clear, "The harsh effects of structural adjustment policies . . . fall disproportionately on women as providers of basic needs, as social welfare programs in areas of health, nutrition, and housing are cut. When government subsidies or funds are no longer available, women in their role as unpaid homemakers and care providers must take over the provision of these basic welfare needs."[36] This, in turn, puts women, especially poor women, even further behind economically. Tickner summarizes this inherent inequality: "Liberal strategies to promote economic growth and improve world welfare that rely on market forces and free trade may have a differential impact on men and women."[37]

As Arne Ruckert explains, this is also the result of a shift in priorities from policies that emphasized the state and the role of government to "put pressure on low-income countries to downsize the role of the state to providing health and other social services as a last resort, coupled with an increased role of the private sector in service delivery for the rich and poor alike."[38] The so-called "retreat of the state" created needs that were often filled by women, especially in the care economy. Not only were women stepping in to fill this need, but the very need itself negatively affected women, especially poor and/or rural women who depended on the state. Runyan and Peterson similarly stress this point when they identify patterns that result from the imposition of SAPs: "the enormous social costs of adjustment, increases in income inequality, tendencies toward social polarization that aggravate conflicts, shifts in control over resources, and 'the existence of class, gender and ethnic biases in the adjustment process.'"[39]

TEXTBOX 4.2

GLOBAL RESTRUCTURING

Jill Steans references Marianne H. Marchand and Anne Sisson Runyan, who coined the term "global restructuring." They did so because "this term better encapsulated the dynamic and inter-related economic and political processes that generated structural transformations in the global economy and changes in globalized social relations." According to Steans, the term "restructuring" "also captured the growing complexity of the global division of labor, the intimate relationship between debt and development (and environmental degradation) and the often uneven and specific effects of these processes across countries and on particular social groups. The impact of restructuring and neoliberal growth strategies in developing countries has been uneven."[40]

What is especially relevant to our intersectional analysis of the global economy and development about this concept is that it has resulted in the growth of economic extremes in the countries of the Global North and those in the Global South, where there are pockets of great wealth while many people in both parts of the world live in extreme poverty. The point here is that these extremes are not confined to one part of the world or one country or another. Rather, this pattern of extremes can be found within countries in all places.

India is an example of these extremes. "Usually, when women work it's a boon to any economy. Most countries develop faster with women in their workforces. That's true for India."[41] According to the World Bank, India has "one of the fastest growing economies of the world" and, during the period from 2011 to 2019, "has halved the share of the population living in extreme poverty." However, the COVID-19 pandemic impacted that progress, such that "the pace of poverty reduction has slowed." While employment indicators have shown progress, "the quality of jobs created" has raised concerns, especially for women in the paid labor force.[42] According to an article broadcast on NPR, India's female labor force participation has been steadily dropping, "from 32% in 2005 to 19% in 2021." While India continues on its path of development, "women are dropping out of its workforce—in record numbers. This is happening among rich and poor women, in urban and rural areas—across social class, religion and age groups. In fact, it's happening even among poor rural women—who might need a paycheck the most." Economists point to a number of reasons for this phenomenon, and these statistics do not account for women who work in agriculture or the informal economy, who are often not included in the statistics. So now India, despite its strong economic growth, has to contend with this economic challenge, which threatens to undermine the country's continued economic growth.[43]

GENDERING DEVELOPMENT: WID, WAD, AND GAD

The very notion of "development" reinforced the advances of the economic sectors that would benefit the state the most, which often ignore the subsistence or caring sectors populated by women. And since the decision-makers are generally men, development programs tend to support projects in areas similarly dominated by men, such as building roads and dams.[44] According to Tickner, "To achieve economic justice for rural women in the Third World, development must target projects that benefit women, particularly those in the subsistence sector. Improvements in agriculture should focus on consumption as well as production; in many parts of Africa, gathering water and fuel, under conditions of increasing scarcity and environmental degradation, are taking up larger portions of women's time and energy."[45] Runyan and Peterson note that "despite greater attention to women and gender relations, contemporary development approaches have done little to alter the gendered divisions of labor or stem poverty and have instead reinforced a range of power relations in the GPE [global political economy] that we associate with the power of gender."[46] As the next section discusses, there have been several approaches to including women in development processes since the 1970s, but today, women around the world still have not achieved gender equality, which is necessary for development and economic growth. For example, while the last few decades have seen a decrease in the gender pay gap around the world, gender pay gaps remain in most countries (men earn more than women).[47] When looking at income groups, women are underrepresented at the top income levels, while they are overrepresented in low-paying jobs.[48] In addition to economic inequalities between men and women with regard to wages, economic inequalities are present when looking at assets, such as land ownership. As Esteban Ortiz-Ospina and Max Rosen's data shows, "in nearly all low and middle-income countries with data, men are more likely to own land than women. Women's lack of control over important household assets, such as land, can be a critical problem in case of divorce or the husband's death."[49]

Thus, when considering the multiple axes of gender, race, class, and so forth in relation to development, one need only note the World Bank's *Gender Equality and Development Report*, published in 2012: "In some areas, however, progress toward gender equality has been limited—even in developed countries. Girls and women who are poor, live in remote areas, are disabled, or belong to minority groups continue to lag behind."[50]

WID, WAD, and GAD

Each of these acronyms—WID (Women in Development), WAD (Women and Development), and GAD (Gender and Development)—emerged in the scholarly literature as terminology referring to the role of women in the development process. As countries "developed," different strategies were devised specifically to address the participation of women in that process. The first, WID, "came into use in the 1970s" specifically to address "the sexual division of labor in the agrarian economies." This led to concerns, especially among American feminists, of the need to rectify the lack of better integration of women into the economy. Eva M. Rathgeber demonstrates that "the WID perspective was closely linked with the modernization paradigm that dominated mainstream thinking on international development from the 1950s into the 1970s. In that period, conventional wisdom decreed that 'modernization,' which usually equated with industrialization, would improve the standard of living in developing countries."[51] This brings us back to the idea that "a rising tide would lift all boats"; specifically, as states experienced economic growth as a result of modernization processes, there would be a concomitant increase in "living conditions, wages, . . . education," and health care that would, in turn, "trickle down" to the rest of society. But when it became apparent "that the relative position of women had, in fact, improved very little over the previous two decades," the assumption that modernization would improve women's conditions became increasingly questionable.[52] While some of the assumptions regarding development noted above helped elevate the position of men, the same was not true of women, who remained in the lowest-paying jobs and were often in the "informal" economy. Hence, structural changes would be needed to offset the disadvantages experienced consistently by women and, conversely, the benefits that accrued to men.

The next evolution was Women and Development (WAD), which has its origins in a Marxist and neo-Marxist feminist approach and which "focuses on the relationship between women and development processes rather than purely on strategies for the integration of women into development."[53] What makes this approach unique is its acknowledgment "that women always have been important economic actors" in their respective economies, both inside and outside the home. WAD recognizes the role of class, consistent with its Marxist framework, but treats women as if they were a monolithic group, as is the case with the WID approach, and thus variables such as "social relations of gender within classes" as well as race and ethnicity are not taken into account. While it acknowledges women's underrepresentation in the critical "economic, political, and social structures," the assumption is that this can and will be addressed as countries develop and become more gender equal—an assumption that has not proven true.[54]

The limitations of WID led to the development of a new approach to considering women and development in the 1980s: GAD (gender-and-development). But GAD differs from the other approaches in that "it is not concerned with women *per se* but with the social construction of gender and the assignment of specific roles, responsibilities, and expectations to women and to men."[55] Further, women are considered "as agents of change" and that it is essential for women to become more empowered politically. Unlike the other approaches, however, GAD highlights the role of the state "to provide some of the social services," such as childcare, that would permit women to engage more actively in the political and economic processes. That said, as countries suffered an economic recession or downturn, those social services were among the first areas to be cut.[56] Another area in which the GAD approach differs from the others has been its emphasis on improving women's rights, such as laws related to inheritance and land ownership, and "in questioning the underlying assumptions of current social, economic and political structures."[57] One of the major flaws in the implementation of this approach, however, is its "commitment to structural change and power shifts," but governments or international organizations are often not willing to make those commitments.[58]

How can this deeply entrenched system, which privileges men at the expense of women or the owner class at the expense of the workers, change and do so in a way that would include and benefit women and other largely disenfranchised groups, two concepts that are directly related? First, the concept of development cannot and will not change unless or until more women, minorities, and/or other disadvantaged groups are included in the process of setting national and even international priorities and policies. As we saw in chapter 2 regarding the passage of UN Security Council Resolution 1325, women had been systematically excluded from the peace process until there was an international agreement specifically to include them. As we also noted in the earlier chapter, passage of the resolution did not guarantee women's inclusion, but did make it a priority to try to do so. What this change suggests is the need to *target the determinants of the gender gaps and not the outcomes.* This would be true for all sectors of the population in which there are gaps—men versus women, minorities, people with disabilities, LGBTQ+ individuals, age, etc.—to focus on the underlying causes of the inequality in order to get to solutions.

Second, increased women's representation and participation in decision-making, particularly in leadership positions, may translate into economic benefits for women as well as other disenfranchised members of a society. The current head of the World Trade Organization, Ngozi Okonjo-Iweala, and IMF Managing Director Kristalina Georgieva have made women's empowerment and gender equality a primary focus of their work (see textbox 4.3).

TEXTBOX 4.3

GENDERING THE GLOBAL ECONOMY AND LEADING THE INTERNATIONAL FINANCIAL INSTITUTIONS

In 1944, during World War II, 730 delegates from countries such as the United States, Belgium, Brazil, Canada, Chile, China, India, the Netherlands, and Russia attended the Bretton Woods conference (officially the United Nations Monetary and Financial Conference) to determine "a system of economic order and international cooperation" in the wake of the major disruptions caused by the war. The goal was also to "foster long-term global growth." Two of the major international economic/financial organizations, the International Monetary Fund (IMF) and the World Bank, were created at that time.[59] The IMF was established to promote international monetary cooperation and stability, while the World Bank was originally designed to help facilitate the postwar reconstruction efforts in Europe and was subsequently expanded to provide loans to assist countries' development efforts. Both these organizations were designed to help foster financial stability, promote international trade and cooperation, and encourage employment and economic growth internationally through their policies. Three years after the IMF and World Bank were created, in 1947 countries signed the General Agreement on Tariffs and Trade (GATT). The World Trade Organization (WTO) came into being in 1995 as a successor to GATT. As the world became more globalized and international trade increased, these international organizations became more important by creating mechanisms for trade and for airing disputes between countries. The leadership of the organizations can tell us much about how they understand the differential impacts on the global economy—and the recognition that the global economy is a gendered one. The current leaders of the World Bank, IMF, and WTO have made clear that economic growth and development of all countries can only come about with women's equality and empowerment.

Traditionally, the World Bank has been headed by an American. The current president is Ajay Banga, who was born in India and is a naturalized American citizen. He was nominated by the Biden administration and took office in June 2023 to serve a five-year term. He has called for "a new playbook" in which "at the center must be women and young people. Without a focus on both we are fighting with a hand behind our back. . . . When [women] do get a seat at the table they aren't paid equally [in the labor force]. We cannot defeat poverty with half the world's population on the sideline. And young people, they can be the engine of our future; but only if we provide quality of life when they're growing up—and then a job."[60]

In contrast to the World Bank, the IMF is always headed by a European. In 2011 Christine Lagarde of France became the first woman managing director of the IMF. She made clear the importance of women's empowerment, noting the IMF's research showing "that if women's employment equaled men's, economies would be more resilient and economic growth would be higher." She further stated, "The IMF's 189 member countries face many different challenges, but empowering women remains a common denominator and a global imperative for all those who care about fairness and diversity, but also productivity and growth of societies and economies that are more inclusive."[61] She was succeeded in 2019 by Kristalina Georgieva of Bulgaria, the first person from an emerging market economy to lead the organization. Georgieva has also focused on the important role that women play in the global economy, noting the research that shows the connection between gender equality and economic growth.[62] She stated, "There is no way for any society to prosper without tapping into the talent of all its people—men and women. It's very simple, if you ignore part of your capabilities, you . . . come up short in terms of economic achievements."[63]

As of 2021, the WTO has been headed by Ngozi Okonjo-Iweala, the first woman and the first African to head that organization. Okonjo-Iweala twice served as Nigeria's finance minister (2003–2006 and 2011–2015) and briefly acted as foreign minister in 2006, the first woman to hold both positions. She also had a twenty-five-year career at the World Bank. Perhaps most important, according to her official biography, "she is a firm believer in the power of trade to lift developing countries out of poverty and assist them to achieve robust economic growth and sustainable development."[64] As the WTO's director-general, Okonjo-Iweala has made it clear that trade and decent jobs can empower women economically, as well as increase economic growth. She stated that "the opportunity costs of gender inequality in the labour market—the economic gains we choose to forego by allowing those inequalities to persist—are immense. . . . They are in the same ballpark as the economic damage from the COVID-19 pandemic."[65]

Third, as illustrated by the differential impact of the COVID pandemic, women's roles as well as those of the traditionally powerless groups must be redefined and elevated to more accurately reflect the critical roles they play. Again, using UNSCR 1325 as a model, making this change successfully will require a change in the power structure or, at the very least, the recognition that "women's work" is critical to the success of the state and the people within it. This will need to take place at both a national and international level, perhaps requiring a resolution similar to 1325. The need for that change will become even more apparent in the case study of COVID-19, provided later in this chapter.

Fourth, gender mainstreaming should be integrated into development projects, such as infrastructure projects, given that "women and men do not benefit equally from public investments." As the OECD report noted, different "social roles, economic status or preferences" indicate that men and women "have diverse needs and use infrastructure differently." The report also stated that "men overwhelmingly dominate infrastructure decision-making, even if the projects are targeted at female end-users."[66]

The Beijing Platform for Action and the Sustainable Development Goals

The Beijing Platform for Action (BPfA) was adopted at the Fourth UN Conference on Women in 1995. It identified "twelve key areas where urgent action was needed to ensure greater equality and opportunities for women and men, girls and boys." Importantly, the BPfA specified policies that states could take "to bring about change" in these areas while also taking into account cultural sensitivities.[67] One of the areas identified that is directly relevant for this chapter was "Women and the Economy," which acknowledges the critical role that women play in the economies of all countries and in all sectors, including business, agriculture, and "unpaid domestic work." It also recognizes a point we have stressed: "Gender discrimination means women often end up in insecure, low-wage jobs, and constitute a small minority of those in senior positions."[68] In highlighting this, the BPfA made visible an economic reality often ignored. It also acknowledged the gender gaps that exist in social protection programs and guaranteeing access to social security systems, which are exacerbated by governments' implementation of austerity programs to deal with their own economic shortfalls. Social protection services must also recognize that these should not only reach women and children but also the elderly, chronically ill, disabled, and others within the society who need extra assistance.[69]

In 2015 the Sustainable Development Goals (SDGs) "completed and broadened the BPfA care agenda by setting concrete redistributive goals" especially for "care policies."[70] In so doing, the SDGs built on the Millennium Development Goals, eight goals that the member states of the UN "agreed to try to achieve by the year 2015." Signed in 2000, "the United Nations Millennium Declaration . . . commits world leaders to combat poverty, hunger, disease, illiteracy, environmental degradation, and discrimination against women. . . . Each MDG has targets set for 2015 and indicators to monitor progress from 1990 levels." While some countries achieved some of the targets, it was clear that these were aspirational, and, according to the World Health Organization, "often the countries making the least progress are those affected by high levels of HIV/AIDS, economic hardship or conflict."[71]

While the MDGs raised important issues and made world leaders aware of the need to address some pressing global problems, the MDGs also fell short in a number of ways. One critical analysis notes, "The MDGs ignore an intersectional analysis of multiple oppressions due to gender, race/ethnicity/caste, class, sexual orientation, age and national origin. . . . If women's poverty is exacerbated by biases due to race, ethnicity or caste, then efforts to end poverty that ignore this reality will fail, and efforts to increase access to education must specifically target the needs of diverse groups of girl [sic]."[72] Hence, the lived experiences of women and girls must take into account the multiple oppressions that they have experienced due to factors such as gender, race, and class, and these should be addressed as part of subsequent policies. It was some of these flaws, and the need to move beyond the aspirational and to more concrete policies, that the SDGs hoped to address.

Thus, in conjunction with the SDGs (textbox 4.4), the UN made important strides to ensuring gender equality in all areas, including the economy. However, as is often the case, the challenges were in the implementation, where the reality once again has deviated from the ways in which changes were envisioned in theory. As Valeria Esquivel and Corina Rodriguez Enriquez assert, the debt relief policies that were designed to redress the inequalities in the SAPs imposed conditions that resulted once again in "the gendered impacts of such policies on poverty, on the deterioration of public care services and on women's unpaid care work."[73] Hence, women continue to be responsible for "unpaid care work, and they are particularly hit when public care services contract and the working conditions of care workers deteriorate."[74] So while the Beijing Platform for Action put the burden on states to implement transformative policies, in general they have failed to do so, challenges made worse by COVID-19. As highlighted by Esquivel and Enriquez, "Achieving economic growth that favors equality goals, as proposed by the BPfA, takes political will, strong regulatory frameworks, and international co-ordination."[75]

It is important to note that these inequities go beyond women and also affect the poor (men and women), disabled, minorities, and any other group that does not have political or economic power and is dependent on the state to redress these inequalities.

TEXTBOX 4.4

SUSTAINABLE DEVELOPMENT GOALS (SDGs)

In 2015 the UN General Assembly adopted the 2030 Agenda for Sustainable Development, which has at its heart seventeen Sustainable Development Goals (SDGs). The successor to the Millennium Development Goals, signed in 2000, the SDGs represent "an urgent call for action" to be embraced by all countries. According to the UN, this "recognize[s] that ending poverty and other deprivations must go hand-in-hand with strategies that improve health and education, reduce inequality, and spur economic growth—all while tackling climate change and working to preserve our oceans and forests."

The SDGs:

1. End poverty in all its forms.
2. End hunger, achieve food security and improved nutrition, and promote sustainable agriculture.

3. Ensure healthy lives and promote well-being for all ages.
4. Ensure inclusive and equitable quality education and promote lifelong learning opportunities for all.
5. Achieve gender equality and empower all women and girls.
6. Ensure availability and sustainable management of water and sanitation for all.
7. Ensure access to affordable, reliable, sustainable and modern energy for all.
8. Promote sustained, inclusive and sustainable economic growth, full and productive employment and decent work for all.
9. Build resilient infrastructure, promote inclusive and sustainable industrialization and foster innovation.
10. Reduce inequality within and among countries.
11. Make cities and human settlements inclusive, safe, resilient, and sustainable.
12. Ensure sustainable consumption and production patterns.
13. Take urgent action to combat climate change and its impacts.
14. Conserve and sustainably use the oceans, seas, and marine resources for sustainable development.
15. Protect, restore and promote sustainable use of terrestrial ecosystems, sustainably manage forests, combat desertification, and halt and reverse land degradation and halt biodiversity loss.
16. Promote peaceful and inclusive societies for sustainable development, provide access to justice for all and build effective, accountable and inclusive institutions at all levels.
17. Strengthen the means of implementation and revitalize the global partnership for Sustainable Development.[76]

CASE STUDY: COVID-19

Ensuring that a population has adequate health care is one of the major requirements for any government (providing for the common good), and access to health care often is tied to economic development. Yet it is also true that access to quality health care differs greatly not only across countries but even within countries. Governments have different understandings of their responsibilities to their populations when it comes to health care, and spending for that sector also reflects different priorities—specifically, guns versus butter trade-offs. For example, the National Health

Service (NHS) was established in Great Britain in 1946 after World War II to ensure that the entire population has access to health care. Anyone who has watched *Prime Minister's Questions* ("Question Time") has heard about the challenges facing the NHS today, including long wait times for some surgeries, growing financial strains on the system, and those who can afford it paying for doctor or hospital visits on their own outside of the NHS, which was recently the case with King Charles's diagnosis of cancer and his rapid treatment. Even in the United States, one of the highest-ranked countries on the Human Development Index (discussed in more detail below), access to health care varies widely by region and wealth. Hence wealthier people in big cities would probably have access to better health care than would poor people and/or those in rural areas where options are more limited. And despite the push by some progressive politicians for "Medicare for all," or the increasing access to health care afforded by the Affordable Care Act (aka Obamacare), the reality is that health care and access to it is not equal within the United States. Yet, as the COVID-19 outbreak showed dramatically, access to health care is important not only for individuals but also for the common good; without it, pandemics spread and the existing health care system is burdened. That is true of all countries, regardless of their level of economic development. However, countries that are more developed economically generally are better positioned to weather health crises.

The Human Development Index (HDI)

In 1990 the United Nations introduced its Human Development Index (HDI), a composite of many socioeconomic variables that, taken together, rank all countries. The HDI uses social data on education and health ("measured by life expectancy at birth"), as well as economic data ("a decent standard of living") to arrive at a composite score for all countries. This allows us to compare "development" across countries using similar measures. Over the years, some critiques of the HDI, such as examining inequality within countries, including gender equality/inequality, have been addressed (for example, the Gender-related Development Index), while others have not, such as environmental sustainability.[77] The HDI does allow for some systematic comparisons and therefore can serve as a surrogate measure for development. This is meaningful in our analysis of global health and development because the HDI explicitly factors in "a long and healthy life, as measured by life expectancy at birth." One of the goals of creating the HDI was to shift the emphasis from a reliance on economic statistics to human outcomes, that is, the impact of policies on individuals.[78]

Not surprisingly, one of the findings in the UN Global Development Report for 2021–22 is that, overall, the HDI value "declined for two years in a row," thereby eliminating "the gains of the preceding five years." Some of this can be attributed to COVID-19 and the impact it had on all countries combined with the war in Ukraine, which affected food and gas availability for some countries and disrupted supply chains; awareness of climate change and environmental uncertainties; and a nagging sense of insecurity felt across the globe.[79] We can speculate that if the HDI is dropping across all countries, then the level of inequality and the differential effects of COVID-19 and the economic disruptions that accompanied it will be felt within countries.

It has been often noted that women, especially poor women, are the backbone of the care economy not only in the developing countries but also in developed ones such as the United States. The health sector especially depends on women's labor, often at little or no remuneration, either because they are expected to fulfill familial responsibilities ("women's work") or because their labor is assumed to be worth less. And, as mentioned in an article in the *New York Times*, one of the ironies is that "when work conditions and pay improve, men often move into the jobs," thereby displacing the women. An example that the article gives is Liberia, which in 2016 began a training program and increasing pay for health workers. But "soon more than 80 percent of the new jobs were held by men."[80]

Men died at higher rates from COVID than did women. Some of the countries in Africa, while poor, were less affected by COVID, as determined by number of deaths per one hundred thousand (see map 4.1), than were countries in the so-called developed world. It can be attributed in part to the extensive experience these countries had with managing previous epidemics/pandemics, such as the spread of Ebola, and therefore were better prepared to address this latest virus. When COVID initially emerged as a global pandemic, the fear was that countries in Africa would be especially hard-hit, given their generally weaker health care systems and infrastructure, high prevalence of other diseases such as malaria, and poverty and malnutrition. However, that did not appear to be the case, at least as indicated by the data.[81] That also raised questions about how accurately each country documented the number of cases and especially deaths due to COVID. Unlike other countries in Africa that did not count every COVID death accurately (many people died at home, having been cared for by relatives), South Africa kept records that can provide important information about the differential impact of the COVID virus, as we document in the case below.[82]

In addition, studies also found "that about two-thirds of the population in most sub-Saharan countries" have the SARS-CoV-2 antibodies while only 14

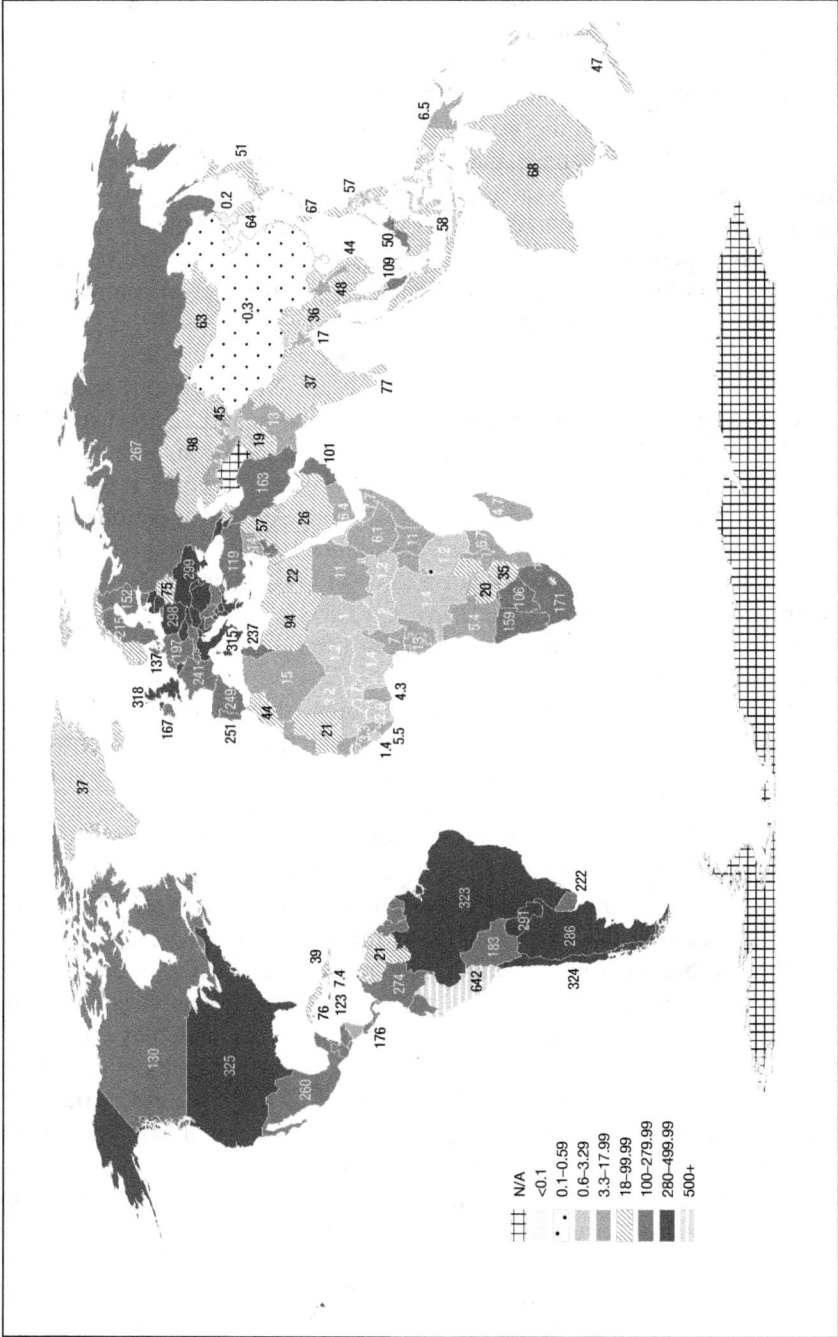

Map 4.1 **Confirmed COVID deaths per 100,000.** *Source:* BBC News, "Covid map: Coronavirus cases, deaths, vaccinations by country," July 5, 2022, https://www.bbc.com/news/world-51235105.

percent of the population have been vaccinated, suggesting that the antibodies were the result of infection.[83] The population of Africa tends to be young compared to Europe and the United States, and thus many in the population have not yet developed comorbidities. This can be contrasted with India, which similarly has a young population, but the Delta variant of COVID caused millions of deaths in India. It should be noted here that the Indian government consistently undercounted (or underreported) the number of COVID deaths.[84] Below, we will look at and compare these two cases, South Africa and India, to see what conclusions we can draw. Again, what the data suggest in both cases is the need to look within a country in order to get a better understanding of who is affected by the spread of a deadly disease and the impact on a state's economy and development.

COVID: A Global Disease Impacting Economies

As Esquivel and Enriquez assert, "The COVID-19 crisis has exposed in one go the fragilities of developing economies, the inequalities and weaknesses of health systems, the vulnerabilities in labor markets, and the failings of social protection systems in plain sight."[85] It is also an example of the impact of globalization as the disease quickly spread around the world. The first case of this new virus, known as SARS-CoV-2, sickened and killed its first victims in the central China city of Wuhan in December 2019. The Chinese government initially attempted to contain the spread by placing the entire province of Hunan, with a population of seventy million, in quarantine. However, in our globalized and interconnected world, people infected with the virus were already on planes heading for Europe and the United States. Outbreaks first in Italy and the city of New York quickly overwhelmed hospitals and health workers. The virus spread far and wide, such that by March 2020, the World Health Organization (WHO) "declared a global pandemic."[86]

It is important to remember that the impact of COVID was not felt by all countries nor by all populations within any country equally. For example, within the United States, there was an increase in deaths across all demographic groups between 2019 and 2020, at the start of the pandemic. Statistics show that "between 2019 and 2020, male deaths increased by 296,061 (20.1%) and female deaths by 232,830 (16.9%). The trend continued in 2021, with 68,208 (3.9%) more male deaths and 12,298 (0.8%) more female deaths," indicating that the pandemic, at least in the United States, had a more deadly impact on men than women.[87] In assessing the data for race and ethnicity, "in 2020, the largest mortality increase occurred in the American Indian and Alaska Native population (36.7%), followed by the Black (29.7%) and Asian (29.4%) populations."[88] The data sources did not break this down further by sex; however, it is clear that the increase in mortality rate could be found among those parts of the US population that are poorer and with less access to health care, or among those parts of the population that generally distrusted the medical care system. We can see a similar pattern globally, where again, statistics show that deaths globally were found disproportionately among the lower-middle- and low-income countries (57 percent) versus 43 percent in high- and upper-middle income countries.[89] While the data show consistently high patterns of death for men versus women, what the aggregate data obscure are the breakdowns within each country (see map 4.1).

The fact that men were disproportionately affected by COVID deaths than women seems to be counterintuitive given the fact that health care responsibilities fall largely on women. However, this apparent contradiction can be explained by the fact that men, especially older men, often suffer from underlying health issues, such as hypertension or other chronic diseases, compared to women. Also, this reinforces the need to look within a country, as the results will vary depending on access to health care and vaccines, which can also be a surrogate for economic well-being.[90]

The Sex, Gender and COVID-19 Project specifically tracked data by sex and gender in national COVID-19 policies.[91] This project affirmed the importance of looking at the data by sex and gender: "Gender influences exposure to risk (air pollution, smoking, alcohol), likelihood of risk reduction (e.g., seeking health care), as well as who benefits from the resources available (e.g., who can access health services, or who is likely to be providing care). Health outcomes and health systems reflect and reinforce gender biases and restrictive gender norms, compromising the safety and well-being of providers and the health of communities. Gender and social inequalities (based on class, race, or ethnicity, etc.) intersect and multiply these negative effects on both the health system and the communities they serve."[92] This report also illustrates the connection between "social and structural inequalities" in the context of "COVID-19 outcomes." Such connections mean that "there is a need for more data that takes other inequalities such as ethnicity, geography, disability, socioeconomic status, etc., into account."[93]

South Africa

Often termed one of the BRICS countries (Brazil, Russia, India, China, South Africa) because of its rapid economic development, South Africa is a country that has been affected by political corruption, unequal economic growth, and disease that has stunted its economic development. Although apartheid (legalized racial segregation) officially ended in 1994 with the creation of a new constitution that guaranteed equality for all, South Africa is a country characterized by inequality. It has a relatively high literacy rate for women (defined as the percentage the population age fifteen and older who can read and write) of 94.5 percent, compared to 95.5 percent for men, and GDP per capita of about $13,500, ranking it 121st in the world, far higher than most other African countries.[94] Yet it also has a high rate of domestic violence and poverty, which is obscured by the data. There is also a significant difference across provinces within the country, and between those who live in the cities and the more remote rural areas. According to the UN Development Report on the country, "South Africa, the most advanced economy in Africa, faces structural limitations including overconcentration of the economy in a few hands, limited skills, power shortages, and deteriorating confidence in the democracy. The COVID-19 pandemic worsened its economic vulnerabilities, leading to a significant output contraction (-6.4%) in 2020, which worsened poverty, unemployment, and inequality, particularly for children, youth and women."[95] In 2021, South Africa ranked 109 out of a total of 191 on the HDI, earning a composite score of 0.71 (with 1 being highest), a decline from the previous high of 0.74 in 2019, which indicates a relatively high level of development.[96] To some extent, the decline reflects the hit that all countries took to their economy and life expectancy due to COVID-19. However, to get a more complete picture of the impact of the disease on the population of South Africa, we have to look within the country at the various groups affected and why the differential impact.

The first case of COVID-19 in South Africa was diagnosed in March 2020. Working women in South Africa were especially vulnerable, not only to the disease but also to the impact it had on the economy and their livelihoods. As Naidoo Saloshni and Naidoo Rajen Nithiseelan observe, "In South Africa most women workers find themselves in vulnerable employment as domestic help in private households, traders in the informal economy, and small-scale agriculture with no employment contracts or health insurance cover." When the pandemic emerged, "women workers had to further deal with the socio-economic vulnerability of their employment, dual domestic and working responsibilities and those infected with COVID-19, with the clinical sequelae of the disease."[97] Unemployment levels increased, having a marked impact on women, many of whom work in the informal economy. Women's unemployment increased "from 31.3% in the 2nd quarter of 2019 to 36.8% in the 2nd quarter of 2021."[98]

As might be expected, women working in the health care sector were especially affected. Data from November 2021 indicated that "of the more than thirty-nine thousand COVID-19 hospital admissions, 2.4% were health care workers. Female health care workers accounted for 67% of all admissions amongst health care workers. . . . Increased infections amongst women workers and slow recovery amongst those with severe morbidity delayed return to work and increased the vulnerability amongst these working women."[99]

In a society in which patriarchy is "deeply entrenched,"[100] women were expected to continue their responsibilities at home to care for children, the sick, and the elderly. Saloshni and Nithiseelan assess the various "workplace and social interventions" to help workers, asserting that "the complicated processes required to achieve the benefits of these interventions proved frustrating for workers and often excluded those most in need such as women workers increasing their vulnerability. The existing vulnerability of working women in South Africa worsened during the COVID-19 pandemic through job losses, increased risk at work and domestic pressures."[101]

As noted earlier, apartheid ended in 1994, yet South Africa continues to remain an unequal society divided by race; COVID made that inequality even more apparent. According to a study of hospitalization and death rates in the country, "Blacks, Indians and Coloreds [people of mixed race] were more likely to die"; the study further reinforces "the interplay between 'race, age, sex and socio-economic status' and how different groups experienced Covid-19."[102] Despite its economic advances as defined by macroeconomic indicators such as the HDI, the legacy of apartheid, with "its history of racial segregation has made it the most unequal of countries for which data are available."[103]

Thus, when we assess the impact of COVID in South Africa, we need to look at more than simply the number of cases of who contracted and died from the disease. We also need to examine the differential impact it had on women, especially poor women and health care workers, as well as the differential impact by race. In so doing, an intersectional analysis offers a more complete understanding of "economic development" in South Africa and how development was impacted by COVID-19.

India

Like South Africa, India is a country that has been characterized by relatively rapid and steady economic growth. It is the world's largest democracy, and its economy has been poised to equal or overtake China's. It is a relatively young country, with 29.8 years the median age. GDP per capita is $7,100, making it lower on the comparison rankings than South Africa.[104] However, that also obscures the bifurcated nature of the economy and the distribution of wealth. According to British-based NGO Oxfam International, inequality increased over the last thirty years, with the richest 10 percent of the population having 77 percent of the national wealth. Government spending on health care is "among the lowest in the world," which clearly was a factor during COVID. Only the wealthiest members of society are able to afford "decent healthcare."[105]

India in many ways is a study in contrasts. According to the UN Human Development Report for 2021–22, like most other countries, India experienced a drop in its HDI from 2019 to 2021 because of decreasing life expectancy rates[106] due to COVID-19, which was diagnosed in India, as in most other countries, in March 2020. The government imposed a lockdown shortly thereafter. Since then, recovery has been uneven and unequal. The UN report also revealed that "developing countries in every region are entering a sharply divergent social, political, and economic period with especially sharp downside risks for the most vulnerable and regression in gender equality."[107] Yet on the whole, India's HDI has been increasing again. According to the UNDP Resident Representative in India: "India is bridging the human development gap between men and women faster than the world. . . . India's growth story reflects the country's investments in inclusive growth, social protection, gender-responsive policies, and push towards renewables to ensure no one is left behind."[108] The Human Development Report stated that "India has also boosted access to social protection for vulnerable sections of society, especially during and after the pandemic."[109]

However, looking within the country tells a different and far bleaker story, and illustrates clearly how the responses to COVID varied not only by gender but also by social class/caste, financial well-being, and even geography. An article about the impact of COVID on India published in *Gender Issues* about six months after the initial outbreak of the disease emphasized the impact of the pandemic in terms of worsening "the already existing gender inequalities with substantial implications on women," and then details the impact of the lockdown "with the most vulnerable and marginalized groups being affected differently due to the already existing social inequalities. . . . Specifically, the lockdown has widened the existing gender inequalities and limited the opportunities for women."[110] Priyanshi Chauhan's analysis demonstrates that the COVID-19 lockdowns added to the burden of unpaid labor on women, for women who were employed as well as those who were not employed outside the home. An intersectional analysis reveals that, as Chauhan concludes, "the burden [of unpaid work] has increased the largest for married women and unemployed women, who already spent the highest time on domestic work even before the lockdown."[111]

During the pandemic lockdown, as older children returned home, some continuing schooling or now working remotely, for many women there were now more people to feed and clean up after, thereby increasing their unpaid work. For the young people who returned home now found themselves in the position of having to take up responsibilities at home (unpaid) such as cooking and cleaning, leading to the conclusion that "the norms of work from home and online education increased the demand for services that were earlier purchased both within and outside the household, and are to be now performed without pay during the lockdown, therefore increasing the burden of unpaid work which is gendered in nature."[112] Hence the impact is not only gendered but there is also a generational/age impact. While it is too soon to know what the longer-term impact of this will be on this generation, the results of this analysis indicate that there was certainly a short-term impact.

A report by Oxfam India, published in July 2021, also highlights some of the data and inequalities in the health care system in the country, which are symptomatic of the larger socioeconomic inequalities that India faces as engrained in the caste system. While these inequalities existed prior to the pandemic, the pandemic brought them forward more dramatically. According to this report, "The health status of a group of people is contingent upon the socioeconomic position it holds. The trends of various health indicators across the socioeconomic groups the report has studied indicates that despite a considerable reduction in the gap between the privileged and the marginalized, inequality persists."[113] Moreover, in looking at religion, class, gender, and geography, "Hindus are better off than Muslims, the rich are better off than the poor, men are better off than women, and the urban population is better off than the rural population on various health indicators."[114] One component of India's caste system is the lack of social mobility beyond the caste you were born into; put another way, "caste should be thought of as a key organizing principle of Indian society."[115]

Rather than just looking at the gap between the "haves" and "have nots," we can put a name to this and ascribe the differences to caste, which encompasses social, economic, and political access. Hence, when the pandemic broke out in India, the Dalits (untouchables, or lowest caste) were "the most vulnerable" for a host of reasons. For example, the creation of community quarantine centers, which isolated the poor and the lower castes, served to reinforce the divisions and prejudices that already existed.[116]

What the data suggest is that looking at broad statistics about India's development cannot address the inherent inequalities that exist within the country, nor can they provide a complete picture of India's economic, social, and political situation. As the COVID case shows, the pandemic had different impacts on groups within the country.

Lessons Learned from the COVID Cases

The COVID-19 pandemic affected all countries around the world, although the impact was experienced differently not only across but also within countries. What examining the case of COVID-19 in general and in the two countries (India and South Africa) in particular reinforces is the importance of looking within countries to get a more complete picture of the impact this disease had on various groups, as it seemed to highlight the differences that already exist within countries. This was especially true of the ways in which the disease exacerbated social inequalities that in some cases were already in place but were often obscured by macro-level economic or development data. And social inequalities are often made worse by government policies—or lack thereof—that do not take into account the powerless and therefore often unseen or ignored members of society.

South Africa and India are held up as examples of countries that are developing rapidly. While a broad picture of both suggests that each is recovering from the impact of COVID-19, looking within each of these two countries illustrates the ways in which the disease not only affected groups differently within each country but also laid bare the flaws and inequalities in their respective health care systems and in their social structures. So despite the fact that broad indicators such as the HDI depict each as a country recovering from the pandemic and becoming more "developed," as evidenced by their scores on a range of variables, the reality is far different and really asks us to think about what "economic development" means.

CONCLUSION

This chapter addressed the important topics of economic development and globalization, using an intersectional lens as a way of supporting the themes we raised in the previous chapters. In so doing, we noted the limitations of mainstream IR approaches to studying the global economy and development. Feminist and postcolonial approaches provide the needed intersectional analysis to account for the differential impacts of the increasingly globalized world. Thus, rather than analyzing broad categories, such as economic development and the ways in which it affects women differently than men, for example, we asked how it affected various groups of women as well as men. Then we used the example of COVID-19 as a case study to illustrate the impact this disease had on different groups within countries, exacerbating the social, economic, and political differences that already existed. Another point that should be highlighted here, and that we raised in the introduction to this chapter, is that there is a relationship between economic development, the empowerment of women and other marginalized people, and ensuring peace and security.

Chapter 5

Intersectionality and the Environment

The year 2023 was declared the hottest on record. Scientists have been keeping records of the global average temperature since the mid-1800s.[1] While there has been variation in terms of some years being warmer than others, alarmingly, according to the World Meteorological Organization, "The past nine years, 2015 to 2023, were the warmest on record."[2] As a result of burning fossil fuels (coal, natural gas, and oil), carbon dioxide and other greenhouse gases are released into the atmosphere, leading to the warming of the Earth's surface temperature. And these hotter temperatures mean more-extreme weather events, such as floods, heat waves, storms, and wildfires.[3] Another impact from the heating of the atmosphere is drought. According to the United Nations, approximately 1.84 billion people around the world lived under drought conditions in 2023. With a global population of 8 billion, that represents almost 25 percent of the world's population. The majority of those people live in what are considered low- and middle-income countries.[4] Ibrahim Thiaw, executive secretary of the United Nations Convention to Combat Desertification, stated:

> Drought knows no boundaries, affecting both developed and developing countries around the world. Its impact goes far beyond the immediate lack of water, as it engulfs communities and ecosystems in a pervasive web of interconnected destruction. While drought affects people from all walks of life, it has a disproportionate impact on vulnerable communities. Rural areas with limited access to water resources and inadequate infrastructure often bear the brunt of drought. Smallholder farmers, indigenous peoples and marginalized groups face immense challenges in sustaining their livelihoods during prolonged dry spells. Studies also revealed that women and girls carry the major burden of such impacts.[5]

When we think of environmental issues as a whole, there is a range we can also consider, such as desertification and deforestation. As stated in the 1994 United Nations Convention to Combat Desertification (UNCCD), desertification is defined as "land degradation in arid, semi-arid and dry sub-humid areas resulting from various factors, including climatic variations and human activities."[6] All around the world people face negative impacts of desertification. Such negative impacts include loss of biodiversity, food insecurity, forced migration, poverty, and water scarcity.[7]

Deforestation occurs when forests are cut down for resources such as "wood for fuel, building materials, or paper." Trees are also cleared for land use, such as "farmland to grow crops; pasture to raise livestock; or land to build roads and cities."[8] The loss of forests has a negative environmental impact, as it leads to biodiversity loss and increase in carbon emissions.[9]

What ties all these environmental issues together is that they are international relations challenges because they often transcend states, and international issues require international solutions, that is, countries working together collaboratively to address them. While deforestation, for example, is often a result of domestic markets for more resources and land, demand for those same resources and land often comes from people in wealthier countries when they import food from poorer states that have cleared their forests for food production, namely crops and meat for export.[10] Data from Hannah Ritchie shows that "most countries across Europe and North America are net importers of deforestation; i.e., they're driving deforestation elsewhere; . . . many subtropical countries are partly cutting down trees to meet this demand from rich countries."[11] In essence, international trade has an impact on deforestation.[12] Additionally, deforestation "intensifies climate change at a dramatic rate," as trees are necessary for absorbing carbon dioxide ("carbon sinks"); without trees, that carbon dioxide stays in the atmosphere and further contributes to the warming of the Earth's temperature.[13] Desertification is an international issue when people are displaced due to land degradation and forced to migrate or emigrate. Such displacement can occur within a country, but also as migration across territorial borders as people seek productive land.[14]

While these are international issues, an intersectional analysis demonstrates the differential impacts on people from a warming climate, drought, deforestation, and so forth. As the quote from Thiaw above makes clear, drought has a particular impact on women and girls, and such gender disparities necessitate an intersectional lens in examining the environment. For example, a recent study showed that deforestation, drought, and land degradation affect women twice as much as men. In large part, domestic work and unpaid care is mostly done by women and girls, and "drought and land degradation tend to increase the burden" of such work.[15] Drought means that women might have to walk farther to access water. Additionally, in many countries, women do not have rights to own land, and "less than one in five landholders worldwide are women," although "nearly half of the global agricultural workforce is female."[16] If we consider Indigenous people, while 20 percent of the Earth's land is Indigenous lands, there is variability around the world as to Indigenous peoples' rights to lands and resources, with some countries, such as the Republic of Congo, Indonesia, Panama, and Norway, passing laws securing those rights while the majority of countries have not.[17]

In this chapter we explore how the environment became an international relations issue, essentially the politics of the environment and the international community's responses to addressing these issues. We demonstrate how the environment relates to conflict and justice as this relates to the differential impacts of environmental problems on people both within and across countries. We apply an intersectional analysis of a specific environmental problem: climate change.

DEVELOPMENT AND EVOLUTION OF
INTERNATIONAL ENVIRONMENTAL POLITICS

Historically there has been concern about aspects of the environment from individuals and states, such as the convention signed in 1918 by "the United Kingdom . . . on behalf of Canada" and the United States to address migratory birds.[18] The mid-twentieth century, however, is when there emerged considerable recognition that environmental issues transcend state boundaries and the need for international action became a priority. Simon Dalby highlights several factors that elevated the environment as an issue for policymakers (and scholars too): "rapid economic growth, political pressure from domestic environmental constituencies worried about pollution population, parks and nature protection, and growing international environmental organizations." In addition, "crucial innovations in science that have focused attention on issues that require international cooperation."[19] Such international cooperation occurred, and continues to occur, primarily through UN conferences. In the late 1960s the UN General Assembly drafted and adopted several resolutions focused on "the problems of human environment." These actions led to the convening of the UN Conference on the Human Environment in Stockholm, Sweden, in 1972.[20] For the first time, the environment was "on the global agenda, articulating its link to human well-being and economic growth."[21] This conference, focused on the connection between the environment and development, "is considered the start of international environmental policy."[22] The Stockholm Declaration and Action Plan for the Human Environment and other resolutions emerged from the conference.[23] The UN General

Assembly then passed a resolution creating the United Nations Environment Programme (UNEP) that same year. UNEP "was conceived to monitor the state of the environment and coordinate responses to the world's greatest environmental challenges."[24] Since its creation, UNEP has utilized scientific research as well as engaging in "public advocacy" in order to "advance the global environmental agenda."[25] With the 1972 conference and the establishment of UNEP, as Hanna Gersmann notes, "the foundation for an active UN role in global environmental protection is in place."[26]

That said, it would be twenty years before another global conference on the environment and development would be convened. The United Nations Conference on Environment and Development (UNCED), the "Earth Summit," was held in Rio de Janeiro in 1992.[27] In terms of participation, "10,000 delegates from 178 countries and more non-state actors than ever before in UN history" attended the conference.[28] The Rio Declaration's Principle 1 states: "Human beings are at the center of concerns for sustainable development. They are entitled to a healthy and productive life in harmony with nature."[29] Principle 4 states: "In order to achieve sustainable development, environmental protection shall constitute an integral part of the development process and cannot be considered in isolation from it."[30]

Particularly noteworthy for an intersectional analysis, which will be discussed later in the chapter, the Rio Declaration included principles on "the vital role of indigenous people in conservation and sustainable management of the environment given their knowledge and traditional practices" (Principle 22), as well as the "vital role" of women "in environmental management and development" (Principle 20). It further noted the importance of women's "full participation,"[31] a theme we have seen before.

In addition to the Rio Declaration, other initiatives resulted from the conference, including Agenda 21, which focused on "new strategies . . . to achieve overall sustainable development in the 21st century," the Convention on Biological Diversity, and the United Nations Framework Convention on Climate Change (UNFCCC) (see the section on climate change below).[32]

While twenty years separated the 1972 UN Stockholm conference and the 1992 Rio conference, in the intervening time period the international community took measures to address various environmental issues. For example, in response to concerns about the status of endangered species, in 1973 states adopted the Convention on International Trade in Endangered Species of Wild Fauna and Flora (CITES).[33] The UN Conference on Desertification (UNCOD) in 1977 "adopted a Plan of Action to Combat Desertification (PACD)." Evident that land degradation and desertification have economic and social impacts, it was not until the early 1990s did "tackling desertification [take] center stage." Following efforts to address the issue at the 1992 UN Conference on Environment and Development in Rio, in 1994 the UN

General Assembly adopted a resolution that established the UN Convention to Combat Desertification.[34]

Signed in 1987, the Montreal Protocol on Substances that Deplete the Ozone Layer ("Montreal Protocol") is one of the most successful international environmental treaties. The Earth's stratospheric ozone layer "protects humans and the environment from harmful levels of ultraviolet radiation from the sun."[35] In 1985 scientists published findings of the discovery of "a gigantic hole above Antarctica"—a hole in the ozone layer.[36] The use of hydrochlorofluorocarbons (HCFCs) in air-conditioning and refrigeration was damaging the ozone layer. The Montreal Protocol "phases down the consumption and production" of those chemicals by both developed and developing states. As noted on the UN website, it is "one of the rare treaties to achieve universal ratification."[37] As of 2024, "the Parties to the Protocol have phased out 98% of ODS [ozone depleting substances] globally compared to 1990 levels . . . [and the Protocol] is contributing significantly to the protection of the global climate system."[38]

Twenty years after the 1992 UN Conference in Rio, representatives gathered at the Rio+20 UN Conference on Sustainable Development in 2012. This conference sought "to develop a global agenda for sustainability."[39] As part of the conference proceedings, the participants "decided to launch a process to develop a set of Sustainable Development Goals (SDGs)."[40] (See chapter 4 for the full list of Sustainable Development Goals.) In 2015 at the UN General Assembly, all member states adopted the 2030 Agenda for Sustainable Development, which included the seventeen SDGs. These SDGs build upon and supersede the UN Millennium Development Goals (MDGs), adopted at the UN Millennium Summit in 2000, which focused on issues such as disease, environmental degradation, hunger, illiteracy, poverty, and women's rights, with a target date of 2015.[41] Several of the SDGs are related to the environment, including "affordable and clean energy" (goal 7), "sustainable cities and communities" (goal 11), "responsible consumption and production" (goal 12), and "climate action" (goal 13).[42]

Continued international attention on the climate that same year (2015) is evident with the signing of the Paris Agreement on Climate Change by 196 states at the Conference of Parties (COP21). (The COP process is discussed in more detail below.) A legally binding treaty—as the text of the agreement makes clear—countries, developed and developing alike, will determine their "contributions to the global response to climate change" in order to "[hold] the increase in the global average temperature to well below 2°C above pre-industrial levels and to pursue efforts to limit the temperature increase to 1.5°C above pre-industrial levels, recognizing that this would significantly reduce the risks and impacts of climate change."[43]

Given this brief overview of the development and evolution of international environmental politics, how might international relations, as a discipline, account for that development and evolution? The next section considers how the mainstream IR theories approach the study of the environment.

INTERNATIONAL RELATIONS AND THE ENVIRONMENT

As discussed in chapter 1, the field of international relations (IR) has, for the most part, studied relations between countries. The "big" topics of IR have tended to focus on understanding international wars (i.e., why and how they start, why they continue, and why and how they end), security, and peace. When considering IR scholarship on the environment, as John Vogler observes, "most of the relevant research before the 1970s was conducted by economists, geographers and others from outside the IR discipline, even if their focus was fixed upon the geopolitics of resource scarcity."[44]

The 1972 UN Conference on the Human Environment became the starting point for placing environmental issues "on the actual agenda of international politics."[45] It is at this time that "substantial theoretical interest amongst IR scholars" emerged.[46] Much of the IR scholarship that followed focused on international cooperation, namely liberal institutionalism.[47] The liberal institutionalist approach, as we discussed in chapter 1, examines how states can cooperate to solve issues of mutual interest. IR scholars in the field of international political economy (IPE) (see chapter 4) developed "the concept of a regime" in order to explain how states, in a world in which there is no world government, could cooperate in the area of economics/trade.[48] In turn, scholars examining state cooperation with regard to environmental issues, such as the 1987 Montreal Protocol as well as other multilateral agreements on the environment, utilized regime theory—essentially, a liberal institutionalist approach.[49] As Vogler makes clear, "Institutions or environmental regimes were seen as significant determinants of government behaviour and sources of learning, leading to potential absolute gains for all concerned and, most significantly, to the joint management of a shared vulnerability to environmental danger."[50]

Constructivists have also studied the environment as an international relations issue, given the focus on the evolution of norms (and how such norms influence state behavior) and state identities.[51] One need only consider the role of "multilateral international environmental governance" institutions, such as the UN conferences, that have utilized science to understand environmental issues and respond to environmental problems. In so doing, as Peter Haas argues, "states are [then] increasingly accountable to domestic and transnational constituencies, thus shifting the locus of enforcement from states toward international institutions and NGOs."[52]

Yet, even with these norms and global governance institutions, states have not done enough to reduce the Earth's temperature, for example. Realists can explain why the major powers (that are also the largest emitters of greenhouse gases) have been unwilling to address climate change in a meaningful way. Stephen M. Walt stresses that "no major power is going to make big sacrifices in the near term to deal with climate change if it thinks that doing so will leave it at a disadvantage relative to others." There's no enforcement mechanism because there's no political authority above states to do so. If a state makes the "sacrifices" required by the terms of an international agreement but other states do not (they cheat), then the state is "worse off yet still facing an overheating planet along with everyone else."[53] He argues that focusing on a state's narrow self-interests rather than "idealistic appeals to our shared humanity" may be the way for states, namely the major states (as the greatest emitters), to act.[54]

In the liberal, realist, and constructivist approaches in IR, states are still the dominant actors and, for the most part, remain the focus of their analysis. Yet recognizing the importance of international governmental organizations (IGOs) and non-governmental organizations (NGOs) in addressing environmental concerns, scholars have also examined how non-state actors matter in the development and implementation of various responses, including multilateral agreements, to different environmental issues. Whether in the form of local protests by civil society actors (i.e., Greenpeace), business practices to reduce pollution, or regional organizations such as the EU's climate and energy targets for 2030, for example, non-state actors are actively engaged in environmental politics at the local, state, regional, and global levels. In essence, the engagement of such actors highlights global governance that transcends states. As Vogler argues, "Global governance theorizing breaks with the state-centric focus of the regime analysis."[55]

Environmental Security and Conflict

As explained in chapter 2, in the 1980s the concept of security, "the overriding concern of IR theory," began to broaden as scholars looked at a range of issues beyond traditional conceptions of security. Rather than focusing narrowly on state security through military means, scholars began to write about human security, of which environmental security was one aspect.[56] Nicole A. Detraz notes that increases in both globalization and population, for example, can have negative impacts on the environment, thereby making states and people less secure.[57] Thus, in considering environmental security, some scholars have looked at the connection between the environment and conflict, namely whether environmental degradation leading to resource scarcities will lead to conflict between groups. Such conflict within countries can, in turn, "threaten the stability of the state."[58] Thomas F. Homer-Dixon explores particular social impacts from environmental scarcities—"population move-ment, economic decline, and the weakening of states"—and the possibility of civil or international conflict.[59] His research findings indicate that violent conflict may result from environmental scarcity and "tends to be persistent, diffuse, and sub-national."[60] Looking at environmental security in this way, that environmental problems can impact "violent conflict and the integrity of the state and its territory," readily fits with mainstream IR concerns about state security.[61] Moreover, with the end of the Cold War, some activists and governments framed environmental problems as national security issues.[62] For example, beginning in 2008 the US national security community noted that climate change is a national security threat. For the US government, and the Department of Defense (DOD) in particular, "extreme heat, floods, rising sea levels, droughts, wildfires and more frequent and intense storms and other natural disasters—compounded by climate change—are reshaping DOD's operating environment, and degrading military readiness."[63]

That the environment is considered a security issue is further illustrated by the issues on UN Security Council agendas. For example, in June 2007 the president of the Security Council issued a statement that included the following: "The Security Council recalls the principles of the Charter of the United Nations and in particular the Security Council's primary responsibility for the maintenance of international peace and security. In this respect, the Security Council recognizes the role that natural resources can play in armed conflict and post-conflict situations."[64] Since then, the UN Security Council has discussed various environmental issues as they pertain explicitly to peace and conflict, including resource extraction, climate change, and deforestation.

Whether realist, liberal, constructivist, or global governance approaches to studying the environment, these approaches are limited in that they do not examine how particular environmental problems and policies to address those problems have differential impacts on people within and across states. As the next section shows, feminist and postcolonial scholars have provided critiques, calling for an intersectional analysis to understand, and respond to, environmental problems.

INTERSECTIONALITY AND INTERNATIONAL/ GLOBAL ENVIRONMENTAL POLITICS

In considering global/international environmental politics, how might gender, race, class, and other categories matter? More specifically, how might we understand the connection between the environment and conflict, for exam-ple, from an intersectional lens? Various approaches utilize intersectionality to study not only the causes but also the consequences of environmental issues.[65] Christina Ergas et al. highlight those approaches, which include ecofeminist, feminist political ecology (FPE), gender and development, and postcolonial feminism and Indigenous studies.[66] Both ecofeminism and feminist political ecology "identify differences across women who are shaped by gendered and racialized histories of colonialism and imperialism."[67]

Emerging in the United States in the 1970s, ecofeminism (with its multiple variants) highlights "that the oppression of women is deeply and critically connected to the domination of nature and that solutions to environmental problems must incorporate feminist perspectives."[68] The patriarchal system "leads to the domination of the 'Other.'"[69] In tracing the evolution of ecofeminist theory, Sonalini Sapra shows that in "the latter half of the 1980s, US ecofeminists started producing literature on Native American and 'Third World Women' as examples of ecofeminist practice. This literature privileges indigenous women as the 'ultimate ecofeminists.'"[70] Here we can see an intersectional analysis that moves beyond women as a monolithic entity.

The FPE approach "reject[s] ecofeminist arguments claiming that there is any 'innate' connection between women and the environment. They argue that the access and distribution of natural resources are differentiated through gender within societies." Given that the bulk of "agricultural and domestic work" is done by women, "particularly in developing countries," they are then "at the frontlines in struggles for health, food, and water."[71] Feminist political ecology scholars explore "how geopolitics and political-economic contexts shape local peoples' gendered access to natural resources, land tenure, property rights, and collective action."[72] Sapra cautions that "although FPE theorists are constantly examining the relationships between men and women, discussion of gender often tends to focus solely on women. Consequently, this can lead to replication of the same problematic essentialized nature of women generated in ecofeminist discourse."[73]

Postcolonial feminists examine the continued impacts of colonialism and the ways in which Western feminists essentialize women in the Global South. In so doing, such women are depicted "as weak, victimized, and traditional."[74] Only by using an intersectional analysis that takes into account categories such as "caste, class, religion, ethnicity, and others" and "acknowledges their [women of the Global South] agency as actors within local social relations and global social movements" can we better understand the causes and the differential impacts of environmental problems.[75] Indigenous studies also direct our attention to understanding how European colonialism led to the exploitation of land, "genocide and relocation . . . forced assimilation."[76]

An intersectional lens shows that "poor, rural, Indigenous women and children in Global South nations are most vulnerable to climate-related disasters."[77] Such vulnerability arises for rural women who rely on agriculture

"to sustain their poverty-stricken livelihoods, families, and communities."
Gender inequality further aggravates women's vulnerability.[78] Without a
focus on adaptation skills, women are further vulnerable when "exposed . . .
to new risks and insecurities."[79] Moreover, studies show "that gender-based
violence typically spikes in the aftermath of disasters, further compounding
vulnerability to disasters for women and girls."[80]

While people in the Global South are vulnerable to environmental disasters, so too are people in the Global North: "Intersecting nodes of inequality
also affect risk and vulnerability for certain sectors of the population in the
face of environmental hazards and disasters."[81] For example, in 1995 Hurricane Katrina made landfall in the Gulf region of the United States, bringing significant devastation to New Orleans, Louisiana, in particular when
"several levee systems caused extensive flooding."[82] The race, gender, and
class dynamics were at play as people tried to flee, but many did not have the
resources (such as a car or money to pay for a hotel away from the path of the
hurricane) to do so. As Jean Ait Belkhir and Christiane Charlemaine assert,
"The poverty and blackness of those most affected by the disaster is obvious
to anyone watching the media in the days following the levy break."[83] Pre-
hurricane policies by the city government, such as failure to fix levees near
areas primarily in which low-income African Americans lived, contributed to
the disproportionate effects of the hurricane.[84]

Environmental Justice

As noted above, in both the Global South and Global North, people experience human insecurity from environmental problems. Recognizing the
impact of such problems of various kinds, both within countries and globally,
activists and scholars have called for *environmental justice*. Environmental
justice is defined "as the multi-dimensional demand for, and/or achievement
of, a healthy environment for all; equal access (across social groups) to environmental goods; equal protection from environmental harms; equal access
to environmental information; and equal participation in environmental
decision-making."[85]

The early scholarship on environmental justice, starting in the 1980s,
"focused almost exclusively on inequities related to environmental racism—spaces where racial/ethnic minorities were exposed to disproportionate
amounts of environmental toxicants and hazards through waste incinera-
tors, hazardous landfills, and other industrial or polluting land uses." As the
research continued to evolve, it explored categories such as age, class, and
gender.[86] Karen Bell states that "women have traditionally been the leaders
and activists in the environmental justice movement." Why this is the case,
according to Bell, is that it may be "because men have more of a vested

interest in the economic and political institutions responsible for environmental harms." Interestingly, Bell also observes that "women involved in the environmental justice movement do not generally seem to assert a gender dimension to the topic or to articulate the gender issues involved."[87] Class figures into the analysis of environmental justice, given that capitalism "causes environmental damage, . . . [and] tends to polarize income and wealth inequalities, creates unemployment and underemployment and is prone to periodic crisis which tend to be borne by the worst off."[88] Bell concludes that "the primary factors driving gender-based environmental injustice" are inequality and poverty.[89]

Global Governance and Intersectionality: Gender Mainstreaming and Representation

According to Charlotte Bretherton, the connection between women and the environment "developed at the global level in the context of the United Nations Decade for Women (1975–85)." One can see these connections clearly when comparing the 1972 Stockholm Declaration, which "referred only to men," to the 1992 Rio Declaration and Agenda 21, both of which included "women's concerns." The inclusion of such concerns resulted from "a well-organized and proactive women's lobby."[90]

One of those women's advocacy groups, the Women's Environment & Development Organization (WEDO), was instrumental in engagement in global environmental politics in the context of global governance. Created in 1991, WEDO, "a global women's advocacy organization," brought together more than fifteen hundred women from eighty-three states at the World Women's Congress for a Healthy Planet, held in Florida in late 1991.[91] The World Women's Congress was "an opportunity to build on the gains of the United Nations Decade for Women."[92] The Women's Action Agenda 21 platform emerged from the meeting in the hopes of inclusion in the upcoming 1992 UN Conference on Environment and Development ("Earth Summit").[93] The Agenda 21 document that resulted from the Earth Summit includes the chapter "Global Action for Women Towards Sustainable and Equitable Development."[94]

As Gunther Handl concludes, "The Rio Declaration was the very first international instrument to explicitly recognize that the empowerment of women and, specifically, their ability to effectively participate in their countries' economic and social processes, is an essential condition for sustainable development."[95] We can see the evolution of feminist engagement in global environmental politics from the period 1980 to the 1990s that emphasized "women, environment and development" (WED). This, in turn, shifted to "women in development" (WID) and "gender, environment and development" (GED), and finally "to an emphasis on feminist political ecology in the 1990s–2000s."[96] That said, Bretherton explains that while there have been attempts over the years "to include gender/development links on the agenda of global environmental politics," such efforts "have been unsuccessful." What we see, instead, is the continued linking of women and the environment.[97] In other words, the emphasis is on women, not gender. As a result, according to Greta Gaard, women were constructed "as *victims* of environmental degradation in need of rescue; their essential closeness to nature, cultivated through family caregiving and through subsistence labor, was argued as providing women with special knowledge, and their *agency* as laborers and leaders in environmental projects was advocated" (emphasis in original).[98] Important to note as well is that this rhetoric, as Gaard remarks, "was also significantly silent on the roles of men, and the ways that gender as a system constructed economic and material resources that produce 'victims.'"[99]

At the same time, as an intersectional analysis shows, women are not a monolithic group. Bretherton makes clear that in "the early years of the UN Decade for Women," there were "significant misunderstandings and tensions between" women in the developed and developing states.[100] And while women environmental activists agreed with much of the UN Conference on Environment and Development processes and the global governance institutions, "differences remain on reproductive rights issues. . . . These reflect cultural/religious factors which cut across racial divisions."[101] In the context of women's roles as reproducers, global environmental policies are then proposed and enacted as a result. In linking the connections between development, population growth, and the environment, solving the population growth problem, as it is framed, means policies that target women's fertility, and often that means women in developing countries.[102] Whether policies put forward by various United Nations agencies, the World Bank, or non-governmental organizations, it is, as Bretherton states, "on the gendered agenda of global environmental politics [that] women are conceptualized primarily in terms of their reproductive roles. . . . Indeed it appears to see reproduction as a process involving women exclusively. This greatly reduces the probability of successful policy implementation."[103]

While women have been, and continue to be, engaged in environmental politics at all levels from the local to the global, that engagement has often faced obstacles in terms of access to financial resources and specialized knowledge. In turn, that limits women's influence in the environmental policy agenda-setting and decision-making.[104] Two related mechanisms to promote women's empowerment and gender equality, whether in terms of local, state, regional, or international levels of governance, are representation and gender mainstreaming.

At the 1995 UN World Conference on Women in Beijing, China, the Beijing Declaration and Platform for Action (see also chapters 2 and 4) called for gender equality and women's empowerment. In order to promote and ensure gender equality and women's empowerment, *gender mainstreaming* became the vital link: "that needs and rights of both men and women are visibly considered in all policies, programmes, strategies, research, and other areas."[105] In terms of gender mainstreaming in international environmental organizations, we see "the shift from inter-governmental politics to a global environmental governance." This shift means that in addition to governments, other actors are participating in developing and implementing environmental politics, such as "networks of experts, environmental organizations, private interests and new agencies set up by governments. International environmental organizations have assumed an increasingly important place in this context."[106] The challenge for gender mainstreaming efforts is that sometimes gender becomes bureaucratized and depoliticized.[107]

With regard to the impact of women's representation in government, studies repeatedly demonstrate that "women's representation in parliaments is associated with stronger environmental policies."[108] A recent study of the European Parliament found that women MEPs (Members of the European Parliament) "are more likely than their male colleagues to advance environmental protection."[109] Yet, at the international level, "women only hold around one-quarter of seats. Despite the fact that women have been at the forefront of environmental activism for decades, women make up only 15 per cent of environment ministers at the national level."[110] For example, in the period 2012–2022, women's participation in the country delegations to the various UN Conferences of the Parties (COPs) on climate increased. In 2012 the percentage of women delegates was 30 percent; by 2022 it was 35 percent. At the same time, "the proportion of delegations headed by women declined slightly from 21 to 20%."[111] Most recently, in mid-January 2024, the president of Azerbaijan, which will host the next COP global climate change summit (COP29), announced the twenty-eight members of the organizing committee. The committee would be an all-male panel.[112] Christiana Figueres, who served as the UN's climate chief in the negotiations on the 2015 Paris agreement, "called the all-male panel 'shocking and unacceptable.'" Following significant public backlash, Azerbaijan's president added twelve women (and another man), so the organizing committee now comprises twenty-nine men and twelve women—not a 50–50 gender balance.[113]

In addition to relatively low levels of women's representation and participation in global environmental governance bodies such as the COPs, the representation and participation of Indigenous peoples are also quite low. This is important to note, given "it is widely agreed that Indigenous participation and knowledge is critical to effective environmental governance."[114] As is the case for women, Indigenous peoples also face barriers in terms of access to financial and other resources and power, and thus have difficulty "accessing environmental governance decision-making processes."[115]

CASE STUDY: CLIMATE CHANGE

According to UN Women, "By 2050, climate change may push up to 158 million more women and girls into poverty and see 236 million more face food insecurity. The climate crisis fuels increases in conflict and migration, as well as exclusionary, anti-rights political rhetoric targeting women, refugees, and other vulnerable groups."[116] As Farhana Sultana makes clear: "Climate change has exacerbated unequal intersectional power relations of gender, class, and other axes significantly in the developing world, but also in the industrialized world (especially in racialized communities and Indigenous communities)."[117] As with environmental justice in general, scholars and activists have called climate justice, which "requires: the recognition and respect of diverse identities, experiences and forms of knowledge, the redistribution of resources; and the representation and meaningful participation of women and marginalized groups in climate-related decision-making."[118] Michael Mikulewicz et al. emphasize, "Climate justice needs intersectionality . . . [because] climate change . . . is a social crisis within which multiple oppressions intertwine and interact."[119]

As this section will show, however, the early decades of global environmental politics related to climate change did not consider women and other marginalized groups, nor did such politics consider gender, race, class, and other factors. Rather, the focus was on technical solutions to address climate change, as well as the economic impacts of policies to reduce emissions from the burning of fossil fuels. Moreover, as Paul G. Harris states, "The politics of climate change have been tortuous and slow, particularly at the international level. . . . It is by far the most prominent challenge in both the practice and study of global environmental politics."[120] In essence, as Jennifer Hadden and Aseem Prakash assert, "Climate change is fundamentally a political problem; it is not merely a technical or economic challenge but rather an arena for sharp conflicts over the distribution of gains and losses and the associated ethical challenges."[121]

In 1979 the World Meteorological Organization (WMO) held the first global conference on the climate, acknowledging "climate change . . . as a serious problem."[122] Representatives and scientists from more than fifty states[123] met to discuss the impact of climate change, with a declaration that called on states in the international system "to foresee and prevent potential man-made changes in climate that might be adverse to the well-being of humanity."[124] In the decade that followed, a series of intergovernmental conferences on climate change were instrumental in increasing awareness internationally about climate change. In addition to scientists and policymakers, environmental activists also attended.[125] The flurry of activity around addressing climate change as a global issue culminated in 1988 with the creation of the Intergovernmental Panel on Climate Change (IPCC) by the UNEP and WMO. The IPCC's mandate was "to assess the state of existing knowledge about the climate system and climate change; the environmental, economic, and social impacts of climate change; and the possible response strategies." Publishing its research findings in its First Assessment Report in 1990 "had a powerful effect on both policymakers and the general public and provided the basis for negotiations on the Climate Change Convention" that was signed two years later at the 1992 UN conference in Rio.[126] The developed states were the focus of the UNFCCC in calling on them "to reduce their emissions of greenhouse gases to 1990 levels by 2000—something that they failed to do." Moreover, they also "agreed to provide 'new and additional' resources to developing states to help them address climate change."[127]

The COP Process and Responding to Climate Change

After the UNFCCC entered into force in 1994, in order "to measure progress and negotiate multilateral responses to climate change," it was determined that the member states that joined the UNFCCC would meet annually. Known as the Conference of the Parties (COP), the first such meeting was held in 1995 in Berlin.[128] Several international agreements have emerged from these conferences. For example, at the COP3 meeting, held in Kyoto, Japan, in 1997, the conference attendees signed the Kyoto Protocol, in which the developed countries committed to reducing their "greenhouse gas emissions for the first time." Developing countries did not have to make such commitments.[129] Harris concludes that "much as developed states failed to do what they promised in the UNFCCC, history shows that collectively they did not actually do what the Kyoto Protocol required."[130]

COPs continued to convene after the Kyoto Protocol was concluded. It was at the Paris COP in 2015, and the Agreement that was concluded, that "was the culmination of efforts to move international climate regulation away from top-down mandates to bottom-up national pledges." Unlike previous agreements that set out requirements for developed states, developing states, "for the first time," were "required . . . to limit their greenhouse gas pollution alongside developed states."[131]

It is also interesting to consider that, according to Hannah Hughes, "in the late 1980s, early 1990s, climate change was largely not identified as a threat in and of itself, but as an issue promising to increase the stress of continuing environmental degradation and population growth."[132] Only in the 2000s was climate change considered a security threat, and hence the concept of *climate security*.[133] For example, the UN's Department of Political and Peacebuilding Affairs (DPPA) made "understanding and responding to climate-related security risks . . . a strategic priority." Its *Strategic Plan for 2023–2026* recognized that climate-related security "risks are highly context-specific, with impacts that vary across regions, countries and communities, requiring integrated analysis and responses as women, men and youth are affected in different ways."[134] Moreover, the "DPPA pays particular attention to the impact on women as well as the potential of women as agents of change."[135] At the same time, as the next section indicates, international climate policy often did not pay attention to gender.[136]

GENDERING CLIMATE CHANGE AND GLOBAL GOVERNANCE

Studies have shown that there are differential impacts of climate on people; and factors "such as race, age, economic status, disability, geographic location, and marital status interact with sex and gender, shaping people's experiences of climate change."[137] For example, as this chapter has noted throughout, women experience "multiple care burdens, including collection of food, water, fuel, cooking, cleaning, and looking after the children, elderly, and the sick," all of which are exacerbated by climate change.[138] At the same time, given that climate change was considered "a techno-scientific problem" and that "environmental politics and institutions were male dominated," the UNFCCC adopted in 1992 "did not pay attention to gender."[139] It was only because of "strong advocacy by gender justice advocates since the UNFCCC Conference of the Parties (COP) 7 in 2001 was this omission slowly remedied."[140]

According to Sapra, it was in 2007 at the COP13 held in Bali, Indonesia, that "marked an important moment for transnational feminist organizing around climate change."[141] In that year, the Global Gender and Climate Alliance (GGCA), which includes various international governmental organizations, NGOs, and UN agencies, seeks "to ensure that all climate change decision-making, policies and initiatives, at all levels, are gender responsive."[142]

This was the same year (2007) that the women's environmental activist group GenderCC-Women for Climate Justice was founded.[143] As its website states, the organization "is a global network of organisations, experts and activists working for gender equality, women's rights and climate justice. GenderCC has evolved in the context of the international climate negotiations

(UNFCCC). It includes women and gender experts working in policy, research and practical implementation at international, national and local levels."[144] In answering the question, "Why gender into climate policy?" the organization makes clear that "different genders contribute differently to the causes of climate change. Individual carbon footprints are a product of gender roles, responsibilities and identities." They also assert that "the impacts of climate change vary by gender" and "climate policies and measures affect people differently, depending on gender and other axes of discrimination. This is due to socio-economic factors, such as disparities in income and occupational choice."[145] GenderCC-Women for Climate Justice recognizes how climate change has differential effects, and thus the need for an intersectional lens to understand and address climate change.

Established in 2009, and one of several constituencies under the UNFCCC, the Women and Gender Constituency (WGC) is "the platform for observer organizations working to ensure women's rights and gender justice within the climate change convention framework . . . [and] ensures that meetings, workshops and conferences include the participation and representation of women's civil society and non-governmental organizations which otherwise would not be able to attend."[146]

TEXTBOX 5.1

WOMEN AND GENDER CONSTITUENCY AT THE UNFCCC "A JUST FRAMEWORK FOR ACTION"

"A just and gender-responsive climate framework can take different forms, but fundamentally it must: respect and promote human rights and gender equality; ensure sustainable development and environmental integrity; require fair, equitable, ambitious and binding mitigation commitments in line with the principles of Common but Differentiated Responsibilities (CBDR); call for urgent and prioritized adaptation action and resources that respond to the most vulnerable countries, communities and populations; demand a sustainable energy paradigm that prioritizes safe, decentralized renewable energy systems that benefit people and communities; ensure adequate, new, additional and predictable climate finance for developing countries; provide resources to reconcile loss and damage already incurred from climate inaction; and ensure full, inclusive and gender-equitable public participation in decision-making, with increased mandatory ex ante and periodic human rights and gender equality impact assessments. It must ensure that gender equality, equal access to decision-making, and benefit sharing are integrated into all its provisions, including through gender-responsive means of implementation. Sex and gender disaggregated data and analysis of the underlying causes of any gender disparities must be mainstreamed in all information, communication and reporting systems."[147]

Considerations of gender and women's participation and representation continued in the context of the UNFCCC's work. For example, "since 2014 the Lima Work Programme on Gender has been guiding gender mainstreaming processes in the UNFCCC."[148] The following year, at the COP21 in Paris, the 2015 Paris Agreement explicitly noted women, as well as other marginalized groups. The text of the agreement states the following: "*Acknowledging* that climate change is a common concern of humankind, Parties should, when taking action to address climate change, respect, promote and consider their respective obligations on human rights, the right to health, the rights of indigenous peoples, local communities, migrants, children, persons with disabilities and people in vulnerable situations and the right to development, as well as gender equality, empowerment of women and intergenerational equity."[149]

Two years later, at the COP held in Bonn, Germany (COP23), the participants established a Gender Action Plan (GAP) that reaffirmed the UN General Assembly's resolution on the 2030 Agenda for Sustainable Development, specifically focused on global governance and climate change. As the UNFCCC report of the COP affirms, "The GAP, . . . seeks to advance women's full, equal and meaningful participation and promote gender-responsive climate policy and the mainstreaming of a gender perspective in the implementation of the Convention and the work of Parties, the secretariat, United Nations entities and all stakeholders at all levels."[150] The GAP lists five priority areas with related activities to ensure gender equality and gender mainstreaming happen at all levels: "Capacity-building, knowledge-sharing and communication"; "Gender balance, participation and women's leadership"; "Coherence"; "Gender-responsive implementation and means of implementation"; and "Monitoring and reporting."[151]

While it is clear that women and gender (and the norm of gender mainstreaming) are increasingly considered in global environmental governance forums, namely the UNFCCC's COPs, as Joanna Flavell argues, "the topic of women and gender tends to get pushed to the background in high-profile years for the UNFCCC more broadly, such as COP21 Paris in 2015." For the members of the Women and Gender Constituency, for example, they "see substantive success only when making arguments based on women's vulnerability to the effects of climate change or about the need to gender balance boards and bodies or national delegations within the UNFCCC."[152] Flavell's observation is reinforced by the most recent COP, COP28, held in December 2023 in Dubai, United Arab Emirates. UN Women issued its "Feminist Climate Justice: A Framework for Action" report on the "gender day" of the conference. The report calls for a "feminist climate justice approach" in "four key areas": "1) Recognizing women's rights, labor, and knowledge"; "2) Redistributing economic resources"; "3) Representation of women's voices"; and "4) Repairing inequalities and historical injustices."[153] In discussing these four areas, the report notes, for example, that "decision-makers need to recognize the expertise that women, including indigenous, rural and young women have" that can inform climate adaptation measures. Additionally, redistributing economic resources means development aid that makes gender equality a priority (currently only 3 percent of such aid goes to these efforts).[154]

As Flavell further demonstrates, "*women*-environment links are mainstreamed into UNFCCC discourse, but *gender*-environment links, including gender in all its complexity, paying attention to both women *and* the workings of masculinity and male power in shaping global climate politics, remain marginalized and resisted" (emphasis in original).[155] It is still the case that climate politics, at least in the UNFCCC, continues to focus on a single axis, women, rather than multiple axes that would include categories such as class, Indigenous peoples, and race.[156]

CONCLUSION

This chapter has looked at how environmental politics is an international relations issue, in terms of both scholarship and practice. Constructivist IR can help us understand how the environment became an international political issue that local, state, regional, and international actors have addressed. Tracing the historical evolution of international environmental politics (i.e., UN conferences, conventions, and treaties) can help us to explain the emergence and diffusion of national and transnational norms about how to manage and perhaps solve environmental problems, including climate change.[157] At the same time, a constructivist approach is limited unless it utilizes an intersectional analysis, as we show in this chapter, and hence the importance of feminist and postcolonial approaches to study the environment. Considering environmental security and environmental justice leads us to delve more deeply into the differential impacts of environmental problems. Without an intersectional lens that takes into account the differential impacts of environmental problems and the role of factors such as political and socioeconomic inequalities, effective adaptation and mitigation measures to address these problems are unlikely to be formulated and implemented.[158]

Chapter 6

Examining IR from an
Intersectional Perspective

LESSONS LEARNED

In chapter 1, as we introduced the main themes of this book, we also asked two important questions: What does traditional IR miss by not including intersectionality in addressing critical issues? How does an intersectional approach change and, in fact, broaden our understanding of international relations and the international system? From that starting point, we reviewed the three traditional approaches used in IR—realist, liberal, and constructivist—to create a framework within which answers to many of the basic questions in IR are addressed, such as why do states go to war, and what is peace? These approaches assume that the state is the primary actor, and the study of the field pertains to the relationships among and between these actors. A traditional levels of analysis framework[1] asks us to look within the state level when answering certain questions that require us to understand the behavior of both the individuals/elites in government and the people within the country in the context of the culture and society within which they live. Concomitant with that are critical concepts such as power, with the realists especially claiming that states will always seek to maximize their power.[2]

Some of the biggest changes in the field came from the feminist scholars who admonished us to ask: "Where are the women?" Injecting women and gender into our understanding of some of these fundamental issues and questions not only changed our answers to these questions but also encouraged us to change the questions we asked. Introducing gender gave rise to a body of literature that expanded the ways in which scholars look at even the most basic questions in international relations. For example, what does peace mean, and how does a country move from war to peace? Their argument is that these broad questions in IR cannot really be answered unless we move beyond the traditional decision-makers, who are usually men, to study the impact of these decisions on all people. Hence, the argument is that by not including women (and gender) in their analysis, traditional IR cannot account for the ways in which these issues are gendered.

Similarly, race and IR offered another perspective in thinking about international relations. The emergence of postcolonial scholarship similarly asked IR scholars to rethink some of the basic power relationships between and among states, including the legacy of colonialism on the developing states in the contemporary period. Each of these perspectives was important for the ways in which they built on the foundations of existing IR theories in order to increase our understanding of international politics.

Intersectional analysis has informed approaches to the study of political science. While intersectionality has been part of the canon in other social sciences, like sociology, it has only recently been introduced into the field of political science in general and IR in particular. The use of an intersectional approach allows us to expand the analysis of international relations. For example, as we note in chapter 1, it is often overlooked that IR has a long history of looking at race as a critical variable. However, the focus on race or gender was generally along a single axis; for example, "women and peace," or "race and IR." An intersectional approach allows us to bring in the *intersection* of a range of categories. So rather than looking at women and peace as a broad category, we can look at the ways in which women of different ages worked for peace in a particular context, or the approaches to peace taken by Black women and White women. Doing so can expand our understanding of the broad category "women and peace." In addition to asking about which women (and which girls), an intersectional lens also leads us to ask about which men (and which boys). One of the important points to keep in mind is that an intersectional analysis does not remove or subvert some of the critical concepts that have long defined the field of IR, such as power. What it does is allow us to consider those concepts in a different way.

In fact, Ange-Marie Hancock considers how an intersectional approach reconceptualizes power. She asks us to think about the unequal power differentials that exist even among women based on race as well as gender.[3] As Patricia Hill Collins and Sirma Bilge describe it, *"The interpersonal domain of power* refers to how individuals experience the convergence of structural, cultural, and disciplinary power. Such power shapes intersecting identities of race, class, gender, sexuality, nation, and age that in turn organize social interactions" (emphasis in original).[4]

ANSWERING THE QUESTIONS

So how does this broader understanding of power and the relationships among categories that affect one's identity change our understanding of international relations? One only need look at the case of Northern Ireland to see how the multiple identities of the people involved in the Troubles conditioned their responses to the conflict situation in which they lived (chapter 2). Or consider the case of Ukraine, and how the multiple identities of the women in that country affected the ways in which they responded to the war—whether they chose to stay or flee—and even the type of welcome they received in the country to which they fled (chapter 1). In both these examples, and there are countless other examples on which we could draw, using an intersectional approach allows us to arrive at different answers to the questions we would ask. When we consciously use an intersectional approach, it allows us to move beyond a one-dimensional analysis to understanding multiple dimensions of concepts such as power.

Thus, one of the most important contributions an intersectional perspective can make to the field of international relations is to force us to move beyond one-dimensional images and the idea that all women (or men) are monolithic categories. Here we need to add a caveat, again drawing on Collins and Bilge: There is a *"complexity* of doing critical intersectional analysis. Using intersectionality as an analytical tool is difficult, precisely because intersectionality itself is multifaceted." As they note, an intersectional analysis "complicates things" by bringing in not only more categories but also the intersection of and/or relationships among them (emphasis in original).[5] Because traditional IR tends to deal with broad categories, it can miss the subtleties that are the result of looking within those categories. In fairness, an intersectional analysis might not be the appropriate approach to take in answering every question in IR. Just as any researcher needs to consider whether to approach a question from a realist, liberal, or constructivist perspective to get the most explanatory value, it is incumbent upon anyone doing IR research also to consider whether or when to examine an issue through an intersectional lens will add knowledge to the answer.

INTERSECTIONALITY AND THE CASE STUDIES

We began this book by looking at Russia's invasion of Ukraine in 2022 as a case study. On the surface, as we note, when we look at this in traditional IR terms, the war is a function of one country, Russia, invading another, Ukraine, in violation of all the basic tenets of international law. But our intersectional analysis illustrated the ways in which the war takes on different dimensions by looking *within* Ukraine at the range of people affected by the invasion and how different groups chose to respond. Women were affected in different ways—some choosing to flee with children; others opting to stay and fight. The fact that there is a gender dimension is not surprising. However, as the case illustrated, we can dig deeper within this group (i.e., women) to see that there is a class dimension that affected not only the ability of some women to leave and others to stay. Of those who left, class, education, and background also affected the options available to them and their children in the new country. These gendered dimensions also impacted men when considering the Ukrainian government's decision to invoke universal conscription, given the assumptions that men are the ones who will fight. Similarly, our case illustrated that race also played a role. While we think of Ukraine as being largely homogeneous racially, what we also found in our case is how even the small number of Blacks who tried to flee were stopped at the borders in a way that White Ukrainians were not. This tells us something not only about emigration from Ukraine but also about the ways in which race is a factor throughout Europe. When we consider the war and its impact on Ukrainians in this way, we get a far more comprehensive picture of the range of people affected by the war, as well as what governed their responses to it, than would be the case using traditional IR approaches.

Even a feminist understanding, with the focus on women and gender alone, would not capture the full complexity of the issue. We used the same approach throughout this book, specifically identifying a critical topic in international relations, such as war, peace, and security (chapter 2), addressing it from a more traditional IR approach and then digging deeper into the topic through an intersectional lens. Included in each chapter is also a case study that explores a particular topic relevant to current thinking in IR but specifically from an intersectional lens. What all these cases illustrate is the importance of looking at relations between states as well as examining factors within a country to assess the impact of economic development, human rights and discrimination, disease, environmental degradation, or any other issue.

The same holds when looking at international agreements such as CEDAW or UNSCR 1325 (chapters 2 and 3). While there is little doubt that CEDAW is an important agreement that helped advance the rights of women internationally, that does not mean we can or should overlook its omissions. For example, the agreement projects an image of women, and the enumerated violations against them, based on sex; and it presumes that a woman will be married to a man, thereby precluding the guarantee of rights of lesbian women. It privileges rural women over urban women, and while it acknowledges that women in general face discrimination, it does not differentiate the discrimination faced by women of color, by women who are poor and/or uneducated, by age, disability, members of a minority group, or other factors.

As we note in chapter 2, UNSC Resolution 1325 recognized the impact of war and conflict on women (including sexual and gender-based violence) and called for women's participation in peace negotiations, an important recognition by the members of the international system of the critical role women can and should play. But in looking at this resolution, it is important to recognize that "women" are not a monolithic category, even though they are treated as a single bloc in this resolution. Even when women are included in formal peace negotiations, it generally is up to the (male) decision-makers to determine which women should be included, and often those women are limited in terms of education, class, and background and generally are similar to the men who make the decisions. This, in turn, eliminates whole categories of women who have much to contribute to the peace process when it is viewed through their eyes, which is often from the bottom up rather than the top down. Again, this is not meant to diminish the importance of this resolution; rather, it is to serve as a reminder that we need to go beyond a single axis that looks at "women" to ask, "Which women?"

We also used the examples of economic development (chapter 4) and the environment (chapter 5) to illustrate not only how each has been approached using traditional IR paradigms but also the richness that is gained when looking at these through an intersectional lens.

CONCLUSION: THE CHALLENGES AND POSSIBLE NEXT STEPS

Since the emergence of feminist IR approaches, there has been a proliferation of books that look at gender and international relations, as well as books and academic journal articles that look at race and IR. But this volume attempts to embrace a broad intersectional approach to the study of the field. In this volume we identified a few major topics that dominate questions within IR: war, peace, and security; human rights; the global economy and development; and the environment. We then sought to address them by moving beyond traditional IR approaches to introduce an intersectional analysis to illustrate how that expands our understanding of the topic, as well as highlighting some of the limitations in the existing approaches. In each of the chapters we identified a case study we think illustrates the added explanatory power gained by introducing an intersectional approach.

That said, in the process of writing this book, the challenges of calling for an intersectional analysis became apparent. Even in looking at international agreements such as CEDAW or UNSCR 1325, as we note in this volume, most focus on gender and especially women; few such agreements move beyond the broad category of "woman" to address race, ethnicity, class, and age, for example, let alone a combination of these categories, which is what an intersectional analysis would require. As scholars of international relations, and as researchers who have focused extensively on feminist perspectives of security issues, it seemed logical to us to expand our perspective further to incorporate intersectionality. In that way, we thought we could move beyond a focus on women and gender to determine how incorporating other categories could broaden our own understanding of many of the issues we had been studying along a single axis of gender. As we discovered in writing this book, it seemed easier in theory than it has been in reality, due in part to the dearth of data on categories that go beyond women and gender and sometimes race to address the issues of concern here. As is apparent from the case of Northern Ireland in chapter 2, we learned that race and ethnicity did play a role in the violence of the Troubles, and in the years that followed the signing of the Good Friday Agreement. But it took a lot of digging as well as analysis to see how and why it is important to go beyond just religion and/or religion and gender to understand more fully the many facets of this conflict.

Clearly this book is just a starting point, a primer on how to introduce intersectionality into the study of international relations. It was never designed to address all major topics in IR, nor to offer a comprehensive understanding of what is admittedly a complex topic. Expanding the research to look at other topics in IR through an intersectional lens is the subject for another book, hopefully building upon the framework we offer here. And given the state of the world today, as well as recent history, there are any number of instances that can be used as the focus of additional cases to see how an intersectional analysis can be applied, and what can be gained by doing so.

We hope that we have done our part in this volume; that said, there is far more work to be done. At a time when the concept of intersectionality has been politicized, it is easy to lose sight of the importance of approaching even basic questions in a new and more capacious way. Doing so will allow us to build on the strong foundation that exists within the field of international relations to help us arrive at different questions we might want to ask, and/ or different ways to answer them. This will allow us to continue to build our body of knowledge in this important area of political science.

Glossary

Beijing Platform for Action (BPfA). Adopted at the Fourth UN Conference on Women in 1995, and identified twelve key areas where urgent action was needed to ensure greater equality and opportunities for women and men, girls, and boys. It also laid out concrete ways for countries to bring about change in those areas (chapter 4).

Bretton Woods. Site of a major conference held in 1944 that resulted in the creation of a new set of financial and monetary institutions, such as the World Bank and the International Monetary Fund (chapter 4).

CEDAW. The Convention on the Elimination of All Forms of Discrimination Against Women was passed in 1979, and is seen by many as the international bill of rights for women (chapter 3).

Conference of the Parties (COP). Member states that are party to the UNFCCC meet annually to discuss implementation of the convention and other international treaties addressing climate change (chapter 5).

conflict. Disagreement over interests or desired outcomes that may be settled peacefully or could lead to war (chapter 2).

constructivism (constructivist theory). Theoretical approach within IR that assumes that states are critical players but that their actions and behaviors are socially constructed or affected by the system(s) within which they operate (chapter 1).

COVID-19. A disease caused by a particular virus called SARS-CoV-2, which was first detected in December 2019 in Wuhan, China, although its particular origins are unclear. The rapid spread of the virus in 2020 quickly led to a global pandemic (chapter 4).

democratic peace. The idea that democratic countries are more peaceful because they do not go to war against other democratic countries (chapter 1).

developing countries. A category used by the United Nations Department of Economic and Social Affairs to identify low-income countries, defined as those with a gross national product per capita of $1,088 or less as of 2024 (chapter 4).

ecofeminism. An approach to studying the environment, noting women's oppression and the link to the domination of nature (chapter 5).

environmental justice. Notion that all people should have a healthy environment and protection from environmental damage (chapter 5).

ethnic cleansing. The systematic extermination of one group by another (i.e., genocide), often with the approval and support of the state (chapter 3).

feminist political ecology. An approach to studying the environment, noting how access to natural resources and land is gendered (chapter 5).

GATT (General Agreement on Tariffs and Trade). Created in 1947 to formalize an international trading system that would be fair and competitive for all countries (chapter 4).

Gender and Development (GAD). Emerged in the 1980s as an alternative to the Women and Development approach; links the relations of production to reproduction, and takes into account all aspects of women's lives (chapters 1 and 4).

globalization. The assumption that all states and international actors interact and are interdependent economically and/or financially in some way (chapter 4).

global restructuring. Growing complexity of the global division of labor, the intimate relationship between debt and development (and environmental degradation), and the often uneven and specific effects of these processes across countries and on particular social groups (chapter 4).

Global South. Refers to countries in the Southern Hemisphere that often were colonies of the Western European countries and/or the United States (chapters 1 and 4).

Human Development Index (HDI). Introduced by the UN in 1990 to evaluate the level of human development by country, the HDI was created to emphasize the people and their capabilities should be the ultimate criteria for measuring development, not just economic growth (chapter 4).

human security. A broad set of issues necessary to human survival, such as protecting the environment, freedom from hunger, and access to potable water. Also known as people-centered security (chapter 2).

International Monetary Fund (IMF). An organization of 188 countries that work together to help stabilize the international economic system. Established in 1944, it grew from the Bretton Woods Conference, which brought together representatives of forty-five countries to arrive at a framework for international economic policy (chapter 4).

International Political Economy (IPE). A subfield of international relations that studies the intersection of politics and economics and focuses especially on the distribution of power and resources (chapter 4).

liberalism (liberal theory). One of the major approaches to international relations that grows from the confluence of economics and politics and believes that all states will benefit from the flourishing of free trade and the open exchange of ideas. It also assumes that countries will benefit from cooperating with one another and advocates pursuing policies that are in the "common good" (chapter 1).

NATO. The North Atlantic Treaty Organization was created in 1949 to link the United States with the countries of Western Europe and Canada to deter aggression by the Soviet Union (chapter 1).

pandemic. An epidemic of an infectious disease that has spread across a large region—for example, multiple continents—affecting a substantial number of people (chapter 4).

peace. A situation characterized by the absence of hostility along with feelings of trust, a sense of security, and cooperation among peoples (chapter 2).

postcolonialism. The ways in which societies, governments, and peoples in the formerly colonized regions of the world experience international relations and their own internal growth and development (chapters 1 and 4).

power. The ability of one country to influence another or to influence the outcome of events in order to achieve desired ends (chapter 2).

realism (realist theory). One of the major approaches to understanding international relations; it assumes that states are the primary actors in the international system and that states will makes decisions based on their national interest, defined by power (chapter 1).

Responsibility to Protect (R2P). Times when one country has the right, or even the obligation, to intervene in the affairs of another sovereign state; for example, to stop genocide or other human rights abuses (chapter 3).

security. The safety and protection of the people and ensuring the continuation of the state (chapter 2).

Structural Adjustment Program (SAP). Often provided by the International Monetary Fund, structural adjustment programs were designed to help a country develop by offering lower interest rates on loans. Often they have had the opposite effect, putting a country into more debt (chapter 4).

The Troubles. A name for the violence in Northern Ireland that started in 1969 and ended with the signing of the Good Friday Agreement in 1998. Usually seen as religious violence between Catholics and Protestants, it had an economic, social, as well as political dimension (chapter 2).

UNFCCC. The United Nations Framework Convention on Climate Change is the main international treaty to address climate change. Since it was signed in 1992, other international agreements have followed, including the 1997 Kyoto Protocol and the 2015 Paris Agreement (chapter 5).

war. Acts of armed violence either within or across states involving two or more parties, designed to achieve a specific outcome (chapter 2).

Women and Development (WAD). Neo-Marxist feminist approach that emerged in the late 1970s to address the limitations of modernization theory and the ways in which it omitted women in development strategies (chapter 4).

Women in Development (WID). Terminology from the 1970s pertaining to the differential impact of modernization on men and women (chapters 1 and 4).

Women, Peace and Security (WPS) agenda. Growing out of UN Security Council Resolution 1325, the WPS agenda offers a broad approach to security that involves women's participation in decision-making, especially pertaining to war and peace and the prevention of conflict; protecting the rights of women and girls especially in times of conflict; and ensuring necessary services for survivors of sexual and gender-based violence (chapters 1 and 2).

World Bank. Like the International Monetary Fund, the World Bank was created as part of the Bretton Woods system and was originally designed to help facilitate the rebuilding of Europe after World War II. It subsequently expanded to provide loans to developing countries and to promote foreign direct investment in those countries (chapter 4).

World Trade Organization (WTO). Created in 1995 as a successor to GATT (chapter 4).

Notes

CHAPTER 1

1. Dominique Arel, "A short history of Ukrainian nationalism—and its tumultuous relationship with Russia," *The Conversation*, March 17, 2022, https://theconversation.com/a-short-history-of-ukrainian-nationalism-and-its-tumultuous-relationship-with-russia-179346.

2. "Ukraine is gaining ground in its counteroffensive, NATO chief says," *Reuters*, September 7, 2023, https://www.reuters.com/world/europe/ukraine-is-gaining-ground-its-counter-offensive-natos-stoltenberg-2023-09-07/; Lou Robinson, Sophie Tanno, Tim Lister, and Byron Manley, "Seeking a breakthrough: A visual guide to Ukraine's counteroffensive," CNN, September 8, 2023, https://www.cnn.com/interactive/2023/09/world/ukraine-war-counteroffensive-maps-guide-dg/.

3. Roger Cohen, "War in Ukraine Has Changed Europe Forever," *New York Times*, February 26, 2023, https://www.nytimes.com/2023/02/26/world/europe/ukraine-russia-war.html.

4. Phelan Chatterjee, "How Sweden and Finland went from neutral to NATO," BBC, July 11, 2023, https://www.bbc.com/news/world-europe-61397478; "Sweden officially joins NATO," North Atlantic Treaty Organization, March 7, 2024, https://www.nato.int/cps/en/natohq/news_223446.htm.

5. Azadeh Moaveni and Chitra Nagarajan, "Another deeply gendered war is being waged in Ukraine," *Al-Jazeera*, March 15, 2022, https://www.aljazeera.com/opinions/2022/3/15/another-deeply-gendered-war-is-being-waged-in-ukraine; Josephine Andrews, Jakob Isanski, Marek Nowak, Victoriya Sereda, Alexandra Vacroux, and Hann Vakhitova, "Feminized forced migration: Ukrainian war refugees," *Women's Studies International Forum* 99 (2023), 1.

6. Andrews et al., "Feminized forced migration: Ukrainian war refugees," 2.

7. Andrews et al., "Feminized forced migration: Ukrainian war refugees," 1.

8. Andrews et al., "Feminized forced migration: Ukrainian war refugees," 8.

9. Andrews et al., "Feminized forced migration: Ukrainian war refugees," 8.

10. Rashawn Ray, "The Russian invasion of Ukraine shows racism has no boundaries," *Brookings*, March 3, 2022, https://www.brookings.edu/articles/the-russian-invasion-of-ukraine-shows-racism-has-no-boundaries/.

11. Andrews et al., "Feminized forced migration: Ukrainian war refugees," 2–3.

12. Nicholas Kristof, "Ukrainian Women Fight for Their Own Liberation," *New York Times*, December 3, 2022, https://www.nytimes.com/2022/12/03/opinion/ukraine-women.html.

13. Simone McCarthy, "China assures Russia it remains 'impartial' on Ukraine war after attending Saudi peace talks," CNN, August 8, 2023, https://www.cnn.com/2023/08/08/china/china-wang-yi-lavrov-ukraine-russia-intl-hnk/index.html.

14. McCarthy, "China assures Russia it remains 'impartial' on Ukraine war after attending Saudi peace talks."

15. United Nations, "UN General Assembly calls for immediate end to war in Ukraine," February 23, 2023, https://news.un.org/en/story/2023/02/1133847.

16. European Council, Council of the European Union, "EU response to Russia's war of aggression against Ukraine," https://www.consilium.europa.eu/en/policies/eu-response-ukraine-invasion/ (accessed June 5, 2024).

17. As of June 4, 2024, the EU has imposed more than a dozen packages of sanctions against Russia. European Council, Council of the European Union, "EU response to Russia's war of aggression against Ukraine," https://www.consilium.europa.eu/en/policies/eu-response-ukraine-invasion/#sanctions.

18. Katharine A. M. Wright, "A feminist perspective on the Russian-Ukraine War: Implications for NATO," London School of Economics, March 8, 2022, https://blogs.lse.ac.uk/wps/2022/03/08/a-feminist-perspective-on-the-russian-ukraine-war-implications-for-nato/; Daniel Boffey, "'Fighting two enemies': Ukraine's female soldiers decry harassment," *The Guardian*, August 4, 2023, https://www.theguardian.com/world/2023/aug/04/fighting-two-enemies-ukraine-female-soldiers-decry-harassment.

19. Moaveni and Nagarajan, "Another deeply gendered war is being waged in Ukraine"; Sean Seddon, "Ukraine fires military conscription officials for taking bribes," BBC, August 11, 2023, https://www.bbc.com/news/world-europe-66478422.

20. Valerie Sperling, Alexandra Novitskaya, Janet Elise Johnson, and Lisa McIntosh Sundstrom, "Vladimir Putin, the czar of macho politics, is threatened by gender and sexuality rights," *The Conversation*, April 11, 2022, https://theconversation.com/vladimir-putin-the-czar-of-macho-politics-is-threatened-by-gender-and-sexuality-rights-180473.

21. See, for example, *The Routledge International Handbook of Intersectionality Studies*, eds. Kathy Davis and Helma Lutz (New York: Routledge, 2023); Marcos S. Scauso, *Intersectional Decoloniality: Reimagining International Relations and the Problem of Difference* (New York: Routledge, 2022).

22. Kimberlé Crenshaw, "Demarginalizing the Intersection of Race and Sex: A Black Feminist Critique of Antidiscrimination Doctrine, Feminist Theory and Antiracist Politics," *University of Chicago Legal Forum*, no. 1, article 8 (1989), 149.

23. Crenshaw, "Demarginalizing the Intersection of Race and Sex," 151.

24. Kimberlé Crenshaw, "Mapping the Margins: Intersectionality, Identity Politics, and Violence Against Women of Color," *Stanford Law Review* 43, no. 6 (July 1991), 1244.

25. Ange-Marie Hancock, "When Multiplication Doesn't Equal Quick Addition: Examining Intersectionality as a Research Paradigm," *Perspectives on Politics* 5, no. 1 (March 2007), 63–64. On intersectionality and class, see Victor Wallis, "Intersectionality's Binding Agent: The Political Primacy of Class," *New Political Science* 37, no. 4 (2015), 604–19.

26. Vrushali Patil, "From Patriarchy to Intersectionality: A Transnational Feminist Assessment of How Far We've Really Come," *Signs* 38, no. 4 (2013), 850.

27. Ange-Marie Hancock, "Intersectionality as a Normative and Empirical Paradigm," *Politics & Gender* 3, no. 2 (2007), 250.

28. Wendy Smooth, "Standing for Women? Which Women? The Substantive Representation of Women's Interests and the Research Imperative of Intersectionality," *Politics & Gender* 7, no. 3 (2011), 437.

29. Anna M. Agathangelou and Heather M. Turcotte, "Reworking postcolonial feminisms in the sites of IR," *Handbook on Gender in World Politics*, eds. Jill Steans and Daniela Tepe-Belfrage (Northampton, MA: Edward Elgar Publishing, 2016), 42.

30. Morton Kaplan, "Is International Relations a Discipline?" *Journal of Politics* 23, no. 3 (August 1961), 463.

31. Hans J. Morgenthau, *Politics Among Nations: The Struggle for Power and Peace*, 5th ed. (New York: Alfred A. Knopf, 1978), 42.

32. Morgenthau, *Politics Among Nations*, 29.

33. Morgenthau, *Politics Among Nations*, 42.

34. The original version of *Politics Among Nations* can be found online at 2015.74487.Politics-Among-Nations-The-Struggle-For-Power-And-Peace.pdf.

35. Daniel Drezner, "Power and International Relations: a temporal view," *European Journal of International Relations* 27, no. 1 (2021), 31.

36. Steven L. Spiegel, Elizabeth G. Matthews, Jennifer M. Taw, and Kristen P. Williams, *World Politics in a New Era*, 6th ed. (New York: Oxford University Press, 2015), 39.

37. There are several variants of realism, including offensive and defensive realism. We focus on classical and neo- or structural realism.

38. Kenneth N. Waltz, *Theory of International Politics* (New York: Random House, 1979); Stephen M. Walt, *Origins of Alliances* (Ithaca, NY: Cornell University Press, 1987).

39. Spiegel et al., *World Politics in a New Era*, 39.

40. Spiegel et al., *World Politics in a New Era*, 40.

41. Spiegel et al., *World Politics in a New Era*, 43.

42. Drezner, "Power and International Relations: a temporal view," 39.

43. On the liberal international order, see, for example, G. John Ikenberry, *After Victory: Institutions, Strategic Restraint, and the Rebuilding of Order after Major Wars*, new edition (Princeton, NJ: Princeton University Press, 2019).

44. Michael Doyle, "Liberalism and World Politics," *American Political Science Review* 80, no. 4 (1986), 1151–69.

45. Christopher Layne, "Kant or Cant: The Myth of the Democratic Peace," *International Security* 19, no. 2 (Fall 1994), 9–10.
46. Joshua S. Goldstein and Jon C. Pevehouse, *Principles of International Relations* (New York: Pearson Longman, 2009), 72. For a critique of democratic peace theory, see Sebastian Rosato, "The Flawed Logic of Democratic Peace Theory," *American Political Science Review* 97, no. 4 (November 2003), 585–602; Layne, "Kant or Cant: The Myth of the Democratic Peace," 5–49.
47. John J. Mearsheimer, "The False Promise of International Institutions," *International Security* 19, no. 3 (Winter 1994–95), 7.
48. Layne, "Kant or Cant: The Myth of the Democratic Peace."
49. Drezner, "Power and International Relations: a temporal view," 41.
50. Alexander Wendt, "Anarchy Is What States Make of It: The Social Construction of Power Politics," *International Organization* 46, no. 2 (Spring 1992), 393.
51. Karen Mingst, *Essentials of International Relations,* 4th ed. (New York: W. W. Norton & Company, 2008), 72.
52. Drezner, "Power and International Relations: a temporal view," 45.
53. Drezner, "Power and International Relations: a temporal view," 43.
54. Bianca Freeman, D. G. Kim, and David A. Lake, "Race in International Relations: Beyond the 'Norm Against Noticing,'" *Annual Review of Political Science* 25 (2022), 177.
55. Kelebogile Zvobgo and Meredith Loken, "Why Race Matters in International Relations," *Foreign Policy* (June 19, 2020), https://foreignpolicy.com/2020/06/19/why-race-matters-international-relations-ir/, 3, 4.
56. Contents for the July 1910, October 1910, and January 1911 *Journal of Race Development.*
57. Zvobgo and Loken, "Why Race Matters in International Relations," 4.
58. Zvobgo and Loken, "Why Race Matters in International Relations," 4.
59. Zvobgo and Loken, "Why Race Matters in International Relations," 4.
60. Freeman et al., "Race in International Relations: Beyond the 'Norm Against Noticing,'" 178.
61. Robert Vitalis, *White World Order, Black Power Politics* (Ithaca, NY: Cornell University Press, 2015), 11.
62. Zvobgo and Loken, "Why Race Matters in International Relations," 4. See also Kelebogile Zvobgo et al. for a recent discussion of how the political science discipline in general and security studies, in particular, continue to ignore race and racism both in terms of the research conducted and representation in the discipline. "Race and Racial Exclusion in Security Studies: A Survey of Scholars," *Security Studies* (2023), 1–29, DOI: 10.1080/09636412.2023.2230880.
63. Roxanne Lynn Doty, "The Bounds of 'Race' in International Relations," *Millennium: Journal of International Studies* 22, no. 3 (1993), 445.
64. Robbie Shilliam, "Race and racism in international relations: retrieving a scholarly inheritance," *International Politics Reviews* 8 (2020), 153.
65. Of the fifteen articles, only one had "women" in the title: "Women and the Afghan peace and reintegration process," by Althea-Maria Rivas and Mariam Safi. None of the other fourteen had women (or gender) in their abstracts either.

66. T. D. Harper-Shipman et al., "Forum: Stripping Away the Body: Prospects for Reimagining Race in IR," *International Studies Review* 23, no. 4 (December 2021), 2019.

67. K. Melchor Quick Hall, "Developing Methodology for the Exploration of Gendered Racialization: Introducing a Plural Capabilities Approach," *International Studies Review* 23, no. 4 (December 2021), 2039.

68. J. Ann Tickner, *Gendering World Politics: Issues and Approaches in the Post-Cold War Era* (New York: Columbia University Press, 2001).

69. Tickner, *Gendering World Politics*, 29.

70. Jacqui True, "Feminism and Gender Studies in International Relations Theory," *Oxford Research Encyclopedias, International Studies* (2010), 8.

71. See, for example, J. Kantola, "The Gendered Reproduction of the State in International Relations," *British Journal of International Relations* 9 (2007), 270–83; Carol Cohn, editor, *Women & Wars: Contested Histories, Uncertain Futures* (Malden, MA: Policy Press, 2013); Cynthia Enloe, *Maneuvers: The International Politics of Militarizing Women's Lives* (Berkeley: University of California Press, 2000); Miranda Alison, *Women and Political Violence: Female Combatants in Ethno-National Conflict* (New York: Routledge, 2009); Donna Pankhurst, editor, *Gendered Peace: Women's Struggles for Post-War Justice and Reconciliation* (New York: Routledge, 2008).

72. Jaqui True, *The Political Economy of Violence against Women* (Oxford, UK: Oxford University Press, 2012).

73. Anne Sisson Runyan and V. Spike Peterson, *Global Gender Issues in the New Millennium*, 4th ed. (Boulder, CO: Westview Press, 2014), 185.

74. Tickner, *Gendering World Politics*, 78.

75. Leslie McCall, "The Complexity of Intersectionality," *Signs* 30, no. 3 (Spring 2005), 1771.

76. Erin Tolley, "Gender Is Not a Proxy: Race and Intersectionality in Legislative Recruitment," *Politics & Gender* 19, no. 2 (2013), 374.

77. V. Spike Peterson, "Thinking Through Intersectionality and War," *Race, Gender & Class* 14, nos. 3–4 (2007), 13.

78. Anne Sisson Runyan, *Global Gender Politics*, 5th ed. (New York: Routledge, 2019), 5.

79. Tickner, *Gendering World Politics*, 78.

80. Sarah Smith and Elena B. Stavrevska, "A different Women, Peace and Security is possible? Intersectionality in Women, Peace and Security resolutions and national action plans," *European Journal of Politics and Gender* 5, no. 1 (2022), 68.

81. While the United States expanded across North America in the eighteenth and nineteenth centuries, it really became an imperialist power with the Spanish-American War in 1898 and its aftermath. Prior to that time, the United States was largely left out of the global power grab engaged in by the European countries. In the aftermath of the Spanish-American War, the United States acquired the Philippines, Guam, and parts of Cuba, thereby giving the country its own colonies as well as a firm place in the Pacific. See chapter 2, "Unilateralism to Engagement," in Joyce P. Kaufman, *A Concise History of U.S. Foreign Policy*, 5th ed. (Lanham, MD: Rowman & Littlefield, 2021), 39–70.

82. Pamela Paxton, Melanie M Hughes, and Tiffany D. Barnes, *Women, Politics and Power: A Global Perspective*, 4th ed. (Lanham, MD: Rowman & Littlefield, 2021), 352.

83. Sheila Nair, "Introducing Postcolonialism in International Relations Theory," E-IR (December 8, 2017), https://www.e-ir.info/pdf/71923, 1.

84. Nair, "Introducing Postcolonialism in International Relations Theory," 2. See also, Phillip Darby and A. J. Paolini, "Bridging International Relations and Postcolonialism," *Alternatives: Global, Local, Political* 19, no. 3 (Summer 1994): 371–97; and Mine Nur Küçük, "Postcolonial Approaches in International Relations," in *Critical Approaches to International Relations*, eds. M. Kursad Ozekin and Engin Sune (Leiden, Netherlands: Brill, 2022): 157–74.

85. Nair, "Introducing Postcolonialism in International Relations Theory," 2.

86. Nair, "Introducing Postcolonialism in International Relations Theory," 2.

87. Navid Pourmokhtari, "A Postcolonial Critique of State Sovereignty in IR: The contradictory legacy of a 'West-centric' discipline," *Third World Quarterly* 34, no. 10 (2013), 1774.

88. Küçük, "Postcolonial Approaches in International Relations," 168.

89. Mia-Lie Nylund, Sandra Hakansson, and Elin Bjarnegard, "The Transformative Potential of Feminist Foreign Policy: The Case of Sweden," *Journal of Women, Politics & Policy* 44, no. 3 (2023), 259.

90. Nylund et al., "The Transformative Potential of Feminist Foreign Policy," 261.

91. Nylund et al., "The Transformative Potential of Feminist Foreign Policy," 261.

92. Gina Koczberski, "Women in development: a critical analysis," *Third World Quarterly* 19, no. 3 (1998), 401.

93. Jill Steans, *Gender and International Relations*, 3rd ed. (Malden, MA: Polity Press, 2013), 204.

94. Nair, "Introducing Postcolonialism in International Relations Theory," 3.

95. Cynthia Cockburn, "The Continuum of Violence: A Gender Perspective on War and Peace," in *Sites of Violence: Gender and Conflict Zones*, eds. Wenona Giles and Jennifer Hyndman (Berkeley: University of California Press, 2004), 24–44.

CHAPTER 2

1. K. J. Holsti, "Scholarship in an era of anxiety: the study of international politics during the Cold War," *Review of International Studies* 24 (December 1998), 18.

2. Holsti, "Scholarship in an era of anxiety," 40–41.

3. Holsti, "Scholarship in an era of anxiety," 45.

4. Georg Sørensen, "IR Theory after the Cold War," *Review of International Studies* 24 (December 1998), 92.

5. Sørensen, "IR Theory after the Cold War," 83–84.

6. Margaret MacMillan, *War: How Conflict Shaped Us* (New York: Random House, 2020), xiv.

7. Charles Tilly, *Coercion, Capital, and European States, AD 990–1992* (Cambridge, MA: Blackwell, 1992), 14.

8. Steven L. Spiegel, Elizabeth G. Matthews, Jennifer M. Taw, and Kristen P. Williams, *World Politics in a New Era*, 6th ed. (New York: Oxford University Press, 2015), 40–41.

9. Adil Ahmad Haque, "The United Nations Charter at 75: Between Force and Self-Defense—Part One," *Just Security*, June 24, 2020, https://www.justsecurity.org /70985/the-united-nations-charter-at-75-between-force-and-self-defense-part-one/.

10. Spiegel et al, *World Politics in a New Era*, 43, 484–85.

11. See, for example, Sebastian von Einsiedel with Louise Bosetti, Cale Salih, Wilfred Wan, and Dr. James Cockayne, "Civil War Trends and the Changing Nature of Armed Conflict," United Nations University Centre for Policy Research, Occasional Paper, March 2017, https://collections.unu.edu/eserv/UNU:6156/Civil_war _trends_UPDATED.pdf.

12. MacMillan, *War: How Conflict Shaped Us*, 42.

13. Elisabeth Prügl, "Gender as a cause of violent conflict," *International Affairs* 99, no. 5 (2023), 1885.

14. Jaqui True, *Women, Peace and Security in Post-Conflict and Peacebuilding Contexts*, NOREF: Norwegian Peacebuilding Resource Centre, Policy Brief, March 2013, 2, http://peacewomen.org/system/files/global_study_submissions/ Jacqui%20True_NOREF%20policy%20brief.pdf.

15. Cynthia Cockburn, "Gender Relations as Causal in Militarization and War," *International Feminist Journal of Politics* 12, no. 2 (2010), 144.

16. Cockburn, "Gender Relations as Causal in Militarization and War," 147–48; see also Prügl, "Gender as a cause of violent conflict," 1887.

17. Joyce P. Kaufman and Kristen P. Williams, *Women at War, Women Building Peace: Challenging Gender Norms* (Boulder, CO: Kumarian Press, 2013), 1.

18. Prügl, "Gender as a cause of violent conflict," 1894.

19. Prügl, "Gender as a cause of violent conflict," 1901.

20. Oliver P. Richmond, "Reclaiming Peace in International Relations," *Millennium: Journal of International Studies* 36, no. 3 (2008), 444.

21. Richmond, "Reclaiming Peace in International Relations," 448.

22. Richmond, "Reclaiming Peace in International Relations," 449.

23. Joyce P. Kaufman and Kristen P. Williams, "Introduction," in *Women, Gender Equality, and Post-Conflict Transformation: Lessons Learned, Implications for the Future*, eds. Joyce P. Kaufman and Kristen P. Williams (London: Routledge, 2017), 1.

24. Elena B. Stavrevska and Sarah Smith, "Intersectionality and Peace," in *The Palgrave Encyclopedia of Peace and Conflict Studies*, eds. O. Richmond and G. Visoka (Springer Nature Switzerland AG, 2020), 3.

25. Stavrevska and Smith, "Intersectionality and Peace," 3.

26. Inger Skjelsbaek, "Gendered Battlefields: A Gender Analysis of Peace and Conflict," PRIO Report 6/97 (Oslo: International Peace Research Institute, 1997), 17.

27. Tami Amanda Jacoby, *Women in Zones of Conflict: Power and Resistance in Israel* (Montreal: McGill-Queen's University Press, 2005), 13.

28. Donna Pankhurst, "The 'Sex War' and Other Wars: Towards a Feminist Approach to Peace Building," *Development in Practice* 13, nos. 2, 3 (May 2003), 161.

29. Jane L. Parpart, "Imagined peace, gender relations and post-conflict transformation: Anti-colonial and post–Cold War conflicts," in *Women, Gender Equality, and Post-Conflict Transformation: Lessons Learned, Implications for the Future*, eds. Joyce P. Kaufman and Kristen P. Williams (New York: Routledge, 2017), 51.

30. Althea-Maria Rivas and Mariam Safi, "Women and the Afghan peace and reintegration process," *International Affairs* 98, no. 1 (2022), 86.

31. Rivas and Safi, "Women and the Afghan peace and reintegration process," 87.

32. Rivas and Safi, "Women and the Afghan peace and reintegration process," 98.

33. Rivas and Safi, "Women and the Afghan peace and reintegration process," 99.

34. Rivas and Safi, "Women and the Afghan peace and reintegration process," 100.

35. Rivas and Safi, "Women and the Afghan peace and reintegration process," 100.

36. Rivas and Safi, "Women and the Afghan peace and reintegration process," 101.

37. "What Is Human Security," United Nations Trust Fund for Human Security, https://www.un.org/humansecurity/what-is-human-security/.

38. Laura J. Shepherd, "Feminist Security Studies," in *Handbook on Gender in World Politics*, eds. Jill Steans and Daniela Tepe-Belfrage (Cheltenham, UK: Edward Elgar Publishers, 2016), 265.

39. Jill Steans, *Gender and International Relations*, 3rd ed. (Malden, MA: Polity Press, 2013), 117.

40. Anne Sisson Runyan and V. Spike Peterson, *Global Gender Issues in the New Millennium*, 4th ed. (Boulder, CO: Westview Press, 2014), 145.

41. Shepherd, "Feminist Security Studies," 269.

42. Steans, *Gender and International Relations*, 118.

43. Katherine E. Brown, "The securitization of human rights," in *Handbook on Gender in World Politics*, eds. Jill Steans and Daniela Tepe-Belfrage (Cheltenham, UK: Edward Elgar Publishers, 2016), 255.

44. Brown, "The securitization of human rights," 255.

45. Runyan and Peterson, *Global Gender Issues in the New Millennium*, 147–48.

46. Runyan and Peterson, *Global Gender Issues in the New Millennium*, 148.

47. UN Security Council Resolution 1325, 1, https://peacemaker.un.org/sites/peacemaker.un.org/files/SC_ResolutionWomenPeaceSecurity_SRES1325%282000%29%28english_0.pdf.

48. United Nations Peacemaker, "Security Council Resolutions on Women, Peace and Security," https://peacemaker.un.org/wps/normative-frameworks/un-security-council-resolutions.

49. United Nations Security Council, "Resolution 1325," October 31, 2000, 2, https://documents.un.org/doc/undoc/gen/n00/720/18/pdf/n0072018.pdf?token=pXeK3wGCOtBrn9ZBKo&fe=true.

50. United Nations Security Council, "Resolution 1820 (2008)," June 19, 2008, 4, https://documents.un.org/doc/undoc/gen/n08/391/44/pdf/n0839144.pdf?token=n2OI5tHSQNq4f0dZjg&fe=true.

51. United Nations Security Council, "Resolution 1888 (2009)," September 30, 2009, 6, https://documents.un.org/doc/undoc/gen/n09/534/46/pdf/n0953446.pdf ?token=pNWBm6IZ9ZC2ub2u5I&fe=true.

52. United Nations Security Council, "Resolution 2122 (2013)," October 18, 2013, 3, https://documents.un.org/doc/undoc/gen/n13/523/44/pdf/n1352344.pdf ?token=onqxS2DojhCVBD6EJU&fe=true.

53. United Nations Security Council, "Resolution 2493 (2019)," October 29, 2019, 2, https://documents.un.org/doc/undoc/gen/n19/339/37/pdf/n1933937.pdf ?token=hTeNVQJ8b7OGz4Lmoq&fe=true (accessed June 10, 2024).

54. Anthony Navone discusses how the United States' Women, Peace and Security Act of 2017 calls for a strategic framework to incorporate the WPS agenda into the various US government agencies tasked with national security. Anthony Navone, "Towards a Gender-Inclusive National Security Strategy," United States Institute of Peace, March 30, 2021, https://www.usip.org/publications/2021/03/toward-gender -inclusive-national-security-strategy.

55. UN Women, "Preventing Conflict: The Origins of the Women, Peace and Security Agenda," *Preventing Conflict, Transforming Justice, Securing the Peace,* 206, https://wps.unwomen.org/pdf/en/CH08.pdf.

56. UN Women, "Preventing Conflict," 206.

57. Marie O'Reilly, Andrea Ó Suilleabhain, and Thania Paffenholz, "Reimagining Peacemaking: Women's Roles in Peace Processes," International Peace Institute, June 2015, 1, https://www.ipinst.org/wp-content/uploads/2015/06/IPI-E-pub-Reimagining-Peacemaking.pdf.

58. Laurel Stone, "Quantitative Analysis of Women's Participation in Peace Processes, Annex II," in Marie O'Reilly, Andrea Ó Suilleabhain, and Thania Paffenholz, "Reimagining Peacemaking: Women's Roles in Peace Processes," International Peace Institute, June 2015, 34, https://www.ipinst.org/wp-content/uploads/2015/06/ IPI-E-pub-Reimagining-Peacemaking.pdf.

59. See O'Reilly et al., "Reimagining Peacemaking."

60. O'Reilly et al., "Reimagining Peacemaking," 2.

61. Elisabeth Porter, "Participatory Democracy and the Challenge of Dialogue across Difference," in *Gender, Democracy and Inclusion in Northern Ireland*, eds. Carmel Roulston and Celia Davis (Basingstoke, UK: Palgrave, 2000), 158.

62. Laura McLeod, "The Women, Peace and Security resolutions: UNSCR 1325 to 2122," in *Handbook on Gender in World Politics*, eds. Jill Steans and Daniela Tepe-Belfrage (Cheltenham, UK: Edward Elgar Publishers, 2016), 274.

63. McLeod, "The Women, Peace and Security resolutions: UNSCR 1325 to 2122," 271.

64. O'Reilly et al., "Reimagining Peacemaking," 1.

65. Danielle Robertson, "If we want to build peace, we can't keep women out," United States Institute of Peace, October 18, 2018, https://www.usip.org/publications /2018/10/if-we-want-build-peace-we-cant-keep-women-out.

66. See Monica McWilliams, *Stand Up, Speak Out: My Life Working for Women's Rights, Peace and Equality in Northern Ireland and Beyond* (Northern Ireland: Blackstaff Press, 2021).

67. Soumita Basu, "The Global South writes 1325 (too)," *International Political Science Review* 37, no. 3 (2016), 363.

68. Basu, "The Global South writes 1325 (too)," 364.

69. Nicola Pratt, "Reconceptualizing Gender, Reinscribing Racial-Sexual Boundaries in International Security: The Case of UN Security Council Resolution 1325 on 'Women, Peace and Security,'" *International Studies Quarterly* 57 (2013), 774.

70. Sarah Smith and Elena B. Stavrevska, "A different Women, Peace and Security is possible? Intersectionality in Women, Peace and Security resolutions and national action plans," *European Journal of Politics and Gender* 5, no. 1 (2022), 74.

71. Smith and Stavrevska, "A different Women, Peace and Security is possible?" 74.

72. Smith and Stavrevska, "A different Women, Peace and Security is possible?" 68.

73. Johan Galtung, "Violence, Peace, and Peace Research," *Journal of Peace Research* 6, no. 3 (1969), 167–91.

74. Marc Mulholland, *Northern Ireland: A Very Short Introduction*, 2nd ed (Oxford, UK: Oxford University Press, 2020).

75. Galtung describes structural violence as a situation in which "violence is built into the structure and shows up as unequal power and consequently as unequal life chances." He elaborates by noting, "*Resources* are unevenly distributed, as when income distributions are heavily skewed, literacy/education unevenly distributed, medical services existent in some districts and for some groups only, and so on. Above all the *power to decide over the distribution of resources* is unevenly distributed" (emphasis in original). Galtung, "Violence, Peace, and Peace Research," 171.

76. Cynthia Cockburn, *The Space Between Us: Negotiating Gender and National Identities in Conflict* (London: Zed Books, 1998), 17.

77. David McKittrick and David McVea, *Making Sense of the Troubles: The Story of the Conflict in Northern Ireland* (Chicago: New Amsterdam Books, 2002), 76.

78. The period from the late 1960s into the mid-1970s was characterized by increased violence on both sides, including bombings in London carried out by members of the IRA and increased Loyalist bombings carried out primarily by Protestant militia groups. For more information about the policy of internment without trial and the increased violence that accompanied it, see Chapter 3, "Descent into Violence, 1969–1971," in McKittrick and McVea, *Making Sense of the Troubles* (52–75).

79. Eilish Rooney, "Women's equality in Northern Ireland's transition: Intersectionality in theory and place," *Feminist Legal Studies* 14 (Spring 2006), 363.

80. Joyce P. Kaufman and Kristen P. Williams, *Women, the State, and War: A Comparative Perspective on Citizenship and Nationalism* (Lanham, MD: Lexington Books, 2007), 169. For more on class and Northern Ireland, see also "Still Troubled," *Economist*, April 12, 2006, https://www.economist.com/britain/2006/04/12/still-troubled.

81. Grainne McCoy, "Women, Community and Politics in Northern Ireland," in *Gender, Democracy and Inclusion in Northern Ireland*, eds. Carmel Roulston and Celia Davies (New York: Palgrave, 2001), 3.

82. McCoy, "Women, Community and Politics in Northern Ireland," 12.

83. Cockburn, *The Space Between Us*, 53.

84. Carmel Roulston, "Women on the Margin: The Women's Movements in Northern Ireland, 1973–1995," in *Feminist Nationalism*, ed. Lois West (New York: Routledge, 1997), 45.

85. The literature on the conflict has not, for the most part, examined the connection between ethnonationalism and LGBT rights. For works that correct for this omission, see Bernadette C. Hayes, "LGBT rights in Northern Ireland: a war by other means" (February 25, 2016), https://blogs.lse.ac.uk/politicsandpolicy/gay-rights-in-northern-ireland-a-war-by-other-means/; Bernadette C. Hayes and John Nagle, "Ethnonationalism and attitudes towards gay and lesbian rights in Northern Ireland," *Nations and Nationalism* 22, no. 1 (2016), 20–41.

86. Eamon Collins, with Mick McGovern, *Killing Rage* (London: Granta Books, 1997), 98.

87. Northern Ireland Women's Coalition, http:/www.niwc.org, accessed June 13, 2007 (site now discontinued).

88. Kate Fearon and Monica McWilliams, "Swimming against the mainstream: the Northern Ireland Women's Coalition," in *Gender, Democracy and Inclusion in Northern Ireland*, eds. Carmel Roulston and Celia Davies (New York: Palgrave, 2001), 125.

89. Colin Coulter, Niall Gilmartin, Katy Hayward, and Peter Shirlow, *Northern Ireland a generation after Good Friday* (Manchester, UK: Manchester University Press, 2021), 224–25.

90. It is important to note that there are a number of articles that focus on race and the Republic of Ireland, which helped provide some context to the issue. However, for purposes of this chapter, we are focusing primarily on the literature that deals with race and ethnicity in Northern Ireland.

91. Northern Ireland Statistics and Research Agency, "Main statistics for Northern Ireland Statistical Bulletin: Ethnic group" (September 22, 2022), 4, https://www.nisra.gov.uk/system/files/statistics/census-2021-main-statistics-for-northern-ireland-phase-1-statistical-bulletin-ethnic-group.pdf (accessed July 22, 2023).

92. Bryan Fanning and Lucy Michael, "Racism and anti-racism in the two Irelands," *Ethnic and Racial Studies* 41, no. 15 (2018), 2657.

93. Fanning and Michael, "Racism and anti-racism in the two Irelands," 2658.

94. Fanning and Michael, "Racism and anti-racism in the two Irelands," 2659.

95. Fanning and Michael, "Racism and anti-racism in the two Irelands," 2658–59.

96. Fanning and Michael, "Racism and anti-racism in the two Irelands," 2667.

97. Fanning and Michael, "Racism and anti-racism in the two Irelands," 2668–69.

98. Robbie McVeigh and Bill Rolston, "From Good Friday to Good Relations: sectarianism, racism and the Northern Ireland state," *Race and Class* 48, no. 4 (2007), 3.

99. McVeigh and Rolston, "From Good Friday to Good Relations," 4.

100. McVeigh and Rolston, "From Good Friday to Good Relations," 10.

101. McVeigh and Rolston, "From Good Friday to Good Relations," 9.

102. McVeigh and Rolston, "From Good Friday to Good Relations," 11.

103. Adele Lee, "'Are you a Catholic Chinese or a Protestant Chinese?' Belfast's ethnic minorities and the sectarian divide," *City* 18, nos. 4–5 (2014), 476.
104. Lee, "'Are you a Catholic Chinese or a Protestant Chinese?'" 476.
105. Lee, "'Are you a Catholic Chinese or a Protestant Chinese?'" 477.
106. Lee, "'Are you a Catholic Chinese or a Protestant Chinese?'" 477.
107. Lee, "'Are you a Catholic Chinese or a Protestant Chinese?'" 477.
108. Lee, "'Are you a Catholic Chinese or a Protestant Chinese?'" 485.
109. Patrick Radden Keefe, *Say Nothing: A True Story of Murder and Memory in Northern Ireland* (New York: Doubleday, 2019), 10.
110. Myrtle Hill, *Women in Ireland: A century of change* (Belfast: The Blackstaff Press, 2003), 153.
111. "Where Women's Lib means guns," *Sunday World*, March 3, 1974, accessed at the Linen Hall Library, Belfast, December 2010.
112. Hill, *Women in Ireland: A century of change*, 172.
113. Azrini Wahidin, *Ex-Combatants, Gender and Peace in Northern Ireland* (Nottingham, UK: Palgrave Macmillan, 2016), 94.
114. Wahidin, *Ex-Combatants, Gender and Peace in Northern Ireland*, 32.
115. Niall Gilmartin, *Female Combatants After Armed Struggle* (New York: Routledge, 2019), 52.
116. Gilmartin, *Female Combatants After Armed Struggle*, 102.
117. Coulter et al., *Northern Ireland a generation after Good Friday*, 165.
118. Coulter et al., *Northern Ireland a generation after Good Friday*, 193.
119. Coulter et al., *Northern Ireland a generation after Good Friday*, 196.
120. See, for example, Stephen Castle, "Northern Ireland Sees Spasm of Violence as Old Tensions Resurface," *New York Times*, April 8, 2021, https://www.nytimes.com/2021/04/08/world/europe/northern-ireland-violence-brexit-covid.html.
121. Coulter et al., *Northern Ireland a generation after Good Friday*, 8.

CHAPTER 3

1. On the emergence of international human rights norms, see Kathryn Sikkink, "Transnational Politics, International Relations Theory, and Human Rights," *PS: Political Science and Politics* 31, no. 3 (September 1998), 517–23.
2. Frans Viljoen, "International Human Rights Law: A Short History," *UN Chronicle* 46, nos. 1, 2 (2009), 8.
3. Jenny S. Martinez, "The Slave Trade and the Origins of International Human Rights Law," *Stanford Lawyer* 85 (Fall 2011), October 28, 2011, https://law.stanford.edu/stanford-lawyer/articles/the-slave-trade-and-the-origins-of-international-human-rights-law-2/.
4. Viljoen, "International Human Rights Law: A Short History," 9.
5. Viljoen, "International Human Rights Law: A Short History," 9.
6. Viljoen, "International Human Rights Law: A Short History," 9.

7. Viljoen, "International Human Rights Law: A Short History," 9.

8. Viljoen, "International Human Rights Law: A Short History," 10–11.

9. Karen A. Mingst, *Essentials of International Relations*, 4th ed. (New York: W. W. Norton & Company, 2008), 310.

10. United Nations, "The Foundation of International Human Rights Law," https://www.un.org/en/about-us/udhr/foundation-of-international-human-rights-law.

11. United Nations, "Universal Declaration of Human Rights: Preamble," https://www.un.org/en/about-us/universal-declaration-of-human-rights.

12. United Nations, "The Foundation of International Human Rights Law," https://www.un.org/en/about-us/udhr/foundation-of-international-human-rights-law; see also Viljoen, "International Human Rights Law: A Short History," 11.

13. United Nations, "The Foundation of International Human Rights Law."

14. "United Nations Charter: Preamble," United Nations, https://www.un.org/en/about-us/un-charter/preamble.

15. Francisca de Haan, "A Brief Survey of Women's Rights from 1945 to 2009," *UN Chronicle* 47, no. 1 (March 2010), 56.

16. "United Nations Charter (full text)," United Nations, https://www.un.org/en/about-us/un-charter/full-text; Rebecca Adami and Dan Plesch, "Women and the UN: a new history of women's international human rights," Open Global Rights, September 10, 2021, https://www.openglobalrights.org/women-and-the-un-a-new-history-of-womens-international-human-rights/.

17. Adami and Plesch, "Women and the UN: a new history of women's international human rights."

18. United Nations, "Twenty-ninth plenary meeting, Tuesday, 12 February 1946," A_PV.29-EN.pdf.

19. United Nations, "Twenty-ninth plenary meeting, Tuesday, 12 February 1946."

20. United Nations, "Twenty-ninth plenary meeting, Tuesday, 12 February 1946."

21. Adami and Plesch, "Women and the UN."

22. United Nations, "The role of women in shaping the Universal Declaration of Human Rights," March 6, 2018, https://www.ohchr.org/en/stories/2018/03/role-women-shaping-universal-declaration-human-rights.

23. United Nations, "The role of women in shaping the Universal Declaration of Human Rights."

24. de Haan, "A Brief Survey of Women's Rights from 1945 to 2009," 56.

25. United Nations, "Women Who Shaped the Universal Declaration," November 2019, https://www.un.org/sites/un2.un.org/files/2019/11/women_who_shaped_the_udhr.pdf.

26. United Nations, "Women Who Shaped the Universal Declaration."

27. United Nations, "Women Who Shaped the Universal Declaration."

28. United States Department of State, Office of the Historian, "Bandung Conference (Asian-African Conference), 1955," https://history.state.gov/milestones/1953-1960/bandung-conf.

29. Roland Burke, "'The Compelling Dialogue of Freedom': Human Rights at the Bandung Conference," *Human Rights Quarterly* 28 (2006), 948.

30. Aziza Ahmed, "Bandung's Legacy: Solidarity and Contestation in Global Women's Rights," in *Bandung, Global History, and International Law: Critical Pasts and Pending Futures*, eds. Luis Eslava, Michael Fakhri, and Vasuki Nesiah (New York: Cambridge University Press, 2017), 450.

31. "Final Communiqué of the Asian-African conference of Bandung (24 April 1955)," CVCE, Luxembourg Centre for Contemporary and Digital History, 4, https://www.cvce.eu/content/publication/1997/10/13/676237bd-72f7-471f-949a-88b6ae513585/publishable_en.pdf (last updated, January 1, 2017).

32. Ahmed, "Bandung's Legacy," 450–51.

33. Ahmed, "Bandung's Legacy," 453.

34. Ahmed, "Bandung's Legacy," 460.

35. Adami and Plesch, "Women and the UN."

36. "Introduction," https://clinton.presidentiallibraries.us/exhibits/show/womens-rights/wr-hr-introduction.

37. Rebecca Turkington, "'Once and For All': The Fourth UN World Conference on Women and the Institutionalisation of Women's Human Rights in American Foreign Policy," *Gender & History* 35, no. 3 (October 2023), 847.

38. United Nations, "Conferences: Women and gender equality," https://www.un.org/en/conferences/women. Since that 1995 conference, there have been five-year reviews to assess the implementation of the Beijing Platform for Action commitments and initiatives.

39. UN, Summary "Gender and racial discrimination: Report of the Expert Group Meeting," https://www.un.org/womenwatch/daw/csw/genrac/.

40. United Nations Division for the Advancement of Women, "Gender and racial discrimination: Report of the Expert Group Meeting, 21–24 November 2000, Zagreb, Croatia," 1, https://www.un.org/womenwatch/daw/csw/genrac/report.htm.

41. United Nations Division for the Advancement of Women, "Gender and racial discrimination: Report of the Expert Group Meeting," 2.

42. United Nations Division for the Advancement of Women, "Gender and racial discrimination: Report of the Expert Group Meeting on gender and racial discrimination," 6.

43. United Nations Division for the Advancement of Women, "Gender and racial discrimination: Report of the Expert Group Meeting," 7.

44. United Nations Division for the Advancement of Women, "Gender and racial discrimination: Report of the Expert Group Meeting," 7.

45. United Nations Division for the Advancement of Women, "Gender and racial discrimination: Report of the Expert Group Meeting," 13.

46. United Nations Division for the Advancement of Women, "Gender and racial discrimination: Report of the Expert Group Meeting," 13.

47. United Nations Division for the Advancement of Women, "Gender and racial discrimination: Report of the Expert Group Meeting," 13.

48. United Nations Division for the Advancement of Women, "Gender and racial discrimination: Report of the Expert Group Meeting," 13–17.

49. Johanne Bouchard and Patrice Meyer-Bisch, "Intersectionality and Interdependence of Human Rights: Same or Different?" *Equal Rights Review* 16 (2016), 193.

50. Bouchard and Meyer-Bisch, "Intersectionality and Interdependence of Human Rights," 194.

51. Bouchard and Meyer-Bisch, "Intersectionality and Interdependence of Human Rights," 194.

52. See Bouchard and Meyer-Bisch, "Intersectionality and Interdependence of Human Rights," especially pages 195–96, for an explanation of the intersection of human rights violations.

53. Bouchard and Meyer-Bisch, "Intersectionality and Interdependence of Human Rights," 196.

54. Bouchard and Meyer-Bisch, "Intersectionality and Interdependence of Human Rights," 196.

55. UN Women, "Intersectionality resource guide and toolkit: An Intersectional Approach to Leave No One Behind" (2022), 3, https://www.unwomen.org/sites/default/files/2022-01/Intersectionality-resource-guide-and-toolkit-en.pdf.

56. UN Women, "Intersectionality resource guide and toolkit," 6.

57. UN Women, "Intersectionality resource guide and toolkit," 8.

58. UN Women, "Intersectionality resource guide and toolkit," 9.

59. An example of how this has become politicized can be found in Florida and Governor Ron DeSantis's Education Department's decision to ban teaching Critical Race Theory. Gov. DeSantis signed a bill restricting how schools can talk about race with students, known as the "Stop WOKE Act," which bars instruction that says members of one race are inherently racist or should feel guilt for past actions committed by others of the same race, among other things. This put the state at odds with the teaching of AP African American Studies. According to the state, "intersectionality" is part of the teaching of "Critical Race Theory," which has been banned. See Anemona Hartocollis and Eliza Fawcett, "The College Board Strips Down Its A.P. Curriculum for African American Studies," *New York Times*, February 1, 2023, updated February 9, 2023, https://www.nytimes.com/2023/02/01/us/college-board-advanced-placement-african-american-studies.html.

60. "Women's Suffrage: A World Chronology of the Recognition of Women's Rights to Vote and to Stand for Election," Inter-Parliamentary Union, http://archive.ipu.org/wmn-e/suffrage.htm; David Ottaway, *Saudi Women Go to the Polls—Finally*, Viewpoints No. 88 (Wilson Center, December 2015), https://www.wilsoncenter.org/sites/default/files/media/documents/publication/saudi_women_go_to_polls_finally.pdf.

61. Christine Chinkin, "The Convention on the Elimination of All Forms of Discrimination against Women," in *Handbook on Gender in World Politics*, eds. Jill Steans and Daniela Tepe-Belfrage (Cheltenham, UK: Edward Elgar Publishing, 2016), 145.

62. United Nations, *Report of the World Conference of the International Women's Year: Mexico City, 19 June–2 July 1975* (United Nations: New York, 1976), iii–iv, https://www.un.org/womenwatch/daw/beijing/otherconferences/Mexico/Mexico%20conference%20report%20optimized.pdf (accessed June 7, 2024).

63. UN Women, "Convention on the Elimination of All Forms of Discrimination against Women: Short History of CEDAW Convention," https://www.un.org/womenwatch/daw/cedaw/history.htm.

64. UN Women, "Convention on the Elimination of All Forms of Discrimination Against Women," https://www.un.org/womenwatch/daw/cedaw/cedaw.htm.

65. UN Women, "Convention on the Elimination of All Forms of Discrimination Against Women."

66. UN Women, "Convention on the Elimination of All Forms of Discrimination Against Women."

67. UN Women, "Introduction," Convention on the Elimination of All Forms of Discrimination Against Women, https://www.un.org/womenwatch/daw/cedaw/text/econvention.htm#intro.

68. See full text of CEDAW: https://www.un.org/womenwatch/daw/cedaw/text/econvention.htm.

69. UN Women, "Convention on the Elimination of All Forms of Discrimination Against Women."

70. Anne Sisson Runyan and Rebecca Sanders, "Prospects for Realizing International Women's Rights Law Through Local Governance: the Case of Cities for CEDAW," *Human Rights Review* 22 (2021), 306.

71. Chinkin, "The Convention on the Elimination of All Forms of Discrimination against Women," 147.

72. UN Women, "Convention on the Elimination of All Forms of Discrimination Against Women."

73. Chinkin, "The Convention on the Elimination of All Forms of Discrimination against Women," 147.

74. Chinkin, "The Convention on the Elimination of All Forms of Discrimination against Women," 148.

75. UN Women, Article 14, "Rural Women," "Convention on the Elimination of All Forms of Discrimination Against Women," https://www.un.org/womenwatch/daw/cedaw/text/econvention.htm#article14.

76. UN Women, "General Recommendations," "Convention on the Elimination of All Forms of Discrimination Against Women," https://www.un.org/womenwatch/daw/cedaw/recommendations/index.html.

77. UN Women, "Convention on the Elimination of All Forms of Discrimination Against Women."

78. UN Women, General Recommendation No. 14 (ninth session, 1990), "Female Circumcision," https://www.un.org/womenwatch/daw/cedaw/recommendations/recomm.htm.

79. United Nations, "General recommendation No. 28 on the core obligations of States parties under article 2 of the Convention on the Elimination of All Forms of Discrimination against Women," 1, https://documents.un.org/doc/undoc/gen/g10/472/60/pdf/g1047260.pdf?token=v9R6QsfVkINNyu45YM&fe=true.

80. Chinkin, "The Convention on the Elimination of All Forms of Discrimination against Women," 150.

81. International Committee of the Red Cross, "What is the difference between IHL and human rights law?" January 22, 2015, 1, https://www.icrc.org/en/document /what-difference-between-ihl-and-human-rights-law.

82. International Committee of the Red Cross, "What is International Humanitarian Law?" April 6, 2022, https://www.icrc.org/en/document/what-international -humanitarian-law.

83. International Committee of the Red Cross, "What is the difference between IHL and human rights law?" 3–4.

84. International Committee of the Red Cross, "The Geneva Conventions of 1949 and their Additional Protocols," January 1, 2014, https://www.icrc.org/en/document/ geneva-conventions-1949-additional-protocols (accessed June 7, 2024).

85. Helen M. Kinsella, "'With all the respect due to their sex': gender and international humanitarian law," in *Handbook on Gender in World Politics*, eds. Jill Steans and Daniela Tepe-Belfrage (Cheltenham, UK: Edward Elgar Publishing, 2016), 171.

86. Jeni Klugman, Robert U. Nagel, Mara Redlich Revkin, and Orly Maya Stern, "Can the Women, Peace and Security Agenda and International Humanitarian Law Join Forces? Emerging findings and promising directions," Georgetown Institute for Women, Peace and Security (2021), 5, https://giwps.georgetown.edu/wp-content/ uploads/2021/01/Can-WPS-and-IHL-Join-Forces.pdf.

87. Klugman et al., "Can the Women, Peace and Security Agenda and International Humanitarian Law Join Forces?" 7.

88. Kinsella, "'With all the respect due to their sex,'" 175.

89. Kinsella, "'With all the respect due to their sex,'" 176.

90. Viljoen, "International Human Rights Law: A Short History," 13.

91. International Criminal Court, *Understanding the International Criminal Court* (2020), 10, https://www.icc-cpi.int/sites/default/files/Publications/understanding-the -icc.pdf.

92. Viljoen, "International Human Rights Law: A Short History," 13.

93. Quoted in Dorothy Q. Thomas and Regan E. Ralph, "Rape in War: Challenging the Tradition of Impunity," *The SAIS Review of International Affairs* 14 (Winter/ Spring 1994), 87.

94. Jennifer Turpin, "Many Faces: Women Confronting War," in *The Women and War Reader*, eds. Lois Ann Lorentzen and Jennifer Turpin (New York: New York University Press, 1998), 5.

95. Global Centre for the Responsibility to Protect, "What Is R2P?" https://www .globalr2p.org/what-is-r2p/.

96. United Nations, "World Summit Outcome Document," October 24, 2005, https://www.un.org/en/development/desa/population/migration/generalassembly/ docs/globalcompact/A_RES_60_1.pdf.

97. Quotes taken from UN Office on Genocide Prevention and the Responsibility to Protect, "Responsibility to Protect," https://www.un.org/en/genocideprevention/ about-responsibility-to-protect.shtml.

98. Global Centre for the Responsibility to Protect, "What Is R2P? The Responsibility to Protect: A Background Briefing," January 14, 2021, https://www.globalr2p .org/publications/the-responsibility-to-protect-a-background-briefing/.

99. Global Centre for the Responsibility to Protect, "What Is R2P?"

100. Global Centre for the Responsibility to Protect, "UN Security Council Resolutions and Presidential Statements Referencing R2P," December 19, 2023, https://www.globalr2p.org/resources/un-security-council-resolutions-and-presidential-statements-referencing-r2p/; "UN General Assembly Resolutions Referencing R2P," December 19, 2023, https://www.globalr2p.org/resources/un-general-assembly-resolutions-referencing-r2p-2/; "UN Human Rights Council Resolutions Referencing R2P," April 5, 2024, https://www.globalr2p.org/resources/un-human-rights-council-resolutions-referencing-r2p/.

101. Global Centre for the Responsibility to Protect, "What Is R2P? The Responsibility to Protect: A Background Briefing."

102. Global Centre for the Responsibility to Protect, "What Is R2P? The Responsibility to Protect: A Background Briefing."

103. Global Centre for the Responsibility to Protect, "What Is R2P? The Responsibility to Protect: A Background Briefing."

104. Jess Gifkins and Dean Cooper-Cunningham, "Queering the Responsibility to Protect," *International Affairs* 99, no. 5 (2023), 2057.

105. In their footnote 3, the authors explain why they use the noun "queer" as opposed to other labels. Gifkins and Cooper-Cunningham, "Queering the Responsibility to Protect," 2057.

106. Mingst, *Essentials of International Relations*, 231.

107. Coralie Pison Hindawi, "Decolonizing the Responsibility to Protect: On pervasive Eurocentrism, Southern agency and struggles over universals," *Security Dialogue* 53, no. 1 (2022), 38–39.

108. Hindawi, "Decolonizing the Responsibility to Protect," 39.

109. Hindawi, "Decolonizing the Responsibility to Protect," 46.

110. Hindawi, "Decolonizing the Responsibility to Protect," 41.

111. United Nations General Assembly, "Resolution adopted by the General Assembly on 15 September 2005," October 24, 2005, 30, https://www.un.org/en/development/desa/population/migration/generalassembly/docs/globalcompact/A_RES_60_1.pdf.

112. Gifkins and Cooper-Cunningham, "Queering the Responsibility to Protect," 2066.

113. Gifkins and Cooper-Cunningham, "Queering the Responsibility to Protect," 2066–67.

CHAPTER 4

1. Kristen Hopewell, "The Liberal International Order on the Brink," *Current History* 116, no. 793 (November 2017), 303.

2. G. John Ikenberry, *After Victory: Institutions, Strategic Restraint, and the Rebuilding of Order after Major Wars*, new edition (Princeton, NJ: Princeton University Press, 2019), 163.

3. The World Bank, "Trade Has Been a Powerful Driver of Economic Development and Poverty Reduction," February 12, 2023, https://www.worldbank.org/en/topic/trade/brief/trade-has-been-a-powerful-driver-of-economic-development-and-poverty-reduction.

4. Douglas A. Irwin, "Globalization enabled nearly all countries to grow richer in recent decades," *Peterson Institute for International Economics*, June 16, 2022, https://www.piie.com/blogs/realtime-economic-issues-watch/globalization-enabled-nearly-all-countries-grow-richer-recent.

5. Irwin, "Globalization enabled nearly all countries to grow richer in recent decades."

6. Irwin, "Globalization enabled nearly all countries to grow richer in recent decades."

7. Zia Qureshi, "Rising inequality: A major issue of our time," *Brookings* (May 16, 2023), https://www.brookings.edu/articles/rising-inequality-a-major-issue-of-our-time/.

8. Qureshi, "Rising inequality."

9. Qureshi, "Rising inequality"; see also Esteban Ortiz-Ospina, "Is globalization an engine of economic development?" *Our World in Data*, August 1, 2017, https://ourworldindata.org/is-globalization-an-engine-of-economic-development.

10. The World Bank, "Trade Has Been a Powerful Driver of Economic Development and Poverty Reduction."

11. Sarah L. Henderson and Alana S. Jeydel, *Women and Politics in a Global World*, 2nd ed. (New York: Oxford University Press, 2010), 242.

12. Violet Bridget Lunga, "Postcolonial Theory: A Language for a Critique of Globalization?" *Perspectives on Global Development and Technology* 7 (2008), 195–96.

13. Michael Mandelbaum, *Mission Failure: America and the World in the Post-Cold War Era* (New York: Oxford University Press, 2016), 39, 40.

14. Thomas Friedman, *The World Is Flat: A Brief History of the Twenty-First Century* (New York: Farrar, Straus & Giroux, 2005), 10.

15. See Robert B. Marks, *The Origins of the Modern World*, 5th ed. (Lanham, MD: Rowman & Littlefield, 2024).

16. Jill Steans, *Gender and International Relations*, 3rd ed. (Malden, MA: Polity Press, 2013), 159.

17. Renée Marlin-Bennett and David K. Johnson, "International Political Economy: Overview and Conceptualization," *Oxford Research Encyclopedias* (January 22, 2021), 1, https://doi.org/10.1093/acrefore/9780190846626.013.239.

18. Marlin-Bennett and Johnson, "International Political Economy," 2.

19. Women's International League for Peace and Freedom, *A WILPF Guide to Feminist Political Economy*, 2nd ed. (August 2018), 4, https://www.wilpf.org/wp-content/uploads/2019/07/WILPF_Feminist-Political-Economy-Guide.pdf.

20. Women's International League for Peace and Freedom, *A WILPF Guide to Feminist Political Economy*, 5.

21. Marlin-Bennett and Johnson, "International Political Economy," 22.

22. J. Ann Tickner, *Gendering World Politics: Issues and Approaches in the Post-Cold War Era* (New York: Columbia University Press, 2001), 79.

146   *Notes*

23. Women's International League for Peace and Freedom, *A WILPF Guide to Feminist Political Economy*, 2.

24. Women's International League for Peace and Freedom, *A WILPF Guide to Feminist Political Economy*, 7.

25. Cheryl McEwan, "Postcolonialism, feminism and development: intersections and dilemmas," *Progress in Development Studies* 1, no. 2 (2001), 94. See also, Marlin-Bennett and Johnson, "International Political Economy," 23.

26. Marlin-Bennett and Johnson, "International Political Economy," 23.

27. Violet Bridget Lunga, "Postcolonial Theory: A Language for a Critique of Globalization?" *Perspectives on Global Development and Technology* 7 (2008), 197–98.

28. Sara Salem, "Capitalism, postcolonialism and gender: Complicating development," *Gender & Development Network*, Thinkpieces (July 2019), 3, https://static1 .squarespace.com/static/536c4ee8e4b0b60bc6ca7c74/t/5d2dd4debb21d40001903ba0 /1563284703863/GADN+Thinkpiece+-+Capitalism%2C+Postcolonialism+and +Gender.pdf.

29. Salem, "Capitalism, postcolonialism and gender," 4.

30. See Robert B, Marks, *The Origins of the Modern World: A Global and Environmental Narrative from the Fifteenth to the Twenty-First Century*, 5th ed. (Lanham, MD: Rowman & Littlefield, 2024).

31. Anne Sisson Runyan and V. Spike Peterson, *Global Gender Issues in the New Millennium,* 4th ed. (Boulder, CO: Westview Press, 2014), 188.

32. Runyan and Peterson, *Global Gender Issues in the New Millennium*, 188–89.

33. Runyan and Peterson, *Global Gender Issues in the New Millennium*, 189.

34. See chapter 3, "Three Models of Man: Gendered Perspectives on Global Economic Security," in J. Ann Tickner, *Gender in International Relations: Feminist Perspectives on Achieving Global Security* (New York: Columbia University Press, 1992), 67–96.

35. Tickner, *Gender in International Relations*, 78.

36. Tickner, *Gender in International Relations*, 78.

37. Tickner, *Gender in International Relations*, 78.

38. Arne Ruckert, "The international financial institutions, structural adjustment and poverty reduction," in *Handbook on Gender in World Politics*, eds. Jill Steans and Daniela Tepe-Belfrage (Northampton, MA: Edward Elgar Publishing, 2016), 423.

39. Runyan and Peterson, *Global Gender Issues in the New Millennium*, 195.

40. Jill Steans, *Gender and International Relations*, 3rd ed. (Malden, MA: Polity Press, 2013), 170.

41. Lauren Frayer and Raksha Kumar, "It's a mystery: Women in India drop out of the workforce even as the economy grows," NPR, *All Things Considered*, updated January 16, 2023, https://www.npr.org/sections/goatsandsoda/2023/01/04/1146953384/ why-women-in-india-are-dropping-out-the-workforce-even-as-the-economy-grows.

42. World Bank, "The World Bank in India," updated September 27, 2023, https://www.worldbank.org/en/country/india/overview.

43. Frayer and Kumar, "It's a mystery: Women in India drop out of the workforce even as the economy grows."

44. OECD, "Gender in infrastructure," https://www.oecd.org/gov/infrastructure-governance/gender-in-infrastructure/; Alexa Blain, "Moving gender-lens infrastructure investment from niche to mainstream: What will it take?" World Bank Blogs, November 25, 2019, https://blogs.worldbank.org/ppps/moving-gender-lens-infrastructure-investment-niche-mainstream-what-will-it-take.

45. Tickner, *Gender in International Relations*, 94.

46. Runyan and Peterson, *Global Gender Issues in the New Millennium*, 193.

47. Esteban Ortiz-Ospina and Max Roser, "Economic Inequality by Gender," *Our World in Data*, https://ourworldindata.org/economic-inequality-by-gender (last updated March 2024).

48. Ortiz-Ospina and Roser, "Economic Inequality by Gender."

49. Ortiz-Ospina and Rosen, "Economic Inequality by Gender."

50. The World Bank, "Gender Equality and Development Report, 2012" (The International Bank for Reconstruction and Development/The World Bank, 2011), xiii, https://documents1.worldbank.org/curated/en/492221468136792185/pdf/Main-report.pdf.

51. Eva M. Rathgeber, "WID, WAD, and GAD: Trends in Research and Practice," *Journal of Developing Areas* 24, no. 4 (July 1990), 490.

52. Rathgeber, "WID, WAD, and GAD: Trends in Research and Practice," 490–91.

53. Rathgeber, "WID, WAD, and GAD: Trends in Research and Practice," 492.

54. Rathgeber, "WID, WAD, and GAD: Trends in Research and Practice," 493.

55. Rathgeber, "WID, WAD, and GAD: Trends in Research and Practice," 494.

56. Rathgeber, "WID, WAD, and GAD: Trends in Research and Practice," 494.

57. Rathgeber, "WID, WAD, and GAD: Trends in Research and Practice," 494–95.

58. Rathgeber, "WID, WAD, and GAD: Trends in Research and Practice," 495.

59. The World Bank, "Bretton Woods and the Birth of the World Bank," https://www.worldbank.org/en/archive/history/exhibits/Bretton-Woods-and-the-Birth-of-the-World-Bank.

60. The World Bank, "Remarks by World Bank Group President Ajay Banga at the 2023 Annual Meetings Plenary," October 13, 2023, https://www.worldbank.org/en/news/speech/2023/10/13/remarks-by-world-bank-group-president-ajay-banga-at-the-2023-annual-meetings-plenary.

61. Christine Lagarde, "A Global Imperative," IMF (March 2019), https://www.imf.org/en/Publications/fandd/issues/2019/03/empowering-women-critical-for-global-economy-lagarde.

62. Andrea Shalal, "'Buckle up': New IMF chief vows 'relentless' focus on gender equality," *Reuters*, October 15, 2019, https://www.reuters.com/article/idUSKBN1WU32P/.

63. As quoted in Shalal, "'Buckle up': New IMF chief vows 'relentless' focus on gender equality."

64. World Trade Organization, "WTO Director General—Dr. Okonjo-Iweala," https://www.wto.org/english/thewto_e/dg_e/dg_e.htm.

65. World Trade Organization, "DG Okonjo-Iweala: Global trade a powerful instrument for improving the lives of women," September 21, 2022, https://www.wto.org/english/news_e/news22_e/dgno_22sep22_e.htm.

66. OECD, "Gender in infrastructure."

67. UN Women, "12 Critical Areas," https://www.unwomen.org/en/news/in-focus/csw59/feature-stories.

68. UN Women, "12 Critical Areas."

69. See Valeria Esquivel and Corina Rodriquez Enriquez, "The Beijing Platform for Action charted a future we still need to bring up: Building feminist economic policy," *Gender and Development* 28, no. 2 (2020), 281–98.

70. Esquivel and Enriquez, "The Beijing Platform for Action charted a future we still need to bring up," 290.

71. World Health Organization, "Millennium Development Goals," February 19, 2018, https://www.who.int/news-room/fact-sheets/detail/millennium-development-goals-(mdgs).

72. Carol Barton, Martin Khor, Sunita Narain, and Victoria Tauli-Corpuz, "Women's Movements and Gender Perspectives on the Millennium Development Goals," in *Civil Society Perspectives on the Millennium Development Goals* (United Nations Development Programme, November 3, 2015), 4, https://www.undp.org/sites/g/files/zskgke326/files/publications/Civil%20Society%20Perspectives%20on%20the%20MDGs.pdf.

73. Esquivel and Enriquez, "The Beijing Platform for Action charted a future we still need to bring up," 284.

74. Esquivel and Enriquez, "The Beijing Platform for Action charted a future we still need to bring up," 284.

75. Esquivel and Enriquez, "The Beijing Platform for Action charted a future we still need to bring up," 287.

76. United Nations Department of Economic and Social Affairs, "The 17 Goals," https://sdgs.un.org/goals.

77. Jeni Klugman, Francisco Rodriguez, and Hyung-Jin Choi, *The HDI 2010: New Controversies, Old Critiques* (United Nations Development Programme Human Development Reports Research Paper 2011/01, April 2011), 11, 35.

78. World Health Organization, "Human development index," https://www.who.int/data/nutrition/nlis/info/human-development-index.

79. United Nations Development Programme, *Human Development Report 2021/2022: Uncertain Times, Unsettled Lives: Shaping our Future in a Transforming World* (United Nations Development Programme, 2022), 3–4, https://hdr.undp.org/system/files/documents/global-report-document/hdr2021-22reportenglish_0.pdf.

80. Stephanie Nolen, "'Only God Can Thank You': Female Health Workers Fight to Be Paid," *New York Times*, September 21, 2023, https://www.nytimes.com/2023/09/21/health/community-health-worker-pay.html.

81. See Stephanie Nolen, "Trying to Solve a Covid Mystery: Africa's Low Death Rates," *New York Times*, March 23, 2022, https://www.nytimes.com/2022/03/23/health/covid-africa-deaths.html.

82. Nolen, "Trying to Solve a Covid Mystery: Africa's Low Death Rates."

83. Nolen, "Trying to Solve a Covid Mystery: Africa's Low Death Rates."

84. Lazaro Gamio and James Glanz, "Just How Big Could India's True Covid Toll Be?" *New York Times*, May 25, 2021, https://www.nytimes.com/interactive/2021/05/25/world/asia/india-covid-death-estimates.html.

85. Esquivel and Enriquez, "The Beijing Platform for Action charted a future we still need to bring up," 293.

86. BBC News, "Covid map: Coronavirus cases, deaths, vaccinations by country," July 5, 2022, https://www.bbc.com/news/world-51235105.

87. Shannon Sabo and Sandra Johnson, "COVID-19 Impacts on Mortality by Race/Ethnicity and Sex," United States Census Bureau, June 22, 2023, https://www.census.gov/library/stories/2023/06/covid-19-impacts-on-mortality-by-race-ethnicity-and-sex.html.

88. Sabo and Johnson, "COVID-19 Impacts on Mortality by Race/Ethnicity and Sex."

89. BBC News, "Covid map: Coronavirus cases, deaths, vaccinations by country."

90. Max Carlos Ramírez-Soto, Gutia Ortega-Cáceres, and Hugo Arroyo-Hernández, "Sex differences in COVID-19 fatality rate and risk of death: An analysis in 73 countries, 2020–2021," National Library of Medicine, published online September 10, 2021, https://www.ncbi.nlm.nih.gov/pmc/articles/PMC8805484/.

91. The Sex, Gender and Covid-19 Project, https://globalhealth5050.org/the-sex-gender-and-covid-19-project/.

92. The Sex, Gender and Covid-19 Project.

93. The Sex, Gender and Covid-19 Project, "Men, sex, gender, and COVID-19," https://globalhealth5050.org/the-sex-gender-and-covid-19-project/men-sex-gender-and-covid-19/.

94. CIA World Factbook, "South Africa," updated May 30, 2024, https://www.cia.gov/the-world-factbook/countries/south-africa/.

95. UN Development Programme, *UNDP South Africa 2022 Annual Report: A Year in Action to achieve Sustainable Development in South Africa* (June 20, 2023), 4, https://www.undp.org/south-africa/publications/undp-south-africa-annual-report-2022.

96. Statista, "Human development index score of South Africa from 2000 to 2021," April 26, 2023, https://www.statista.com/statistics/1236017/human-development-index-of-south-africa/.

97. Naidoo Saloshni and Naidoo Rajen Nithiseelan, "Vulnerability of South African women workers in the COVID-19 pandemic," *Frontiers in Public Health* (September 9, 2022), 1, https://www.ncbi.nlm.nih.gov/pmc/articles/PMC9507001/pdf/fpubh-10-964073.pdf.

98. Saloshni and Nithiseelan, "Vulnerability of South African women workers in the COVID-19 pandemic," 2.

99. Saloshni and Nithiseelan, "Vulnerability of South African women workers in the COVID-19 pandemic," 2.

100. Tsoaledi Thobejane, "South Africa needs a strong feminist movement to fight patriarchy," *The Conversation*, May 7, 2015, https://theconversation.com/south-africa-needs-a-strong-feminist-movement-to-fight-patriarchy-40508.

101. Saloshni and Nithiseelan, "Vulnerability of South African women workers in the COVID-19 pandemic," 4.

102. Antony Sguazzin, "Story of South Africa's Inequality Highlighted by Covid-19 Statistics," *Bloomberg Law*, June 14, 2022, https://news.bloomberglaw.com/coronavirus/story-of-south-africas-inequality-told-by-covid-19-statistics.

103. Sguazzin, "Story of South Africa's Inequality Highlighted by Covid-19 Statistics."

104. CIA World Factbook, "India," updated May 31, 2024, https://www.cia.gov/the-world-factbook/countries/india/.

105. Oxfam International, "India: extreme inequality in numbers" (n.d.), https://www.oxfam.org/en/india-extreme-inequality-numbers.

106. UN Development Programme, "India Ranks 132 on the Human Development Index as global development stalls," September 8, 2022, https://www.undp.org/india/press-releases/india-ranks-132-human-development-index-global-development-stalls.

107. UN Development Programme, "India Ranks 132 on the Human Development Index as global development stalls."

108. UN Development Programme, "India Ranks 132 on the Human Development Index as global development stalls."

109. UN Development Programme, "India Ranks 132 on the Human Development Index as global development stalls."

110. Priyanshi Chauhan, "Gendering COVID-19: Impact of the Pandemic on Women's Burden of Unpaid Work in India," *Gender Issues* 38 (2021), 395, 396.

111. Chauhan, "Gendering COVID-19," 408.

112. Chauhan, "Gendering COVID-19," 409.

113. Oxfam India, *Inequality Report 2021: India's Unequal Healthcare Story* (July 2021), 9, https://d1ns4ht6ytuzzo.cloudfront.net/oxfamdata/oxfamdatapublic/2021-07/India%20Inequality%20Report%202021_single%20lo.pdf?nTTJ4toC1_AjHL2eLoVFRJyAAAgTqHqG.

114. Oxfam India, *Inequality Report 2021: India's Unequal Healthcare Story*, 80.

115. Sandip Mondal and Ranjan Karmakar, "Caste in the Time of the Covid-19 Pandemic," *Contemporary Voices of Dalit* (2021), 2.

116. Mondal and Karmakar, "Caste in the Time of the Covid-19 Pandemic," 2–3.

CHAPTER 5

1. Rebecca Hersher, "'Frankly astonished': 2023 was significantly hotter than any other year on record," NPR, January 12, 2024, https://www.npr.org/2024/01/12

/1224398788/frankly-astonished-2023-was-significantly-hotter-than-any-other-year-on-record; Rachel Ramirez, "2023 will officially be the hottest year on record, scientists report," CNN, December 6, 2023, https://amp.cnn.com/cnn/2023/12/06/climate/2023-hottest-year-climate/index.html.

2. World Meteorological Organization, "2023 shatters climate records, with major impacts," November 30, 2023, 2, https://wmo.int/news/media-centre/2023-shatters-climate-records-major-impacts.

3. Hersher, "'Frankly astonished': 2023 was significantly hotter than any other year on record."

4. Somini Sengupta, "Drought Touches a Quarter of Humanity, U.N. Says, Disrupting Lives Globally," *New York Times*, January 11, 2024, https://www.nytimes.com/2024/01/11/climate/global-drought-food-hunger.html.

5. United Nations, *Global Drought Snapshot 2023: The Need for Proactive Action* (United Nations Convention to Combat Desertification, 2023), 7, https://www.droughtglobal.org/_files/ugd/184219_4dcb7a4451514f2281981f604c3848cc.pdf?index=true.

6. United Nations, *United Nations Convention to Combat Desertification in those countries experiencing serious drought and/or desertification, particularly in Africa* (1994), 4, https://catalogue.unccd.int/936_UNCCD_Convention_ENG.pdf.

7. "Desertification," United Nations Convention to Combat Desertification (UNCCD), https://www.unccd.int/land-and-life/desertification/overview.

8. Hannah Ritchie, "Deforestation and Forest Loss," *Our World In Data* (2021), https://ourworldindata.org/deforestation.

9. United Nations, "Sustainable Development Goal 15: Life on Land," https://www.un.org/sustainabledevelopment/biodiversity/.

10. Ritchie, "Deforestation and Forest Loss."

11. Ritchie, "Deforestation and Forest Loss."

12. Ritchie, "Deforestation and Forest Loss."

13. Martina Igini, "How Does Deforestation Affect the Environment?" Earth, April 6, 2023, https://earth.org/how-does-deforestation-affect-the-environment/.

14. "UNCCD thematic fact sheet series No. 3: Migration and desertification," United Nations Convention to Combat Desertification, https://catalogue.unccd.int/22_loose_leaf_Desertification_migration.pdf.

15. Evelyn Kpadeh Seagbeh, "Women at More Risk of Effects of Deforestation, Land Degradation, Drought, New UNCCD Study Reveals," *Earth Journalism Network*, June 6, 2022, https://earthjournalism.net/stories/women-at-more-risk-of-effects-of-deforestation-land-degradation-drought-new-unccd-study.

16. Shihana Mohamed, "Breaking Down Barriers to Women's Land Rights Starts in Our Homes," *Global Issues*, March 22, 2024, https://www.globalissues.org/news/2024/03/22/36300.

17. The United Nations Permanent Forum on Indigenous Issues, "Indigenous peoples' collective rights to land, territories and resources," UN Department of Public information, https://www.un.org/development/desa/indigenouspeoples/wp-content/uploads/sites/19/2018/04/Indigenous-Peoples-Collective-Rights-to-Lands-Territories-Resources.pdf.

18. Simon Dalby, "Environment and International Politics: Linking Humanity and Nature," E-IR (May 23, 2016), 2, https://www.e-ir.info/2016/05/23/environment-and-international-politics-linking-humanity-and-nature/.

19. Dalby, "Environment and International Politics: Linking Humanity and Nature," 2.

20. United Nations, "Declaration of the United Nations Conference on the Human Environment," *United Nations Audiovisual Library of International Law* (2012), https://legal.un.org/avl/pdf/ha/dunche/dunche_ph_e.pdf.

21. United Nations Environment Programme, "Frequently Asked Questions: When was UNEP founded?" https://www.unep.org/who-we-are/frequently-asked-questions.

22. Hanna Gersmann, "International environmental policy—a timeline," Heinrich Boll Stiftung, May 28, 2022, 1, https://www.boell.de/en/2022/05/28/international-environmental-policy-timeline.

23. United Nations, "Conferences/Environment and sustainable development: Stockholm 1972," https://www.un.org/en/conferences/environment/stockholm1972.

24. United Nations Environment Programme, "Frequently Asked Questions: When was UNEP founded?"

25. United Nations Environment Programme, "Frequently Asked Questions: What does UNEP do?" https://www.unep.org/who-we-are/frequently-asked-questions.

26. Gersmann, "International environmental policy—a timeline," 1.

27. Gunther Handl, "Declaration of the United Nations Conference on the Human Environment (Stockholm Declaration), 1972, and the Rio Declaration on Environment and Development, 1992," *United Nations Audiovisual Library of International Law* (2012), 1, https://legal.un.org/avl/pdf/ha/dunche/dunche_e.pdf.

28. Gersmann, "International environmental policy—a timeline," 5.

29. United Nations General Assembly, "Report of the United Nations Conference on Environment and Development, Annex 1: Rio Declaration on Environment and Development" (August 12, 1992), 1, https://www.un.org/en/development/desa/population/migration/generalassembly/docs/globalcompact/A_CONF.151_26_Vol.I_Declaration.pdf.

30. United Nations General Assembly, "Report of the United Nations Conference on Environment and Development, Annex 1: Rio Declaration on Environment and Development," 2.

31. United Nations General Assembly, "Report of the United Nations Conference on Environment and Development, Annex 1: Rio Declaration on Environment and Development," 4.

32. United Nations, "United Nations Conference on Environment and Development, Rio de Janeiro, Brazil, 3–14 June 1992," https://www.un.org/en/conferences/environment/rio1992.

33. Gersmann, "International environmental policy—a timeline," 2; CITES: Convention on International Trade in Endangered Species of Wild Fauna and Flora, "What is CITES?" https://cites.org/eng/disc/what.php.

34. United Nations Convention to Combat Desertification, "The history of UNCCD," https://www.unccd.int/convention/history-unccd.

35. United Nations Environment Programme, "About Montreal Protocol," https://www.unep.org/ozonaction/who-we-are/about-montreal-protocol.

36. Gersmann, "International environmental policy—a timeline," 4.

37. United Nations Environment Programme, "About Montreal Protocol."

38. United Nations Environment Programme, "About Montreal Protocol."

39. Gersmann, "International environmental policy—a timeline," 10.

40. United Nations, "United Nations Conference on Sustainable Development, Rio+20," https://sustainabledevelopment.un.org/rio20.html.

41. World Health Organization, "Millennium Development Goals (MDGs): Key facts," February 19, 2018, https://www.who.int/news-room/fact-sheets/detail/millennium-development-goals-(mdgs); United Nations Department of Economic and Social Affairs, "Sustainable Development: The 17 Goals," https://sdgs.un.org/goals.

42. United Nations Department of Economic and Social Affairs, "Sustainable Development: The 17 Goals."

43. United Nations Department of Economic and Social Affairs: Sustainable Development, "Paris Agreement" (2015), https://sdgs.un.org/frameworks/parisagreement.

44. John Vogler, "International relations theory and the environment," in *Global Environmental Politics: Concepts, Theories and Case Studies*, eds. Gabriela Kutting and Kyle Herman, 2nd ed. (London: Routledge Publishers, 2018), 10.

45. Vogler, "International relations theory and the environment," 10.

46. Vogler, "International relations theory and the environment," 10.

47. Vogler, "International relations theory and the environment," 11.

48. Vogler, "International relations theory and the environment," 11–12.

49. Vogler, "International relations theory and the environment," 11–12.

50. Vogler, "International relations theory and the environment," 13.

51. Vogler, "International relations theory and the environment," 14.

52. Peter M. Haas, "Abstract," https://www.taylorfrancis.com/chapters/edit/10.4324/9781315717906-16/social-constructivism-evolution-multilateral-environmental-governance-peter-haas.

53. Stephen M. Walt, "The Realist Guide to Solving Climate Change," *Foreign Policy*, August 13, 2021, https://foreignpolicy.com/2021/08/13/realist-guide-to-solving-climate-change/.

54. Walt, "The Realist Guide to Solving Climate Change."

55. Vogler, "International relations theory and the environment," 16. On Greenpeace's work on the climate, see https://www.greenpeace.org/international/. On an analysis of multinational firms and pollution, see Itzhak Ben-David, Yeejin Jang, Stefanie Kleimeier, and Michael Viehs, "Exporting pollution: where do multinational firms release CO_2?" *Principles for Responsible Investment* (March 18, 2020), https://www.unpri.org/pri-blog/exporting-pollution-where-do-multinational-firms-release-co2/5592.article. On the European Union's efforts at addressing environmental issues, see the European Environment Agency, https://www.eea.europa.eu/en.

56. Vogler, "International relations theory and the environment," 18. See also Hannah Hughes, "Environmental Security," in *Global Environmental Politics:*

Concepts, Theories and Case Studies, eds. Gabriela Kutting and Kyle Herman, 2nd ed. (London: Routledge, 2018), 66–68.

57. Nicole A. Detraz, "The genders of environmental security," in *Gender and International Security: Feminist Perspectives,* ed. Laura Sjoberg (London/New York: Routledge Publishers, 2010), 106.

58. Detraz, "The genders of environmental security," 104–5.

59. Thomas F. Homer-Dixon, "Environmental Scarcities and Violent Conflict: Evidence from Cases," *International Security* 1, no. 1 (Summer 1994), 36.

60. Homer-Dixon, "Environmental Scarcities and Violent Conflict," 39.

61. Vogler, "International relations theory and the environment," 19.

62. Vogler, "International relations theory and the environment," 18.

63. Jim Garamone, "Hicks Defines Need to Focus DOD on Climate Change Threats," DOD News, August 30, 2023, https://www.defense.gov/News/News -Stories/Article/Article/3510772/hicks-defines-need-to-focus-dod-on-climate-change -threats/.

64. United Nations Security Council, "Statement by the President of the Security Council," S/PRST/2007/22, June 25, 2007, https://www.securitycouncilreport.org /atf/cf/%7B65BFCF9B-6D27-4E9C-8CD3-CF6E4FF96FF9%7D/NRC%20SPRST %202007%2022.pdf.

65. Christina Ergas, Laura McKinney, and Shannon Elizabeth Bell, "Intersectionality and the Environment," in *Handbook of Environmental Sociology,* eds. Beth Schaefer Caniglia, Andrew Jorgenson, Stephanie A. Malin, Lori Peek, David N. Pellow, and Xiaorui Huang (Springer Nature Switzerland AG, 2021), 16.

66. Ergas et al., "Intersectionality and the Environment," 16–20.

67. Ergas et al., "Intersectionality and the Environment," 17.

68. Ergas et al., "Intersectionality and the Environment," 17–18.

69. Sonalini Sapra, "Feminist Perspectives on the Environment," *Oxford Research Encyclopedias, International Studies* (November 30, 2017), 2, https://doi .org/10.1093/acrefore/9780190846626.013.49.

70. Sapra, "Feminist Perspectives on the Environment," 4.

71. Sapra, "Feminist Perspectives on the Environment," 2.

72. Ergas et al., "Intersectionality and the Environment," 17.

73. Sapra, "Feminist Perspectives on the Environment," 12.

74. Ergas et al., "Intersectionality and the Environment," 19.

75. Ergas et al., "Intersectionality and the Environment," 19.

76. Ergas et al., "Intersectionality and the Environment," 19.

77. Ergas et al., "Intersectionality and the Environment," 21.

78. Bethuel Sibongiseni Ngcamu, "Climate change effects on vulnerable populations in the Global South: a systemic review," *Natural Hazards* 118 (2023), 981.

79. Ngcamu, "Climate change effects on vulnerable populations in the Global South," 982.

80. Ergas et al., "Intersectionality and the Environment," 21.

81. Ergas et al., "Intersectionality and the Environment," 21.

82. Jean Ait Belkhir and Christiane Charlemaine, "Race, Gender and Class Lessons from Hurricane Katrina," *Race, Gender & Class* 14, nos. 1–2 (2007), 123.

83. Belkhir and Charlemaine, "Race, Gender and Class Lessons from Hurricane Katrina," 129.

84. Sarah R. Lowe, Kara Lustig, and Helen B. Marrow, "African American Women's Reports of Racism during Hurricane Katrina: Variation by Interviewer Race," *New School Psychology Bulletin* 8, no. 2 (2011), 46.

85. Karen Bell, "Bread and Roses: A Gender Perspective on Environmental Justice and Public Health," *International Journal of Environmental Research and Public Health* 13 (2016), 1.

86. Stephanie A. Malin and Stacia S. Ryder, "Developing deeply intersectional environmental justice scholarship," *Environmental Sociology* 4, no. 1 (2018), 2.

87. Bell, "Bread and Roses," 4.

88. Bell, "Bread and Roses," 11.

89. Bell, "Bread and Roses," 11.

90. Charlotte Bretherton, "Global environmental politics: putting gender on the agenda?" *Review of International Studies* 24, no. 1 (January 1998), 86.

91. Women's Environment & Development Organization, "Our Story: Timeline," https://wedo.org/about-us/.

92. Greta Gaard, "Ecofeminism and climate change," *Women's Studies International Forum* 49 (2015), 21. See also Women's Environment & Development Organization, "Our Story: Timeline"; Women's Major Group, "History of the Women's Movement and Sustainable Development," January 2018, 1, https://womensmajorgroup.org/wp-content/uploads/2018/01/History-of-the-Women%E2%80%99s-Movement-and-Sustainable-Development.pdf.

93. Gaard, "Ecofeminism and climate change," 21; Women's Major Group, "History of the Women's Movement and Sustainable Development," 1.

94. Women's Major Group, "History of the Women's Movement and Sustainable Development," 1.

95. Handl, "Declaration of the United Nations Conference on the Human Environment (Stockholm Declaration), 1972, and the Rio Declaration on Environment and Development, 1992," 7.

96. Gaard, "Ecofeminism and climate change," 21.

97. Bretherton, "Global environmental politics: putting gender on the agenda?" 86.

98. Gaard, "Ecofeminism and climate change," 21–22.

99. Gaard, "Ecofeminism and climate change," 22.

100. Bretherton, "Global environmental politics: putting gender on the agenda?" 94.

101. Bretherton, "Global environmental politics: putting gender on the agenda?" 94.

102. Bretherton, "Global environmental politics: putting gender on the agenda?" 88.

103. Bretherton, "Global environmental politics: putting gender on the agenda?" 99–100.

104. Bretherton, "Global environmental politics: putting gender on the agenda?" 92–94.

105. UN Women, "Five big wins ushered in by the landmark Beijing Platform for Action," March 20, 2020, https://www.unwomen.org/en/news/stories/2020/3/compilation-five-wins-ushered-in-by-beijing-platform-for-action.

106. Seema Arora-Jonsson and Bimbika Basnett Sijapati, "Disciplining Gender in Environmental Organizations: The Texts and Practices of Gender Mainstreaming," *Gender, Work and Organization* 25, no. 3 (May 2018), 310.

107. Arora-Jonsson and Sijapati, "Disciplining Gender in Environmental Organizations," 322.

108. UN Women, "Press Release: As climate change pushes millions of women into poverty, UN Women calls for a new feminist climate justice approach," December 4, 2023, https://www.unwomen.org/en/news-stories/press-release/2023/12/as-climate-changes-pushes-millions-of-women-into-poverty-un-women-calls-for-a-new-feminist-climate-justice-approach.

109. Lena Ramstetter and Fabian Habersack, "Do women make a difference? Analysing environmental attitudes and actions of Members of the European Parliament," *Environmental Politics* 29, no. 6 (2020), 1077.

110. UN Women, "Press Release: As climate change pushes millions of women into poverty, UN Women calls for a new feminist climate justice approach."

111. UN Women, "Press Release: As climate change pushes millions of women into poverty, UN Women calls for a new feminist climate justice approach."

112. Damian Carrington, "Azerbaijan appoints no women to 28-member Cop29 climate committee," *The Guardian*, January 15, 2024, https://www.theguardian.com/environment/2024/jan/15/cop29-climate-summit-committee-appointed-with-28-men-and-no-women-azerbaijan.

113. Damian Carrington, "Women added to Cop29 climate summit committee after backlash," *The Guardian*, January 19, 2024, https://www.theguardian.com/environment/2024/jan/19/women-cop29-climate-summit-committee-backlash.

114. Melanie Zurba and Anastasia Papadopoulos, "Indigenous Participation and the Incorporation of Indigenous Knowledge and Perspectives in Global Environmental Governance Forums: a Systematic Review," *Environmental Management* 72 (2023), 88.

115. Zurba and Papadopoulos, "Indigenous Participation and the Incorporation of Indigenous Knowledge and Perspectives in Global Environmental Governance Forums," 89.

116. UN Women, "New report shows how feminism can be a powerful tool to fight climate change," December 2, 2023, https://www.unwomen.org/en/news-stories/feature-story/2023/12/new-report-shows-how-feminism-can-be-a-powerful-tool-to-fight-climate-change.

117. Farhana Sultana, "Climate change, COVID-19, and the co-production of injustices: a feminist reading of overlapping crises," *Social & Cultural Geography* 22, no. 4 (2021), 454.

118. Laura Turquet, Constanza Tabbush, Silke Staab, Loui Williams, and Brianna Howell, "Feminist Climate Justice: A Framework for Action," Conceptual framework prepared for *Progress of the World's Women* series (New York: UN Women, 2023), 12.

119. Michael Mikulewicz, Martina Angela Caretta, Farhana Sultana, and Neil J. W. Crawford, "Intersectionality & Climate Justice: A call for synergy in climate change scholarship," *Environmental Politics* 32, no. 7 (2023), 1281.

120. Paul G. Harris, "Climate change: Science, international cooperation and global environmental politics," in *Global Environmental Politics: Concepts, Theories and Case Studies*, eds. Gabriela Kutting and Kyle Herman, 2nd ed. (London: Routledge Publishers, 2018), 123.

121. Jennifer Hadden and Aseem Prakash, "Symposium: What Scholars Know (and Need to Know) about the Politics of Climate Change," *PS: Political Science and Politics* 57, no. 1 (January 2024), 17.

122. United Nations Framework Convention on Climate Change, "Climate Change Information Sheet 17: The international response to climate change: A history," https://unfccc.int/cop3/fccc/climate/fact17.htm (last modified: July 18, 2000).

123. Gersmann, "International environmental policy—a timeline," 2–3.

124. Quoted in the United Nations Framework Convention on Climate Change, "Climate Change Information Sheet 17," 1.

125. United Nations Framework Convention on Climate Change, "Climate Change Information Sheet 17," 1.

126. United Nations Framework Convention on Climate Change, "Climate Change Information Sheet 17," 1.

127. Harris, "Climate change: Science, international cooperation and global environmental politics," 130.

128. United Nations, "Climate Action: UN Climate Change Conferences," https://www.un.org/en/climatechange/un-climate-conferences.

129. Gersmann, "International environmental policy—a timeline," 7.

130. Harris, "Climate change: Science, international cooperation and global environmental politics," 131.

131. Harris, "Climate change: Science, international cooperation and global environmental politics," 135.

132. Hughes, "Environmental security," 76.

133. Hughes, "Environmental security," 76.

134. UN Department of Political and Peacebuilding Affairs, "Addressing the Impact of Climate Change on Peace and Security," https://dppa.un.org/en/addressing-impact-of-climate-change-peace-and-security.

135. UN Department of Political and Peacebuilding Affairs, "Addressing the Impact of Climate Change on Peace and Security."

136. Anna Kaijser and Annica Kronsell, "Climate change through the lens of intersectionality," *Environmental Politics* 23, no. 3 (2014), 427.

137. Irene Dankelman and Kavita Naidu, "Introduction: Gender, development, and the climate crisis," *Gender & Development* 28, no. 3 (2020), 448.

138. Dankelman and Naidu, "Introduction," 449.

139. Dankelman and Naidu, "Introduction," 452.

140. Dankelman and Naidu, "Introduction," 452.

141. Sapra, "Feminist Perspectives on the Environment," 14.

142. Women's Environment & Development Organization, "Global Gender & Climate Alliance," December 24, 2008, https://wedo.org/global-gender-and-climate-alliance/.

143. Sapra, "Feminist Perspectives on the Environment," 14.

144. GenderCC—Women for Climate Justice, "Who are we," https://www.gendercc.net/who-are-we.html.

145. GenderCC—Women for Climate Justice, "Who are we."

146. Women and Gender Constituency, "Our background," https://womengenderclimate.org/our-background/.

147. Women and Gender Constituency, "About us: A Just Framework for Action," https://womengenderclimate.org/about-us/.

148. Dankelman and Naidu, "Introduction," 452–53.

149. United Nations Department of Economic and Social Affairs: Sustainable Development, "Paris Agreement."

150. United Nations Framework Convention on Climate Change, "Report of the Conference of the Parties on its twenty-third session, held in Bonn from 6 to 18 November 2017," FCCC/CP/2017/11/Add.1 (February 8, 2018), 15, https://unfccc.int/resource/docs/2017/cop23/eng/11a01.pdf.

151. United Nations Framework Convention on Climate Change, "Report of the Conference of the Parties on its twenty-third session, held in Bonn from 6 to 18 November 2017," 15–16.

152. Joanna Flavell, "From Gender-Blind to Gender Bind: Foregrounding Gender in the History of the UNFCCC," *Global Environmental Politics* 24, no. 1 (February 2024), 33.

153. UN Women, "As climate change pushes millions of women into poverty, UN Women calls for a new Feminist Climate Justice Approach."

154. UN Women, "As climate change pushes millions of women into poverty, UN Women calls for a new Feminist Climate Justice Approach."

155. Flavell, "From Gender-Blind to Gender Bind," 43.

156. Flavell, "From Gender-Blind to Gender Bind," 45.

157. For a discussion of IR theory and norm life cycle in the context of climate change, see Kathryn Sikkink, "How International Relations Theory on Norm Cascades Can Inform the Politics of Climate Change," *PS: Political Science & Politics* 57, no. 1 (January 2024), 36–39.

158. Ngcamu, "Climate change effects on vulnerable populations in the Global South," 977.

CHAPTER 6

1. For the classic description of "levels of analysis" see J. David Singer, "The Level of Analysis Problem in International Relations," *World Politics* 14, no. 1 (October 1961), 77–92. See also Kenneth Waltz, *Man, The State, and War: A Theoretical Analysis* (New York: Columbia University Press, 1954).

2. For the classic description of power and the role it plays regarding nations, see Hans J. Morgenthau, *Politics Among Nations: The Struggle for Power and Peace*, brief edition (Boston: McGraw-Hill, 1993).

3. Ange-Marie Hancock, *Intersectionality: An Intellectual History* (New York: Oxford University Press, 2016), 35, 63, 107.

4. Patricia Hill Collins and Sirma Bilge, *Intersectionality*, 2nd ed. (Malden, MA: Polity Press, 2020), 15.

5. Collins and Bilge, *Intersectionality*, 34.

Index

activism: peace, 11, 20; of women,
34–35, 106–7, 112–13
Affordable Care Act (Obamacare), US,
86
Afghanistan, 20–22
Africa, *51–52*, 55, 87, 89–92. *See also*
specific countries
African Americans, 106
age, 23, 34, 40–42, 93–94, 114, 120–21;
in Africa, 89; in India, 89, 92;
military conscription and, 2–3
agency, 13, 105, 108
agriculture, agricultural labor and, *77*,
77–78, *84*, 91, 98–99
Ahmed, Aziza, *51*
Andrews, Josephine, 2
androcentricism, 37
apartheid, 90, 92
armed conflicts, 21, 26, *26*, 61, 67, 104.
See also violence; wars
Asia, 13, 24, *51–52*, 72, 89
austerity programs, 83
authoritarianism, 8
automation, 70
Azerbaijan, 109

Bandung Conference (1955), *51*
Banga, Ajay, *81*
Basu, Soumita, 29–30

Begtrup, Bodil, 50
Beijing Conference (Fourth World
Conference on Women, 1995), UN,
25, 52, 82–84, 109, 123, 140n38
Beijing Platform for Action (BPfA),
UN, 82–84, 123, 140n38
Belkhir, Jean Ait, 106
Bell, Karen, 106–7
Bernardino, Minerva, 49–50
Bilge, Sirma, 118–19
biodiversity loss, *85*, 98
Black people, 5, 10; Black women, 5,
118; in Ukraine, 2, 120; in the US,
89, 106
bombings, in Northern Ireland, 40,
136n78
Bosnia, 45, 62–64
Bouchard, Johanne, 54
boundaries/borders, national, 2, 12, *70*,
72
BPfA. *See* Beijing Platform for Action
Bretherton, Charlotte, 107–8
Bretton Woods Conference, 7–8, *80*,
123–24, 126
Brexit, 33, 42
British government (the Crown),
32–33
Brown, Katherine, 24
Bulgaria, *81*

Canada, 99, 125
capitalism, 39, 69, 74, 107
carbon emissions, 98
care economy, 76, 87
Carter, Jimmy, 58
caste system, Indian, 94
Catholicism, 15, 23, 31–42, 125
ceasefires, in Northern Ireland, 33, 37
CEDAW. *See* Convention on the
    Elimination of All Forms of
    Discrimination Against Women
Charlemaine, Christiane, 106
Chauhan, Priyanshi, 93
childcare, 29, 34, 79
children, 2–3, 74, 93, 120
China, 3, 6, 16, 37, *71*, 128n13;
    COVID-19 associated with, 24, 89,
    123
Chinkin, Christine, 57–60
circumcision, female, 59–60
CITES. *See* Convention on International
    Trade in Endangered Species of Wild
    Fauna and Flora
citizenship status, 19, 23–24, 49, *81*
civil rights, 32–33, 40, 56
civil wars, 19, 45
class, 4, 53, 75, 90, 107; gender and,
    34–37, 79, 120–21; middle, 22–23,
    34–35, 118; working, 22–23, 34–35
climate change, 23, *85*, 92, 97, 103,
    156n108; gender and, 112–15,
    113–14; intersectionality and, 16,
    98, 110–12; Montreal Protocol
    addressing, 103; UNFCCC
    addressing, 100, 111–15, *114–15*,
    125–26
Clinton, Hillary, 52
Cockburn, Cynthia, 15, 19, 32–34
Cold War, 7, 13, 23, 25, *51*, 104;
    globalization following, 69, *71*;
    intrastate conflicts since, 19; post–
    Cold War period, 16, 17, 61
Collins, Eamon, 35
Collins, Patricia Hill, 118–19
colonialism, 4, 50, *72*, 74–75, 124,
    131n81; European, 13, 105; racism

and, 9–10, 37–39; state power and,
    118
Commission on Human Rights, UN,
    46, 50
Commission on the Status of Women,
    UN, 58
communication technologies, *70–71*
Conference of Parties (COP) process,
    101, 111–12, 114, 123
Conference on the Human Environment,
    UN, 99, 102
Conference on Women, UN (1995), 25,
    82–84, 109, 123, 140n38
conscription, 2–3, 120
constructivism, 6, 8–9, 21, 46, 117,
    123; environmental issues and,
    102–3, 115
Convention on Consent, Minimum Age,
    and Registration for Marriage, UN,
    52
Convention on International Trade in
    Endangered Species of Wild Fauna
    and Flora (CITES), UN, 100
Convention on the Elimination of All
    Forms of Discrimination Against
    Women (CEDAW), 15, 123;
    intersectional analysis on, 45, 52–60,
    67–68, 120–22
Convention on the Political Rights of
    Women (CPW), UN, 52
Convention on the Prevention and
    Punishment of the Crime of
    Genocide (1948), UN, 48
cooperation, 16; international, *80*, 99,
    102; state, 7–8, 20
Cooper-Cunningham, Dean, 65, 67
COP. *See* Conference of Parties
Coulter, Colin, 37
COVID-19, 24, *77*, 82, 84, 123; as
    case study for intersectionality, 70,
    85–87, *88*, 89–95; data on, 87, *88*,
    89–90; economies impacted by, 16,
    89–94
CPW. *See* Convention on the Political
    Rights of Women
Crenshaw, Kimberlé, 5, 52–53

Dalby, Simon, 99
DDR programs. *See* disarmament, demobilization, and reintegration programs
deaths: COVID, 87, *88*, 89–90, 92; during the Troubles, 33, 41
debt, 75, *76*, 84
decision-making, 17, 65–66, 73, 108–10; gender and, 25, *25–26*, 27, 29, 77, 82, 117–18, 121–22; WPS addressing, 126
Declaration of Independence, US, 46
Declaration of the Rights of Man and Citizen, France, 46
Declaration on the Rights of Indigenous Peoples, UN, 47
Declaration on the Rights of Persons belonging to Ethnic, Religious and Linguistic Minorities, UN, 47
deforestation, 98
democracies, 8–9, 17, 47, 92
democratic peace, 8, 20, 123
Democratic Republic of Congo, 55
Deng, Francis, 66
Department of Economic and Social Affairs, UN, 124
Department of Political and Peacebuilding Affairs (DPPA), UN, 112
DeSantis, Ron, 141n59
desertification, 97–98, 100
Detraz, Nicole A., 103
developing countries, 26, *82*, 89–94, 101, 111, 124, 126; women in, 14, *76–77*, 87, 108, 118
disabilities, 55, 90, 112, 120–21
disarmament, demobilization, and reintegration (DDR) programs, 21
discrimination, 52–55, 73, 113; gender, 3, 5, 57–60, 83, 120–21; racial, 5, 48
disease, 120, 123, 125. *See also* COVID-19
Division for the Advancement of Women, UN, 52
division of labor, 12, 74–75, *76–77*, 124

domestic violence, 11, 20, 34, 37, 91
Doty, Roxanne Lynn, 10
Doyle, Michael, 8
DPPA. *See* Department of Political and Peacebuilding Affairs
Drezner, Daniel, 6–7, 9
droughts, 97–99
dual nationality, 41–42
Dubai, United Arab Emirates, 114–15
Du Bois, W. E. B, 10

Ebola, 87
ecofeminism, 105, 124
economic: inequalities, *51*, 78, 94, 115; status, 2, 16, 37, 75, 82, 90, 92, 112
economic development, 70, 120–21; COVID-19 and, 85–87, *88*, 89
economy, global, 16, 72–76, *76–77*; COVID-19 impacting, 89–95; gendering the, 12, *80–82*
education, 2, 10, 27, *85*, 120–21
endangered species, 99–100
England, 8, 46, 85–86
Enriquez, Corina Rodriguez, 84, 89
environmental: degradation, 77, 83, 103–4, 108, 111–12, 120; justice, 106–15, 124
environmental politics, international, 16, 98, 102–3, 111–15, 120; intersectionality and, 99–101, 104–10
Ergas, Christina, 105
Esquivel, Valeria, 84, 89
ethnic cleansing, 25, 62–64, 124
ethnicity, 21, 23, 37–40, 137n90. *See also* race
ethnonationalism, 35, 137n85
EU. *See* European Union
Eurocentrism, 74
Europe, 10, 89, 98, 109, 120, 126, 131n81; balance of power in, 3; colonialism via, 13, 105; Thirty Years' War in, 1. *See also specific countries*
European Union (EU), 1, 15, 128; the Troubles and, 32, 37, 39

Fanning, Bryan, 37–38
Fearon, Kate, 36
female circumcision, 59–60
femininity, 11, 19, 41, 73
feminism, 3, 21, 49–52, 78,
    117–18, 120, 122; feminist IR,
    4–5, 11–13, 19–20, 95, 115, 121;
    feminist security studies, 11–12,
    23–24; postcolonial, 13–14, 105;
    transnational, 40, *51*, 112
feminist political ecology (FPE), 73,
    105, 124
Figueres, Christiana, 109
Finland, 1
Flavell, Joanna, 114–15
food insecurity, *84*, 98, 110
forced migration, 2, 98, 105
Foreign Affairs (journal), 10
foreign policies, 7
fossil fuels, 97
FPE. *See* feminist political ecology
France, 8, 46
Freeman, Bianca, 10
free trade agreements, 75, 125
Friedman, Thomas, *71*

Gaard, Greta, 108
GAD. *See* Gender and Development
Galtung, Johan, 30, 32, 136n75
Gani, Jasmine, 10
GAP. *See* Gender Action Plan
GATT. *See* General Agreement on
    Tariffs and Trade
GED agenda. *See* gender, environment
    and development agenda
gender, 127n5, 128n20, 130n65,
    135n54, 156n108; class and, 34–37,
    79, 120–21; climate change and,
    112–15, *113–14*; conscription and,
    2, 120; decision-making and, 25,
    25–26, 27, 29, 77, 82, 117–18, 121–
    22; discrimination, 3, 5, 57–60, 83,
    120–21; environmental issues and,
    98–100, 106–15; equality, 21–22, 26,
    49–52, 82–84, *85*, 109, 123–24, 126;
    forced migration and, 2; identity,

12, 23–24, 60; IHL and, 61–62;
    inequality, 73–74, *82*, 90, 106;
    international environmental politics
    and, 107–10; mainstreaming, 82,
    107–10, 114; norm, 20, 34, 90; pay
    gaps, 77–78; race and, 118, 121–22;
    violence based on, 11–13, 19–20,
    106, 121, 126. *See also* division of
    labor
gender, environment and development
    (GED) agenda, 107–8
Gender and Development (GAD)
    agenda, UN, 14, 78–80, 124
GenderCC-Women for Climate Justice,
    112–13
*Gender Equality and Development
    Report* (2012), World Bank, 78
Gender Issues (journal), 93
General Agreement on Tariffs and Trade
    (GATT), *81*, 124, 126
generations, 23, 34, 40–42, 93–94, 114
Geneva Conventions (1949), 61
genocides, 62–64
Georgieva, Kristalina, 80, *81*
Germany, 2, 8, 46, 114
Gersmann, Hanna, 100
GFA. *See* Good Friday Agreement
GGCA. *See* Global Gender and Climate
    Alliance
Gifkins, Jess, 65, 67
Gilmartin, Niall, 41
Global Centre for the Responsibility to
    Protect, 64
Global Gender and Climate Alliance
    (GGCA), 112
globalization, 16, 17, 23, *70*, *72*, *81*, 95,
    124; COVID-19 and, 89; economic,
    69–70, *71*
Global North, 13, 30, *51*, 76, 106
global political economy (GPE), 69,
    72–73, 77
Global South, *51*, 66, 74, *76*, 105–6,
    124; gender and, 13–14, 29–30;
    UNSCR 1325 and, 29–30
Good Friday Agreement (GFA) (1998),
    32–33, 36–37, 39, 41–43, 122, 125

governance, global, 103, 107–15, *113–14*
government, 18, 75–76, 85, 120; British, 32–33; India, 89, 93
GPE. *See* global political economy
Great Depression, 69
great powers, 8–9, 13, 20–21

Haas, Peter, 102
Hadden, Jennifer, 110
Hall, K. Melchor Quick, 11
Hancock, Ange-Marie, 5, 118
Handl, Gunther, 107
Harris, Paul G., 110
hate speech, 67
HDI. *See* Human Development Index
health care, 85–87, 89–95
Henderson, Sarah L., *70*
heterosexuality, 35
Hill, Myrtle, 41
Hindawi, Coralie Pison, 66
Hindu people, 94
History of the Peloponnesian War (Thucydides), 6
Hitler, Adolf, 46
Holocaust, 48, 61
Homer-Dixon, Thomas F., 104
Hughes, Hannah, 111–12
Human Development Index (HDI), UN, 95, 124; COVID-19 and, 86–87, 92–93
human insecurity, 23, 106
humanitarian interventions, 13, 15, 45, 60–68
human rights, 15, 24, 46–51, *47–48*, *51*, 120; intersectional perspective on, 52–56; violations of, 45, 54–55, 63, 66
Human Rights Watch, 62–63
human security, 15, 18, 23–25, 43, 124
Hurricane Katrina, 106

ICC. *See* international criminal court
ICCPR. *See* International Covenant on Civil and Political Rights

ICESCR. *See* International Covenant on Economic, Social and Cultural Rights
identity, 11, 39, 42, 118–19; gender, 12, 23–24, 60; intersectional, 5, 54–55; national, 3–4, 62–63; religious, 32–33; social, 9, 53; state, 8–9, 21, 102
IGOs. *See* international governmental organizations
IHL. *See* international humanitarian law
Ikramullah, Begum Shaista, 50
ILO. *See* International Labor Organization
IMF. *See* International Monetary Fund
imperialism, imperialist powers and, 10, 38, 131n81
income inequality, 69–70, 76
India, 70, *71*, *76–77*, 89, 92–95
Indigenous peoples, 13, 89, 99–100, 109–10, 115; Declaration on the Rights of Indigenous Peoples, 47; ecofeminism and, 105; racial ideologies suppressing, 38
Indonesia, 112
industrialization, *71*, 74–75, 78, *85*
inequalities, *85*, 86, 91–92; economic, *51*, 78, 94, 115; gender, 73–74, *82*, 90, 106; global, 69, 73; income, 69–70, 76–78; social, 11–12, 14, 90, 93–95
informal economy, 73, *77*, 78–79, 91
interest rates, loan, 75, 125
Intergovernmental Panel on Climate Change (IPCC), 111
international: cooperation, *80*, 99, 102; institutions, 7–9, 20, *26*, 65, 73, 102; law, 1, 3, 45–46, 119–20; order, 8, 16, 17, *71*; trade, 69–70, 73, *80–81*, 98, 100
International Affairs (journal), 10
International Convention on the Elimination of All Forms of Racial Discrimination (1965), 48
International Covenant on Civil and Political Rights (ICCPR), 45–46, 57

International Covenant on Economic, Social and Cultural Rights (ICESCR), 46, 57
international criminal court (ICC), 62
international governmental organizations (IGOs), 103
international humanitarian law (IHL), 31, 45–46, 61, 68
International Labor Organization (ILO), 46
International Monetary Fund (IMF), 7–8, 69, *80–81*, 124, 125, 126
International Peace Institute, 27–28
international political economy (IPE), 16, 72–74, 102, 125
international relations (IR): study of, 4, 6, 9, 16, 17, 19, 31–32, 122. *See also specific topics*
International Studies Review journal, 11
intersectionality, intersectional analysis and, 5, 20, 21–22, 49, 65–68, 83, 117–19; CEDAW case study, 45, 52–60, 67–68, 120–22; climate change and, 16, 98, 110–12; COVID-19 case study, 70, 85–87, *88*, 89–95; division of labor and, 74–76, *76–77*; international environmental politics and, 99–101, 104–10; the Troubles in Northern Ireland and, 33–42; UNSCR 1325 and, 24–31, *25–26*, 43
"Intersectionality resource guide and toolkit," UN, 55–56
interstate wars, 17, 19–20, 31–32
IPCC. *See* Intergovernmental Panel on Climate Change
IPE. *See* international political economy
IR. *See* international relations
Irish Republican Army (IRA), 35, 40–41, 136n78
Islam, 59, 94

Jewish people, 37
Jeydel, Alana S., *70*
Johnson, David K., 73
Journal of International Relations, 10

Journal of Race Development, 10
Just War Doctrine, 19, 61

Kant, Immanuel, 8
Kaplan, Morton, 6
Kennan, George, 7
Kinsella, Helen, 61–62
Kissinger, Henry, 7
Klugman, Jeni, 61
Kosovo, 28
Kristof, Nicholas, 2
Küçük, Mine Nur, 13
Kyoto Protocol (1997), 111, 125–26

Lagarde, Christine, *81*
land: degradation, *85*, 97–99; rights, 75, 78–79, 99
League of Nations, 46
Lee, Adele, 39
Lefaucheux, Marie-Hélène, 50
LGBT people, 3, 59, 120, 137n85
liberalism (liberal theory), 6–8, 20, 45–47, 102–3, 117, 125
Liberia, 87
literacy rates, in South Africa, 90–91
Lithuania, 37, 39
Local Ulster Volunteer Force (UVF), 38
Loken, Meredith, 9–10
Lunga, Violet Bridget, *70*, 74
Lutz, Bertha, 49

MacMillan, Margaret, 18–19
Magna Carta, 46
Mandelbaum, Michael, *71*
marginalized people and groups, 5, 22, 38, 93, 97, 110, 115. *See also* minorities, minority groups and
Marks, Robert, *71*, 74
Marlin-Bennett, Renée, 73
Marshall, Jenna, 10
Marxism, 79
masculinity, 11, 12, 19, 20, 41, 115
McCall, Leslie, 12
McCoy, Grainne, 34
McLeod, Laura, 28
McVeigh, Robbie, 38

McWilliams, Monica, 29, 36
MDGs. *See* Millennium Development
   Goals
Medicare, US, 86
Mehta, Hansa, 50
men, 2–3, 11–12, 19, 29, 120–21;
   COVID-19 deaths for, 87, 89–90;
   as decision-makers, 27, 77, 82;
   division of labor and, 74–75;
   environmental justice and, 106–9,
   115; modernization benefiting,
   78–79; during the Troubles, 33,
   40–42
Menon, Lakshmi, 50, 67, 77
Meyer-Bisch, Patrice, 54
Michael, Lucy, 37–38
middle-class, 22–23, 34–35, 118
Middle East, *51–52*
Mikulewicz, Michael, 20, 110
military, 18, 23, 29; conscription, 2–3,
   129
Millennium Development Goals
   (MDGs), UN, 83, *84*, 101
Mingst, Karen, 9, 47, 66
minorities, minority groups and, 50–51,
   71–72, 78–80, 83–84, 120–21; R2P
   framework addressing, 65, 67; racial/
   ethnic, 37–39, 47, 106
modernization, 74–75, 78, 216
Montreal Protocol (1987), 101
Morgenthau, Hans, 6–7

Nair, Sheila, 13
NAM. *See* Non-Aligned Movement
National Action Plans (NAPs), UNSCR
   1325, 28
National Health Service (NHS), 85–86
nationalism, 1, 3–4, 11, 19
national security, 7, 26, 104, 135n54
nation-states, 16, 18, *71*, 74. *See also*
   state
Native Americans, 89, 105. *See also*
   Indigenous peoples
NATO. *See* North Atlantic Treaty
   Organization
natural resources, 73, 104–5, 124

Navone, Anthony, 135
neoliberalism, 7, 9, 16, *76*
neo-Marxism, 79, 126
neorealism, 7, 16, 18
NGOs. *See* non-governmental
   organizations
NHS. *See* National Health Service
Nigeria, *82*
Nithiseelan, Naidoo Rajen, 91–92
NIWC. *See* Northern Ireland Women's
   Coalition
Nixon, Richard, 7
Non-Aligned Movement (NAM), *51*
non-governmental organizations
   (NGOs), 62–64, 103, 108, 112–13
North Atlantic Treaty Organization
   (NATO), 1, 125
Northern Ireland, 19; race and ethnicity
   in, 23, 34, 37–40, 137n90; The
   Troubles in, 15, 18, 22–23, 31–43,
   119, 125
Northern Ireland Women's Coalition
   (NIWC), 27–29, 36–37
nuclear weapons, 17
Nuremburg trials, 61

Obamacare (Affordable Care Act), US,
   86
Office of the High Commissioner for
   Human Rights (OHCHR), UN, 52
Okonjo-Iweala, Ngozi, 80, *82*
organized violence, 6, 14–15, 18–20
Origins of the Modern World (Marks), *71*
Ortiz-Ospina, Esteban, 78

pandemics, 87, 89, 123, 125. *See also*
   COVID-19
Pankhurst, Donna, 21
Paris Agreement (2015), 101, 109, 111,
   114, 125–26
Paris Agreement on Climate Change,
   COP21, 101
Parpart, Jane, 21
participation of women in peace
   negotiations, 12–13, 22, 24–31, *25–
   26*, 57, 80, 121; NIWC and, 36–37

patriarchy, 3, 28, 35, 65, 75
pay gaps, gender, 77–78
peace, 4, 12, 14–15, 17, 30, 118, 125–
    26; activism, 11, 20; durable, 18, 21;
    gendered, 21–22, *25–26*; negotiations
    and processes, 3, 12–13, 21–22, 25,
    25–26, 27, 112, 121; the Troubles
    and, 22–23, 31–36, 41–43. *See also*
    participation of women in peace
    negotiations
Peterson, V. Spike, 12, 23–24, *71*, 74–77
Poland, 2, 37, 39
political: access, 5, 94; neglect, 34–35;
    science, 2–3, 118
political violence, 11, 20, 34, 42–43
politicization, 33, 40–41, 56, 122,
    141n59
Politics Among Nations (Morgenthau), 6
pollution, 99, 103, 106
population growth, 108, 111–12
Porter, Elisabeth, 27
post–Cold War period, 16, 17, 61
postcolonialism, postcolonial scholars
    and, 4, 13–14, 95, 105, 115, 118,
    125; global economy and, 73–74; on
    human rights, 46
postwar reconstruction, 8, *80*
poverty, 17, 34–35, 73, 83, 98, 106–7,
    156n108; climate change and, 110;
    COVID-19 and, 70; in India, *76–77*;
    poor women in, 75, *77*, 87, 92; in
    SDGs, *84*; in South Africa, 91; World
    Bank on, 69, *81–82*
power, 4, 11, 13, 24, 82, 110, 117–19;
    balance of, 3, 7, 9, 20–21, 38, 65–66;
    capitalism and, 74; distribution of,
    7–8, 125; gender and, 19, 30; GPE
    and, 77; imperialist, 38, 131n81;
    Morgenthau on, 6; unequal, 66, 118,
    136n75
Prakash, Aseem, 110
Pratt, Nicola, 30
Price, Dolours, 40–41
Price, Marian, 40–41
privilege, 5, 12, 14–15, 30, 74, 79–80
protectionism, 69, 74

Protestantism, 15, 23, 31–42, 125
Prügl, Elisabeth, 19–20
Putin, Vladimir, 1, 128n20

Qureshi, Zia, 69–70

R2P. *See* Responsibility to Protect
race, 4, 9–11, 108, 141n59; gender and,
    118, 121–22; in Northern Ireland,
    23, 34, 37–40, 137n90; in Ukraine,
    2, 120
racialization, 13–14, 20, 24, 38–39, 65
racism, 9–10, 37–39, 90, 128n10,
    130n62, 141n59
rape, 19, 25, 37, 62–63
realism (realist theory), 6–8, 117, 125,
    129n37; on environmental issues,
    102–3; peace and, 20–21
refugees, 2, 3, 25, 54, 110
religions, 15, 23, 32–34, 108, 122, 125.
    See also specific religions
representation, 5, *26*, 27–29, 74, 107–
    10, 115, 130n62
reproductive rights, *51*, 58, 108
Republic of Ireland, 32–37
Resolution 1325 (UNSCR 1325), UN
    Security Council, 12–13, 15, 18, 80,
    121–22; intersectionality and, 24–31,
    25–26, 43
resources, 102, 115; distribution of, 72,
    74, 136n75; natural, 73, 104–5, 124
Responsibility to Protect (R2P), 45,
    60–68, 125
Richmond, Oliver, 21
rights, human, 46; economic, 75, 78–79;
    civil, 32–33, 40, 56, 99; reproductive,
    51, 58, 108; of women, 15, 45, 52,
    58–59, 67, 79, 113, 120, 126. *See
    also* human rights
Rio Declaration, UNCED, 100–101,
    107, 111
Ritchie, Hannah, 98
Rivas, Althea-Maria, 22
Rolston, Bill, 38
Roman Empire, *70*
Rooney, Eilish, 33–34

Roosevelt, Eleanor, 49–50

Rosen, Max, 78

Roulston, Carmel, 35

Ruckert, Arne, 76

Runyan, Anne Sisson, 12, 23–24, 74, 76, 76–77

rural, 86, 97–98; women, 59, 76–77, 77, 105–6, 120–21

Russia, Ukraine invaded by, 1–4, 14, 119–20, 128n10, 128n17

Rwanda, 45, 62–64

Safi, Mariam, 22

Sahnoun, Mohamed, 66

Salem, Sara, 74

Saloshni, Naidoo, 91–92

Sapra, Sonalini, 105, 112

SAPs. *See* structural adjustment programs; Structural Adjustment Programs

Saudi Arabia, 56

Schumpeter, Joseph, 8

SDGs. *See* Sustainable Development Goals

sectarianism, 37–39

security, 1, 14–15, 24, 28, 125; climate, 112; economic, 11, 73; environmental, 103–4, 115; human, 18, 23, 24, 43; national, 7, 26, 104, 135n54; state, 17–18, 23, 43, 103–4

Security Council, UN, *25–26*, 25–31, 126

security studies, 16, 17, 130n62; feminist, 11–12, 23–24

segregation, 34, 90, 92

Serbia, 28

Sex, Gender and COVID-19 Project, 90

sexuality, 35, 53, 59–60, 120

sexual violence, 19–20, 24, *25–26*, 37, 55, 61–62

Shariah law, 59

slavery, 46

Smith, Sarah, 12–13, 21, 30, 46

Smooth, Wendy, 5

social mobility, 94

social welfare programs, 75–76

Somalia, 64

Sørensen, Georg, 17

South Africa, 52, 70, 87, 89–92, 95

Soviet Union (USSR), 1, 7, 13, *51*, 125; collapse of the, 17, *71*

Spanish-American War (1898), 131n81

Sperling, Valerie, 3

Sri Lanka, 55

Stalinska, Mariia, 2

state, 7–8, 13, 16, 75–76; identities, 8–9, 102; power, 117–18; sovereignty, 1, 3, 17, 19–20, 63–64, 125

Stavrevska, Elena B., 12–13, 21, 30

Steans, Jill, 23–24, 72, *76–77*

stereotypes, 14, 24, 28, 34, 59

structural, 90; realism, 7, 18; violence, 30, 32, 36, 136n75

structural adjustment programs (SAPs), 75–76, 84, 125

study of IR, 4, 6, 9, 16, 17, 19, 31–32, 122

Sultana, Farhana, 110

Sun Tzu, 6

sustainability, *84–85*, 100–101

Sustainable Development Goals (SDGs), UN, 55, 83–84, *84–85*, 101

Sweden, 1

Syria, 19

Taliban, 21–22

technological changes, 70, *70–71*

Thiaw, Ibrahim, 97–98

Third World Conference on Women, UN, 21

"Third World" designation, 72–73, 77

Thirty Years' War, 1

Tickner, J. Ann, 11–12, *71*, 73, 75, 77

Tilly, Charles, 18

traditional IR, 4, 21, 31, 117–18, 120; feminist IR in response to, 19–20, 43; security in, 23–24

transnational feminism, 40, *51*, 112

Treaty of Westphalia (1648), 1

tribunals, criminal, 62

the Troubles, 15, 18, 31–32, 119, 122, 125; violence related to, 22–23,

33–38, 40–43; working-class women during, 22–23
True, Jacqui, 11–12
Trump, Donald, 24
Turpin, Jennifer, 63

UDF. *See* Ulster Defense Force
UDHR. *See* Universal Declaration of Human Rights
Ukraine, 1–4, 14, 119–20, 127n2, 127n5
Ulster Defense Force (UDF), 136n78
UN. *See* United Nations
UNCCD. *See* United Nations Convention to Combat Desertification
UNCED. *See* United Nations Conference on Environment and Development
underrepresentation, 14, 35, 78–79
UNEP. *See* United Nations Environment Programme
UNFCCC. *See* United Nations Framework Convention on Climate Change
UNIFEM. *See* United Nations Development Fund for Women
United Arab Emirates, 114–15
United Kingdom, 32, 56, 99
United Nations (UN), 21, 23, 47, 97–98; Charter, 18, 45–46, 49–52, 63–64; Conference on the Human Environment, 99, 102; COP process, 101, 111–12, 114, 123; GAD agenda, 14, 78–80, 124; General Assembly, 3, 46, *47–48*, 49–50, 57, 99–101; HDI developed by, 86–87, 92–93, 95, 124; MDGs, 83, *84*, 101; SDGs, 55, 83–84, *84–85*, 101; Security Council, *25–26*, 25–31, 126; UDHR, 45–46, *47–48*, 48–57, *51*, 67–68; UNCED, 100–101; WAD approach, 78–80, 124, 126; WID agenda, 14, 78–80, 107–8, 126; WPS agenda, 12–13, 15, 18, 24–31, *25–26*, 43, 126, 135n54. *See also specific commissions*; *specific conferences*; *specific conventions*; *specific resolutions*

United Nations Conference on Environment and Development (UNCED), 100–101, 107–8
United Nations Convention to Combat Desertification (UNCCD), 97–98, 100–101
United Nations Decade for Women (1975–85), 107–8
United Nations Development Fund for Women (UNIFEM), 52
United Nations Environment Programme (UNEP), 99–100
United Nations Framework Convention on Climate Change (UNFCCC), 100, 111–15, *114–15*, 125–26
United States (US), 7–8, 15–16, *71*, 99, 118, 131n81, 135n54; access to health care in, 86, 89–90; Afghanistan invaded by, 20–22; CEDAW not ratified by, 58; colonialism of, 13; COVID-19 in, 24, 86, 89; Declaration of Independence, 46; ecofeminism in, 105; Great Depression, 69; Hurricane Katrina in, 106; in NATO, 125; Soviet Union and, 17, *51*; the Troubles and, 32; Ukraine and, 1, 3; voting rights in, 56; "war on terror," 20, 24
Universal Declaration of Human Rights (UDHR), UN, 45–46, *47–48*, 48–57, *51*, 67–68
unpaid work/labor, 72, 93–94
urban women, 50, 120–21
US. *See* United States
USSR. *See* Soviet Union
UVF. *See* Local Ulster Volunteer Force

Vietnam War, 40
Viljoen, Frans, 46, 62
violence, 4, 122, 125, 136n78; domestic, 11, 20, 34, 37, 91; gender-based, 11–13, 15, 19–20, 106, 121, 126; organized, 6, 14–15, 18–20; political, 11, 20, 34, 42–43; sexual, 19–20, 24, *25–26*, 37, 55, 61–62; structural,

30, 32, 36, 136n75; of the Troubles, 22–23, 33–38, 40–43
Vogler, John, 102–3
voting, voting rights and, 42, 46, 56

WAD approach. *See* Women and Development
Wahidin, Azrini, 41
Walt, Stephen M., 103
War of 1812, 8, 25
wars, 1–4, 6, 8, 11–15, 18, 119–20, 126; civil, 19, 45; interstate, 17, 19–20, 31–32; intrastate, 15, 17–21, 31–32, 42, 61, 68. *See also specific wars*
water scarcity, *85*, 97–99
WED agenda. *See* women, environment and development
WEDO. *See* Women's Environment & Development Organization
Wendt, Alexander, 8–9
Western Europe, 125
WGC. *See* Women and Gender Constituency
White people, 2, 9–10, 15, 37–40; women, 5, 118
WID. *See* Women in Development
WMO. *See* World Meteorological Organization
women, 18, 25, 40–41, 74, 89, 122; activism of, 34–35, 106–7, 112–13; Afghani, 21–22; of color, 5, 30, 59, 121; in developing countries, 14, *76–77*, 87, 108, 118; empowerment of, 52, 80, *81–82, 85*, 108–9, 114; exclusion of, 3, 35–36, 80, 117–18; poor, 75, *77*, 87, 92, 120–21; racialization of, 13–14; reproductive rights for, *51*, 58, 108; rights of, 15, 45, 52, 58–59, 67, 79, 113, 120, 126; rural, 59, 76–77, *77*, 105–6, 120–21; Ukrainian, 119–20; UN Charter and, 49–52; urban, 50, 120–21; working-class, 22–23, 34–35. *See also* gender; participation of women in peace negotiations
women, environment and development (WED) agenda, UN, 107–8

Women, Peace, and Security Act (2017), US, 135n54
Women, Peace and Security (WPS) agenda, UN, 12–13, 15, 18, 24–31, *25–26*, 43, 135n54; decision-making addressed by, 126. *See also* Resolution 1325, UN Security Council
Women and Development (WAD) approach, UN, 78–80, 124, 126
Women and Gender Constituency (WGC), UNFCCC, 113, *114–15*
Women in Development (WID) agenda, UN, 14, 78–80, 107–8, 126
Women's Environment & Development Organization (WEDO), 107
World Bank, 7–8, 69, *76–77*, 78, *80–82*, 108, 126
World Conference against Racism, Racial Discrimination, Xenophobia and Related Intolerance, UN, 52–54
World Health Organization, 83, 89
World Meteorological Organization (WMO), 97, 110–11
World Trade Organization (WTO), *81–82*, 126
World War I, 6, 8
World War II, 2, 6, 10, 46, 48, 61, 126; Bretton Woods conference during, *80–81*; economic order following, 69, *71*; health care following, 85–86; international economic order following, 16; rise in intrastate conflicts following, 19
World Women's Congress, 107
WPS agenda. *See* Women, Peace and Security agenda
WTO. *See* World Trade Organization
Wuhan, China, 89, 123

xenophobia, 52–53

Yugoslavia, 28, 62, 64

Zelenskyy, Volodymyr, 1
Zvobgo, Kelebogile, 9–10, 130n62

About the Authors

Joyce P. Kaufman is professor emerita of political science and founding director of the Center for Engagement with Communities at Whittier College. She is currently serving as director of the Women, Peace and Security Program of the Institute of World Affairs in Washington, DC. She is the author of *NATO and the Former Yugoslavia: Crisis, Conflict, and the Atlantic Alliance* (2002) and numerous articles and papers on US foreign and security policy. She is also the author of *A Concise History of U.S. Foreign Policy* (5th edition, 2021) and *Introduction to International Relations: Theory and Practice* (3rd edition, 2022). With Kristen Williams, she is coauthor of *Women at War, Women Building Peace: Challenging Gender Norms* (2013), *Women and War: Gender Identity and Activism in Times of Conflict* (2010), and *Women, the State, and War: A Comparative Perspective on Citizenship and Nationalism* (2007). Joyce P. Kaufman received her BA and MA from New York University and her PhD from the University of Maryland.

Kristen P. Williams is professor of political science at Clark University. She has published journal articles, chapters in edited volumes, and several books on hegemony and international relations, nationalism and ethnic conflict, and gender and war. Her books include *Despite Nationalist Conflicts: Theory and Practice of Maintaining World Peace* (2001); *Identity and Institutions: Conflict Reduction in Divided Societies*, coauthored with Neal G. Jesse (2005); and *Ethnic Conflict: A Systematic Approach to Conflict* (2011). With Joyce P. Kaufman, she coauthored *Women, the State, and War: A Comparative Perspective on Citizenship and Nationalism* (2007) and *Women at War, Women Building Peace: Challenging Gender Norms* (2013). Williams has coedited *Beyond Great Powers and Hegemons: Why Secondary States Support, Follow, or Challenge* (2012) and *Women, Gender Equality, and Post-Conflict*

Transformation: Lessons of the Past, Implications for the Future (2017). Her academic articles have been published in journals including *Political Psychology, International Feminist Journal of Politics, Journal of Research in Gender Studies, International Politics,* and *Oxford Bibliographies in International Relations.* She published a chapter in the *Oxford Handbook of Gender, War and the Western World since 1600* (2020).

www.ingramcontent.com/pod-product-compliance
Lightning Source LLC
Chambersburg PA
CBHW052008270326

41929CB00015B/2835